INVENTING VIETNAM

IN THE SERIES

Culture and the Moving Image

EDITED BY ROBERT SKLAR

INVENTING VIETNAM

The War in Film and Television

EDITED BY

Michael Anderegg

TEMPLE UNIVERSITY PRESS Philadelphia

Temple University Press, Philadelphia 19122
Copyright © 1991 by Temple University, except Chap. 3, which is
© 1982 American Studies Association, and Chap. 11, which is
© 1988 Arizona Quarterly. All rights reserved
Published 1991
Printed in the United States of America

The paper used in this publication meets the minimum requirements
of American National Standard for Information Sciences—
Permanence of Paper for Printed Library Materials,
ANSI Z39.48–1984 ∞

Library of Congress Cataloging-in-Publication Data
Anderegg, Michael A.
    Inventing Vietnam : the war in film and television / edited by
Michael Anderegg.
        p.   cm. — (Culture and the moving image)
    Includes bibliographical references.
    ISBN 0-87722-861-2 (cloth). 0-87722-862-0 (paper).
    1. Vietnamese Conflict, 1961–1975–Motion pictures and the
conflict.   2. War films—United States—History and criticism.
3. Television plays, American—History and criticism.   I. Title.
II. Series.
DS557.73.A5   1991
791.43'658—dc20   91-11392

This book is for Niles

Contents

Acknowledgments

I particularly thank Robert Sklar for helping me pilot this collection of essays to a safe harbor and Janet Francendese for her careful editorial labors. Help and useful advice of various kinds came from Barbara Timmons, Robert Slabey, Ursula Hovet, and Sandra Holmgren. The students in my "Vietnam and Film" class at the University of North Dakota in the fall of 1987 provided the initial impetus for this collection. My wife, Jeanne, as always, lent both moral support and her skills as a reader and an editor. I am grateful to the editors of *Arizona Quarterly* and *American Quarterly* for permission to reprint, respectively, Susan White's "Male Bonding, Hollywood Orientalism, and the Repression of the Feminine in Kubrick's *Full Metal Jacket*" and John Hellmann's "Vietnam and the Hollywood Genre Film: Inversions of American Mythology in *The Deer Hunter* and *Apocalypse Now*."

INVENTING VIETNAM

Michael Anderegg

Introduction

T he essays here collected testify to the unique relationship between the U.S.–Vietnam War and the images and sounds—on celluloid and videotape—that have been employed to represent it. Whereas World War II, despite all the cinematic treatments it inspired, found its most characteristic depictions in historical writings, memoirs, and novels, the Vietnam War, though it has produced a number of brilliant novels and nonfictional prose accounts, has thus far been given its imaginative life primarily through film. The most compelling statements about the war, for many people, have been *The Deer Hunter* (1978), *Apocalypse Now* (1979), *Platoon* (1986), and *Full Metal Jacket* (1987). Significantly, except for the last mentioned, these films were made from original screenplays, and all were released after the war had ended. Cinematic representations, in short, seem to have supplanted even so-called factual analyses as *the* discourse of the war, as the place where some kind of reckoning will need to be made and tested. Even those for whom film can only be a tendentious and cynical product of American capitalism respond passionately to whatever it is they feel Hollywood seems to be saying about the war.

1

Why should this be? Why should films and, to a lesser extent, teledramas of various kinds seem to be so intimately associated with the reality of what has come to be known as the Vietnam experience? One, perhaps obvious, answer is that the Vietnam War was the most visually represented war in history, existing, to a great degree, as moving image, as the site of a specific and complex iconic cluster. As even the novels and memoirs insist, the Vietnam War was itself a movie. Certainly, the war became a television event, a tragic serial drama stretched over thousands of nights in the American consciousness. Those nights presented Vietnam as a tactile video-audio construct, a tight matrix of specific, easily recognized signs: the sight and sound of Huey helicopters, the green of dense jungles, the helmets with plastic bottles taped to their sides, villagers in conical hats.

These images and sounds, furthermore, were produced with an immediacy never before experienced in the history of warfare. The film footage of World War II and Korea, however vivid or powerful, nevertheless carried with it an aura of Hollywood classicism, a distance that resulted—with some exceptions—from an attempt, under difficult conditions, to present "well-made" footage. Film images from the forties and fifties have the look and feel of the already done, the lost moment. The footage from Vietnam, whether on film or videotape, was produced by a generation of filmmakers imbued with the style and technique of cinema verité and direct cinema. One-day relay of film and other forms of rapid dissemination gave much of what Americans watched on the evening news an immediacy and intensity that was new and that forever shaped America's experience of warfare. No previous war had been—and, if the Gulf War is any indication, no subsequent war would be—as visually and aurally "present," as thoroughly documented on film and tape, as was the Vietnam War. At their best, the fictional representations of the Vietnam War recapture and reenact that painful immediacy, that crazed energy, that stylistic roughness associated with what was seen on television for so many nights.

Another factor contributing to the importance of cinematic and video representations of Vietnam was, ironically, the very absence of Vietnam films contemporaneous to the war. Unlike World War II, during which Hollywood, in a sense, created its own war that ran parallel to, but seldom could be mistaken for, the real war, the Vietnam films were produced with sufficient distance from the war that they could reasonably be considered meditations on and explications of America's military and political involvement in Indochina. Vietnam films benefit from an authority of hindsight that few World War II or Korean War films could claim. Not that the combat and other war-related films of the earlier period lacked imaginative force or power; indeed, several Korean War films of the mid to late fifties prefigure the narrative and ideological ambiguities characteristic of Hollywood's Vietnam. The propaganda purpose of most such films, however, was obvious to all: they were meant to boost morale or to promote the necessity of sacrifice or to bring the nation together or to vilify the enemy. After the war, World War II films either celebrated wartime heroism and reasserted wartime values or concerned themselves with problems of postwar readjustment, the rebuilding of America, and reintegration of soldiers and wartime workers into peacetime society for the common good. The ambitions of such films seldom went much further.

The importance of Vietnam films, in particular, may also be related to the way films in general have achieved the status of art, a phenomenon that certainly postdates the World War II and Korean period. Precisely when film ceased to be the primary form of mass entertainment it came to be recognized as perhaps the dominant art form of the twentieth century. Filmmakers were now expected to go beyond the superficialities of a mass cultural form and to "say something," to comment significantly on the subjects they treated. In this context, *The Deer Hunter* and *Apocalypse Now*, when released in the late seventies, were received not simply as movies but as important cultural events, as intellectually respectable statements, however "right" or "wrong" they might be, about the war. Both films called forth a passionate intensity that suggests as much as anything the new status movies had come to occupy with middle- and highbrow audiences, pundits, and commentators of various kinds.

Beyond this, we may also consider that, with the total abolition of the Hollywood Production Code and the virtual elimination of all forms of censorship, movies were no longer seen as a semiofficial arm of the dominant ideology. Filmmakers, it was widely believed, could say what they wanted, could express virtually any point of view. As the Vietnam War continued to be a living part of the political, social, and cultural life of the decades following its official end, the films about the war could contribute multiple voices to the ongoing conversation. From this vantage point, it becomes clear that Vietnam films were not merely retrospective; rather, they became and continue to be barometers of current attitudes. In the Vietnam cinema, the war is not presented so much in the realm of history or memory as it is projected beyond history and memory into the present. The Vietnam War, one feels, never really ends.

The chapters that follow have been organized to construct a roughly chronological structure for the texts they discuss. My consideration of John Wayne and Jane Fonda provides an oblique mapping of much of the territory that follows in this book through an analysis of how two film stars have functioned in the discourse of Vietnam. Both Wayne and Fonda, I suggest, embody a set of meanings that represent, in a mythical way, the polarization of American society during as well as after the war, but, in each instance, a reconstruction of these meanings reveals greater ambiguity and complexity than might be initially apparent. In Wayne's case, the myth has served to disguise some of the contradictions inherent in his action and behavior and has at the same time flattened out his richly detailed screen persona. Fonda, for her part, emerges on close inspection as a figure more conventionally centered in the American mainstream than her radical activities suggest. As cultural symbols, they represent not the opposite ends of a wide field of discourse but rather the two facets of a conflict that lies at the core of the American psyche.

In centering on stars more than on specific films, my chapter reflects the difficulty American culture had in actually representing the war during the sixties and early seventies. As a consequence of the "unrepresentability" of Vietnam, a number of the most significant commentaries on the war did not show—and in some cases did not even mention—Vietnam. *Taxi Driver* (1976), Cynthia Fuchs suggests, is a film precisely about the inability to represent the war. Martin Scorsese's film constructs a "patent metaphoric commentary on America's Vietnam experience in the place of direct representation." We can deduce, without being explicitly told, that Travis Bickle, the film's protagonist, is a Vietnam veteran, and his experiences as a Manhattan cab driver replay many of the thematic issues that have become associated with Vietnam, revealing in the process both "the disordering effects and the disordered foundation of Vietnam" by representing "not the war, but its dispersion"; not its historic or "narrative" coherence, but its culturally constructed madness. Just as race, sex, and class assume crucial importance in any consideration of the Vietnam War and in understanding the war's meaning in postwar America, so the same issues are central to the narrative drive and thematic texture of *Taxi Driver*. Travis's inability to sort out the complexities of his environment leads to a focus on "the mission" as a redemptive act, a focus that ultimately transforms Travis into an image of the enemy Other he so fears and despises. That Travis, the psychopathic loner, should end up, in the film's coda, apotheosized into a popular hero nicely prefigures the trajectory of media representation of Vietnam veterans over the decade following *Taxi Driver*.

By the late seventies, Hollywood was able, for the first time since *The Green Berets* (1968), to engage the war directly. In a close analysis of the two most important Vietnam films of the period, *The Deer Hunter* and *Apocalypse Now*, John Hellmann argues that both films take their narrative cues from popular forms of American literature: the western in *The Deer Hunter* and the hard-boiled detective story in *Apocalypse Now*. In both instances, the myth underlying the genre is radically inverted and critiqued. "*The Deer Hunter*," he writes, "through the western formula, presents Vietnam as yet another historic projection of an internal struggle of white American consciousness, but one where the dream of mastery over nature and the unconscious, or alternatively of benign communion with them, is turned upside down into a nightmare of captivity." Associating *The Deer Hunter* with the literary tradition of James

Fenimore Cooper as well as cinematic versions of the western myth, Hellmann shows the extent to which Cimino's film both incorporates and radically transforms the concept of "regeneration through violence" that lies at the heart of both sources. In *Apocalypse Now*, the traditional hard-boiled detective hero who, though himself pure, moved through a corrupt world has now become corrupt as well, the object of his quest not some external source of evil but his own impure soul. Both films employ romance formulas and "couch the terror of Vietnam in American myths" in order to examine an experience that, as we see again and again in the cinema of Vietnam, seemingly resists more direct forms of representation.

David Desser's chapter, " 'Charlie Don't Surf,' " engages in a broad-ranging analysis of the Oriental "other" in the discourse of Vietnam, both fictional and nonfictional. As Desser notes, "the image of the VC-as-woman, the ubiquity of women who are VC, is a near-hysterical reaction to the shock to the (masculine) American psyche that this physically smaller, technologically inferior race could defeat the hypermasculinized, hypertechnologized American soldier." The Vietnam War, whether conceived of as a fictional or a factual discourse, has nearly always been considered in the West as a predominantly American experience. In this context, the Vietnamese people and their experiences are excluded or are included only negatively in most of the texts discussed in this book. Placing the issue in historical perspective, Desser shows that the enemy was usually invisible, or only present as an externalized Other, in World War II films as well. The treatment of the Asian in the Vietnam cinema, in fact, can be seen as a continuation of the "yellow menace" propaganda of half a century ago. Focusing on *The Boys in Company C* (1978) and, especially, *Go Tell the Spartans* (1978), Desser finds both films notably ambivalent in their treatment of the Vietnamese. As he argues, it is not merely the enemy—the Vietcong and the North Vietnamese—who are posited as an inexplicable Other, but, more notably, the Americans' South Vietnamese allies. Frequently, in fact, the enemy is granted more respect, though not necessarily more humanity, than the "host country nationals" for whom the Americans are supposedly fighting. Desser finds, ultimately, an "essential cultural myopia" in the American discourse of Vietnam that goes beyond racism, extending to an inability to conceive of other people as essentially different.

Ellen Draper, too, illuminates the question of the enemy Other in the Vietnam discourse by examining a postwar cinema that displaces or represses the war altogether. Draper discusses two action/sci-fi films of the eighties, *Aliens* (1986) and *Predator* (1987), neither explicitly about Vietnam, to show how Hollywood dealt retrospectively with the war's "suicidal legacy." As she sees it, both films—and there are others with a similar thrust—manage simultaneously to critique America's past involvement in Indochina (and, by obvious analogy, continuing involvement in other areas of the third world) and to comment on the failure of Hollywood representation itself. In contemporary action films, Draper writes, "Vietnam recurs as a symbol of the failure of American culture." Both *Aliens* and *Predator* present a series of violent actions in a way that defies narrative coherence. At the same time, each film provides a resolution whereby the enemy is revealed as some manifestation of the self, an internal rather than an external version of the Other. "This is ultimately the point of the Vietnam films," Draper adds, "that the alien we engaged with in that war was not foreign but familiar." In such action films as *Aliens* and *Predator*, the point is made perhaps more forcefully, and certainly less sentimentally, than in films that, like *Platoon*, seem to address America's schizophrenia in a more direct fashion.

In an overview that embraces both direct and indirect representations of the Vietnam War, Tony Williams suggests a continuity from the 1970s to the 1980s Vietnam films that may be more significant than their perceived differences. "All Vietnam films," in his view, "attempt to impose some form of narrative order upon a conflict that refuses, both historically and fictionally, any form of convenient definition." Ranging freely over a large group of films, Williams shows how a small set of narrative and mythic patterns is constantly reworked and refurbished in film after film. Both seventies and eighties Vietnam films exhibit such mythic structures as the bildungsroman and the captivity narrative. Additionally, the films rely on recurring motifs that tend toward the feminization of the enemy, the demonization of the media, and the valorization of patriarchy. Stylistically, too, Williams suggests, the body of Vietnam films draws on a limited range of possibilities, with comic-book imagery at one end and a hallucinatory fantasy world at the other. What is most characteristic of the Vietnam cinema, however, is "the hold of binary oppositional motifs that separate Vietnam as a foreign landscape of the mind or geography from whatever protagonist the narrative may want us to conveniently identify with." Williams calls for a Vietnam cinema that will eschew binary structures and motifs for a "polyphonic interplay of codes and experiences" that can allow for a questioning of—rather than an acquiescence to—the limited set of paradigms with which the culture industry has thus far imagined the Vietnam era.

Although no such polyphonic interplay can be said to characterize the "Rambo" films of the 1980s, John Hellmann, in an intriguing reevaluation of *First Blood* (1982) and *Rambo: First Blood, Part II* (1985), extending his discussion of *Apocalypse Now* and *The Deer Hunter*, suggests that, rather than seeing Rambo as an image of right-wing revisionism scourging liberals, peaceniks, and the media, we should consider his "superhuman masculine power" and cathartic use of violence as a response to the dominant American majority of the early 1960s, whose political philosophy and moralism sent young Americans to fight in Vietnam in the first place. What has been "betrayed" in these films is the legacy of John F. Kennedy's New Frontier. *First Blood*, in particular, reverses the classic western paradigm in order to expose the bankruptcy of the American wilderness myth. The western hero (in this case, Vietnam veteran John Rambo) is almost immediately associated in the narrative with the victims of American imperialist ambitions— blacks, Native Americans, and third-world peoples in general. In the film's major irony, the Vietnam vet, chased and harassed like a wounded animal, is "driven into positions that iconographically associate him with the Vietcong and Indians against American society." In the sequel to *First Blood*, the much-maligned *Rambo*, the enemy of the American hero is not so much the dark-skinned

Other as the technocrats and bureaucrats whose soulless greed have betrayed the traditional values enshrined in American mythology. Judy Lee Kinney's essay, though it concentrates specifically on three films from 1987—*Gardens of Stone, Platoon,* and *Hamburger Hill*—concerns itself with a theme that embraces virtually every text touched upon in this book: how the war should be remembered. The Vietnam films of the late eighties, Kinney argues, engage in an attempt to memorialize the war through strategies that incorporate the individual into "a readily accepted cultural matrix of meaning." Employing the realistic effect as a primary stylistic method, *Platoon* and *Hamburger Hill* in particular paradoxically bring about a highly symbolic reconciliation of individual experience with a universalizing theme. In part bildungsroman and in part morality play, *Platoon* relies for its effect on meanings and symbols brought in from the outside; *Hamburger Hill,* touted, like *Platoon,* as a "realistic" combat film, the war from the grunts' point of view, manipulates a set of internally generated symbols and rituals. Both films treat the experiences of soldiers as if they took place in a political-cultural vacuum. This has become one of the primary myths of Vietnam, that the soldier in the field had no understanding of politics, no sense of why the war was being fought, no awareness of the complexities the war represented. In order to absolve the individual soldier from responsibility, these films turn the GIs into little more than mindless robots or total innocents, characterizations neither true to history nor even credible as fictional constructs. All three films contribute to a "collective evasion of Vietnam's tough questions," an attempt at reconciliation that flattens out all specific experience into a dishonest, albeit poignant, act of memorialization.

Daniel Miller's chapter on CBS Television's *Tour of Duty* (1987–90) extends Kinney's argument into the matrix of television programming. What Kinney sees as characteristic of *Platoon* and *Hamburger Hill*—the erasure of politics, the incorporation of the individual into a unified field of meaning—Miller identifies as the structuring principle of *Tour of Duty.* He argues that the significance of *Tour of Duty* transcends its status as a specific television program and becomes the site for an examination of the conception, promotion, and dissemination of meaning in our culture. *Tour of Duty* intensifies as well the myth that the Vietnam War can only truly be represented from the point of view of the individual soldier, a point of view simplistically constructed as politically innocent and fundamentally "heroic" in the traditional mode of American mythology. Valorizing the experience of veterans in this manner becomes a way of denying or co-opting their "real, full, and complex experience" of the war. As Judy Kinney also notes of the films she discusses, Miller finds that *Tour of Duty* serves to memorialize war "as a crucible, leading to heterogeneity, natural camaraderie, male bonding across racial or ethnic barriers, and paternal and fraternal love." All internal difficulties and conflicts combat troops may have encountered—racism, drugs, and the like—are resolved by the military patriarchy. Here, one may add, the television-series format, which at once demands a continuing openness and a definite, weekly closure, although in a sense it imitates the war's seeming endlessness, nevertheless works in an especially pernicious manner to close off or silence complexity.

Another prime-time television series, *China Beach* (1988–91), which quickly followed in the wake of *Tour of Duty*, claims to honor the experience of the women who served in Vietnam. But, as Carolyn Reed Vartanian argues, *China Beach*, by adopting the "structure, style, and tone" of television melodrama, fails to address women as subjects in Vietnam and instead produces a feminized spectator with the purpose of "refiguring the war and its impact on the psyche of the general public." The women of *China Beach*, like the women of melodrama generally, are constructed primarily by their relationships to men. The continuing characters in the series have roles related to serving men's needs, "be they physical (nurse and prostitute), emotional (Red Cross volunteer and USO entertainer), or spiritual (base commander)." Even in a special episode that incorporates the experiences of actual veterans, the emphasis falls on the women's emotional relationship to men. Through this process, Vartanian suggests, the men are newly constructed in terms of "heroism" and the complexities of America's involvement in Vietnam are once again elided via generic conventions that undermine the fiction's stated purpose.

The tyranny of genre may, however, be overcome to some extent through inversion. Stanley Kubrick's *Full Metal Jacket*, for instance, while ostensibly structured in line with the combat-film paradigm, projects a powerfully symbolic satire of the genre it is imitating. Adapted from Gustav Hasford's *Short-Timers* and co-written by Hasford, Kubrick, and Michael Herr, *Full Metal Jacket* clearly participates in the postmodernist mode of Vietnam literary texts identified by other contributors to this book. The collapse of the individual into the group, which Judy Kinney identifies as characteristic of late-eighties Vietnam films, here is replayed ironically, according to Susan White, in the image of the film's protagonist, Private Joker, melting into an "irrevocably infantalized" group. The creation of young killing machines, as Kubrick delineates the process, involves a form of male bonding that comes about through a repression of homoerotic desire coupled with a violent ejection of the feminine. White's chapter expands outward from Kubrick's film to incorporate not only other Kubrick meditations on war—*Paths of Glory* (1957), *Dr. Strangelove* (1964)—but various examples of *film noir*, old and new, from *The Big Sleep* (1946) to *Year of the Dragon* (1985), in order to link femininity with the Oriental "other" of Hollywood cinema, a cinema that tends "to conflate Eastern culture with corrupt sexuality, a degraded or treacherous femininity and male homoeroticism."

The film and television programs of Vietnam, though sometimes treated in isolation from other Vietnam-inspired texts, necessarily derive from, parallel, comment on, or rework themes, motifs, and formal strategies to be found in literary texts inspired by the war. Owen W. Gilman, Jr., compares Ward Just's novel *Stringer* to *Good Morning, Vietnam* and finds in both that "the dark act of improvisation" provides an ideal vehicle for reading the Vietnam experience. In *Stringer*, Just found his primary metaphoric core in Chicago jazz and in the improvisational routines of Mike Nichols and Elaine May. Similarly, Gilman argues, the improvisational routines of Robin

Williams and director Barry Levinson's willingness to give up control to Williams come to suggest paradigms for the war itself. "By having Robin Williams go into the broadcast booth without a script, Levinson represented a fundamental truth of the war," in part because the experience of Vietnam involved a situation where authority was absent and where the individual became cut off and isolated from any recognizable context. "The great texts of Vietnam," as Gilman sees it, "have one thing in common: a pulsating, scintillating, rhetorically charged hard-driving rhythm of language in overdrive, pursuing frenetically the hope of life." Gilman thus associates *Good Morning, Vietnam* with a number of the significant literary texts of the war—not only *Stringer,* but the work of Caputo, Hasford, Herr, and O'Brien as well.

Thomas Doherty, in "Witness to War: Oliver Stone, Ron Kovic, and *Born on the Fourth of July,*" also juxtaposes literary and cinematic texts as he reexamines the relationship between the Vietnam experience as it has been mediated in film and literature and the cinematic structures and images that underlie and provide a "backstory" for that mediation. Stone, the first Vietnam veteran to write and direct Hollywood feature films based, at least in part, on his own war experiences, reinvents Vietnam initially as a World War II combat film in *Platoon* and then as a post–World War II vet-rehabilitation film in *Born on the Fourth of July* (1989). In each instance, as Doherty shows, the genre conventions cannot be sustained. No World War II film could have included the My Lai–like sequence that is so central to the meaning and emotional resonance of *Platoon.* In *Born on the Fourth of July,* Stone goes much further in both borrowing and simultaneously undermining genre conventions. Though the film (and Ron Kovic's memoir on which it is based) may echo William Wyler's *Best Years of Our Lives* (1946) and Fred Zinnemann's *The Men* (1950), "none of the comforts of Hollywood's World War II is available to Kovic—not the reconstituted ethnic diversity of the platoon, not the sympathy of a girl back home, not the honor and understanding of an appreciative home front." Vietnam, even in film, is not a World War II movie; and neither, of course, was World War II. The point always to bear in mind about media is that they mediate: a representation of war—or of any other human experience—is never the thing itself. Understanding the ways in which media filter and transform experience is especially crucial as Vietnam—and, particularly, film and television representations of Vietnam—is more and more entering the curriculum of America's high schools and universities. As anyone who has taught such a course knows, young people today have a hunger to know more about Vietnam and to understand the relationship between current and past representations of the war and the "reality" of the war itself. In "Teaching Vietnam," Thomas J. Slater places a number of key documentary films in a specific pedagogic context and indirectly shows that documentaries present a viewer with issues of representation and invention similar to those that other essayists discover in the "fictional" discourse. Each documentary, whether *A Face of War* (1967), PBS's *Vietnam* (1983), *Television's Vietnam* (1985; Accuracy in Media's critique of PBS's *Vietnam*), or Peter Davis's *Hearts and Minds* (1975), can only be an artful construct, shaping and presenting, usually in the guise of exposing the "truth," a preselected and carefully arranged set of images and sounds. The bringing together of texts produced from differing viewpoints offers a useful lesson regarding the essential nature of film, video, and, indeed, all media. As Slater's analysis demonstrates, neither the traditional Right nor the traditional Left has produced, or indeed can produce, definitive statements on the war.

These contributions, like a number of others in the literature that has formed around media depictions of Vietnam, make much of the *unrepresentability* of the war. Another way of looking at this issue would be to suggest that the war is not so much unrepresentable as represented multiply in film and television. One finds little resemblance between Coppola's war and Cimino's, Stone's and Kubrick's; Vietnam does not look, sound, or feel the same in *Hamburger Hill* as it does in television's *Tour of Duty*. We are dealing here with something more than different aspects of the war, or different locations "standing in" for Vietnam, or different moments in the war's history. Simply put, no construction of the Vietnam War can be anything more than a highly limited facet of a many-surfaced object. These chapters, like the texts they discuss, individually illuminate specific areas of interaction between the audiovisual media and the Vietnam War. Taken as a group, they present a more rounded discussion of the subject than any single author can suggest. Nevertheless, no group of essays, no melding of voices, can be final or comprehensive. Quite simply, there is no last word to be written about either Vietnam or its representations. Each author invents Vietnam anew, discovers this or that meaning or significance while leaving open the possibility for other inventions, other discoveries. Vietnam, as fact and as myth, remains a central, contested area in the American consciousness. Those who claim that the U.S.–Iraq War, or any event in recent American history, has laid to rest the "Vietnam syndrome" only reveal the extent to which that war's most important lessons have still to be learned.

Michael Anderegg

Hollywood and Vietnam
John Wayne and Jane Fonda as Discourse

CHAPTER 1 Hollywood's failure to participate imaginatively in America's war against Vietnam has been often noted: only one wartime film, John Wayne's *Green Berets* (1968), took as its primary subject the combat in Southeast Asia. Other films of the period use the war as background or premise for characters and situations located within some other, non-Vietnam context. We can find, as well, films that allude to the war obliquely or indirectly; indeed, some would say that a Vietnam allegory underlies virtually every significant American film released from the mid sixties to the mid seventies, from *Bonnie and Clyde* (1967) and *Night of the Living Dead* (1968) to *Ulzana's Raid* (1972) and *Taxi Driver* (1976). It remains true, nevertheless, that the film industry had little interest in the Vietnam War as such. At the same time, what might be termed "the matter of Vietnam," both during the war and after, intersects in a number of ways with the discourse of Hollywood. Not only are Hollywood movies—in particular, World War II combat films—themselves texts frequently alluded to in the literature and postwar films of Vietnam, but throughout the 1960s the politics of Hollywood as a community of specific individuals and as an imagined world revolved around and expressed itself through attitudes toward the war.

Almost as if to compensate for the absence of movies about Vietnam, movies themselves quickly became a central motif in the Vietnam mythology. "We are starring in our very own war movie," writes Philip Caputo in *A Rumor of War*, characterizing his first, "romantic" months in Vietnam.[1] Caputo had gone to OCS and Officer Basic School, his head filled with Hollywood fantasies. "For me, the classroom work was mind-numbing. I wanted the romance of war, bayonet charges, and desperate battles against impossible odds. I wanted the sort of thing I had seen in *Guadalcanal Diary* [1943] and *Retreat, Hell!* [1952] and a score of other movies."[2] Michael Herr in *Dispatches* sees "life-as-movie, war-as-(war) movie, war-as-life."[3] "One day," Herr recalls, "at the battalion aid station in Hue a Marine with minor shrapnel wounds in his legs was waiting to get on a helicopter, a long wait with all of the dead and badly wounded going out first, and a couple of sniper rounds snapped across the airstrip, forcing us to move behind some sandbagging. 'I *hate* this movie,' he said, and I thought, 'Why not?' "[4] "Vietnam: The Movie" emerges as a key catchphrase for the war and for its imaginative reconstructions.[5]

One soon notes a pervasive intertextuality in the Vietnam discourse, where everything seems to refer to everything else, allusions bouncing from text to text in a seemingly endless sequence. So, for example, Graham Greene's *The Quiet American*, published in 1955, probably the first Vietnam novel, comes up several times in Michael Herr's *Dispatches*, and Herr's description of a soldier with "Born to Kill" inscribed on his helmet next to a peace symbol becomes a key image in Stanley Kubrick's *Full Metal Jacket* (1987; Herr worked on the screenplay of Kubrick's film). Gustav Hasford's novel *The Short-Timers*, from which *Full Metal Jacket* derives, refers back to *Dispatches*, both in its epigraph and in the comment the novel's protagonist, Private Joker, makes as he reacts to boot camp: "I think I'm going to hate this movie."[6] Even the advertising copy for *Full Metal Jacket*—"In Vietnam, the wind doesn't blow, it sucks"—echoes a passage from Tim O'Brien's novel *Going after Cacciato*. One begins to wonder, after a while, just where the striking images and allusions originate; not simply where fact begins and fiction leaves off but, more intriguingly, which of the two—fiction or fact—derives from the other. In this sense, at least, the novels, memoirs, and films of Vietnam, in blurring the line between the fictive and the factual, replay the confusions and contradictions that were and continue to be central to America's experience of the Vietnam War.

The reciprocal relationship between real life and the movies, which is a crucial aspect of this intertextuality, is exemplified by two Hollywood stars, John Wayne and Jane Fonda, who can be seen as spokespersons for and representatives of the "right" and "left" extremes of the political response to the war. In real life—and sometimes even in film—such polarizations are simplistic; both Wayne and Fonda stand in a much more complex and ambiguous relationship to Hollywood, the war, and that phenomenon conveniently labeled "the sixties" than the terms Right and Left (or "conservative" and "liberal") can account for easily. Both stars operate in the discourse in multiple ways: iconographically, as performers in particular films; ideologically, in terms of specific statements each made and specific acts each engaged in; and, as well, as imaginary constructs that innocently or deliberately efface the distinction between person and performer, actor and role.

John Wayne and Jane Fonda, furthermore, represent a discourse operating within the film industry itself: "Old" versus "New" Hollywood. Here, too, both stars functioned in a complex manner. Although Wayne might reasonably be seen, by age, experience, associations, and so forth, as an archetypal representative of Old Hollywood, his iconic power, throughout the sixties and up to and indeed beyond his death in 1979, operated on young filmgoers with at least as much if not more effect as on their middle-aged or older counterparts. And Fonda, for her part, though clearly associated with the new, post–Production Code, post–studio-system Hollywood, provided a strong and significant link to the Old Hollywood through the star image of her father, Henry Fonda, whose presence not only made itself felt via her physical resemblance to him but

tended to emerge as well as part of a phenomenon known as "The
Fondas," with the career of Jane's brother Peter and his even stronger association with New Hollywood (*Easy Rider* [1969], etc.) serving
as catalyst for the generational conflicts on which the press regularly
commented.

A "generation gap" of sorts can in part account for the ideological differences separating John Wayne and Jane Fonda, but politics
also distinguished Wayne from Henry Fonda, well known in Hollywood as a liberal. Wayne and the elder Fonda were about the same
age (as are Jane Fonda and Wayne's second son, Patrick). Both
Henry Fonda and John Wayne remain associated in film history as
crucial members of director John Ford's professional "family," each
virtually alternating as protagonist in Ford's films in the late 1930s
and throughout the 1940s: Wayne in *Stagecoach* (1939), *The Long
Voyage Home* (1940), *They Were Expendable* (1945), *Three God-
fathers* (1948), and *She Wore a Yellow Ribbon* (1949); Fonda in
Young Mr. Lincoln and *Drums along the Mohawk* (both 1939), *The
Grapes of Wrath* (1940), *My Darling Clementine* (1946), and *The
Fugitive* (1947). They starred together only once, however, in Ford's
Fort Apache (1948), where they played characters in constant conflict. Ironically, it is Fonda, the liberal, who portrays the harsh,
unbending, racist Custer-surrogate Owen Thursday, while Wayne
plays the softer, more human and humane, near-liberal Kirby York.
In the course of the narrative, the Wayne character moves from a
relatively untroubled, blunt honesty to a position of affirming the
useful lie over the unpleasant reality. Kirby York is thus fundamentally compromised, ending up a far more ambivalent character than
the film-text had constructed him at the outset. In this context, it
seems particularly notable that *Fort Apache* evokes thematic issues
that would become central to the Vietnam discourse—America's
historic role, imperialism, militarism, genocide, truth to image
versus truth to fact—and thus becomes, as Michael Herr noticed,
"more a war movie than a Western, [a] Nam paradigm."[7]

The complex, equivocal character John Wayne played in *Fort
Apache* bears very little resemblance to his popular image, particularly as that image was appropriated by various voices in the

Vietnam discourse. Most of the allusions to Wayne in the war novels, memoirs, and films of the era construct a simple, one-dimensional heroism: Wayne as Captain America, a hero undivided in his loyalties and emotions and indestructible in his encounters with the enemy.[8] If Vietnam was a war movie, John Wayne was its star. In *A Rumor of War*, Philip Caputo reflects on the illusion that he, a young marine second lieutenant hoping for glory and fame, carried into battle: "Already I saw myself charging up some distant beachhead, like John Wayne in *Sands of Iwo Jima*, and then coming home a suntanned warrior with medals on my chest."[9] Ron Kovic, too, in his memoir *Born on the Fourth of July*, remembers the impact the film made on him as a boy: "Like Mickey Mantle and the fabulous New York Yankees, John Wayne in *The Sands of Iwo Jima* became one of my heroes."[10] Michael Herr writes of the grunts whose motives or justifications for being in Vietnam range "from the lowest John Wayne wetdream to the most aggravated soldier-poet fantasy."[11] Gustav Hasford's *Short-Timers* is imbued with Wayne allusions, from "John Wayne cookies" to Private Joker's vocal impressions. A soldier who goes berserk and performs a suicidally "heroic" act is characterized as having done "a John Wayne." Adapted into *Full Metal Jacket*, the Wayne presence seems even stronger, a constant subtext in Matthew Modine's enactment of Private Joker.

By the 1960s, when Wayne's image had hardened into a cliché-laden icon of the uncomplicated warrior hero, his film persona began to be confused with and seemingly contaminated by his public statements. Reciprocally, his roles began to take on the coloration of his offscreen activities. Wayne's various "patriotic" remarks in speeches and interviews, and in particular his support of Richard Nixon, turned him into, depending on one's point of view, either a noble superpatriot or a neolithic ultraconservative. Wayne's middle-American, lower-middle-class roots could be posited as in some ways explaining his response to the turmoil of the sixties. Wayne exemplified the archetypal self-made man Americans are supposed to value. Unlike Jane Fonda, who was born a kind of acting princess, and a wealthy one at that (her mother was an heiress), Wayne's parents were poor midwesterners: his father, according to most sources, was a charming ne'er-do-well who moved his family from Iowa to the golden land of California, where he signally failed to improve his lot; Wayne's mother eventually divorced him. John Wayne's rise to stardom was lengthy and frequently painful. In a number of ways, his career paralleled that of his political hero, Richard Nixon. Both men knew defeat and failure and both carried with them, even in success, a streak of anger and meanness that often expressed itself in a seemingly contrary mode: the mouthing of sentimental platitudes and pieties.

Jane Fonda, in her thirty-year film career, has not constructed anything like John Wayne's iconic film persona. As a representative of the New Hollywood, she did not enjoy the advantages or suffer the disadvantages of the studio system, a system that encouraged the casting of performers according to type and within a fairly narrow range of generic conventions. Her roles have been far fewer than Wayne's for an equivalent period (from 1930 to 1960, Wayne appeared in well over a hundred films), and she has evidently made an effort to choose a variety of roles, creating a persona that identifies her as an actress as much as a star. From Neil Simon to Ibsen, from Barbarella to Lillian Hellman, from Kitty Twist to Cat Ballou, her roles trumpet her versatility; only in recent years has it been possible to speak of a "Jane Fonda character." Her political beliefs and associations have undoubtedly determined her choice of films in the 1970s and 1980s, and filmgoers are free to read ideological significance in virtually any character she plays; nevertheless, she has tried to establish herself as a serious actress, choosing roles that both broaden her range and associate her name with projects that could be regarded as much as significant cultural or political events as movies.

The Jane Fonda acting persona took some time to develop, however. From her movie debut as a high-school cheerleader in *Tall Story* (1960) at the very beginning of the sixties, through her Roger Vadim phase up to *Klute* in 1971, one can trace a growing maturity, a coming of age both in Jane Fonda the actress and in Jane Fonda the public figure. Her initial progress was gradual and erratic, almost as if she were searching for a role that would encapsulate the essential elements of her acting personality. Her early films project her as a naïve, though at times comically self-aware, sex object. By the mid 1960s, her subjectivity appeared to have become dominated by Vadim, who attempted to mold her into an American blend of Brigitte Bardot and Catherine Deneuve, his previous star-lovers. She ultimately freed herself of both his influence and the image that came with it, finding her voice in the political arena. With *They Shoot Horses, Don't They?* (1969) and *Klute*, she successfully brought into productive tension key ingredients from earlier roles, creating a richly nuanced screen persona, one that combined sensuousness and vulnerability with toughness and strength of character. In France, her professional move from Vadim to Godard, from *Barbarella* (1968) to *Tout va bien* (1972), though not as liberating as she might have hoped, was from this point of view as much a political as an aesthetic choice. Her more or less simultaneous involvement with social causes can thus be seen as a personal act of liberation as well as the expression of a political commitment. [12]

Fonda's roles in such "socially conscious" films of the later seventies as *Julia* (1977), *Coming Home* (1978), and *The China Syndrome* (1979) play out compressed versions of her professional life. In the latter two films in particular, the Fonda character is initially seen as a naïve, politically unaware, conventionally bourgeois, unliberated woman. The narrative drive in each case becomes a tracing of her journey to maturity, awareness, involvement, action. At the beginning of each film, she serves as a stand-in for the average American and audience member who, in the very process of viewing, has her or his consciousness raised and learns that radical action, far from being a threatening or foreign concept, is as American as apple pie. In *Coming Home*, Fonda's only explicitly Vietnam-related commercial film, this trajectory is severely compromised by the conventional pieties and romantic demands of the fiction. Inevitably, given the institutional constraints that governed the film's production, the political is quickly, and with a complete absence of subtlety, reduced to the personal. In the very act of making political awareness respectable, *Coming Home* sanitizes politics, substituting sentimentalism and unobjectionable compassion for obvious victims for any kind of broader commitment to social justice. In this sense, *Coming Home* functions both as a courageous reminder, and as an opportunistic reinterpretation, of Fonda's notorious journey to Hanoi in the summer of 1972.

The culmination and logical outcome of several years of antiwar activities, including tours of stateside military bases with her F.T.A. ("Free the Army" or "Fuck the Army") troupe, Jane Fonda's trip to Vietnam has come to symbolize the extreme lengths to which the antiwar movement in America was willing to go in order to register its total rejection of U.S. actions in Southeast Asia. For many Americans, the act was a brave gesture by someone with little to gain and much to lose; for many others, it remains an unforgivable act of treason. It was not so much the trip itself that aroused vehement condemnation—other more or less notable Americans had gone to North Vietnam without creating as much of a stir—as some of the images the event generated, particularly a short film clip of Fonda sitting at the firing position on an antiaircraft gun, clapping her hands with seeming joy. Equally damning, perhaps, she made several radio broadcasts to U.S. troops, thereby earning the nickname "Hanoi Jane," an allusion to Tokyo Rose of World War II infamy. She also agreed to talk to American POWs, who later claimed that they would have been punished if they had refused to see her.

The uproar over Fonda's Vietnam visit was, in part, a matter of who she was and what she represented. As a film star, Fonda was especially vulnerable to attack. Actors and actresses, traditionally, have had a difficult time being taken seriously outside of their profession. (The recent political career of Ronald Reagan may turn out to be the exception that not only proves the rule but carves it indelibly in stone.) For the former POWs who later recalled the visit, that she was not just any actress but specifically Jane Fonda seemed particularly disturbing. "I felt betrayed," Major Ted Gostas remembered. "I had seen a movie years ago when Henry was young. It was about Drums on the Mohawk or something. . . . Well, Henry ran away from Indians chasing him with tomahawks. They poop out and he gets safely to reinforcements. How often I thought of that in prison."[13] Another former POW, Colonel George Day, interviewed for the television documentary *Unauthorized Biography: Jane Fonda* (1988), echoed the sentiment: "that's not what anyone would expect from Henry Fonda's daughter."[14] Henry Fonda's daughter—by implication, America's daughter. Young, pretty, and rebellious, a child of privilege, a starlet who had romped half-naked through several naughty French films, Fonda clearly distilled the central generational conflict of the sixties. Even with her clothes off, perhaps especially with her clothes off, Jane Fonda had always seemed fundamentally innocent, thoroughly wholesome. Clearly, her actions triggered a powerful network of feelings, many of them undiscerned or unacknowledged.

That Fonda was a woman—an attractive, wealthy, famous woman—constitutes a definite subtext to how her Vietnam journey was perceived. If Paul Newman or Marlon Brando had done what Jane Fonda was doing, they probably would have been vilified as well (as they had been on other, less touchy, issues), but not, one suspects, in the same tone. In the remarkable short film *Letter to Jane* (1972), made by the French left-wing filmmaking team of Jean-Luc Godard and Jean-Pierre Gorin, the issue is directly addressed. *Letter to Jane* makes clear the extent to which Fonda's political act opened her to attack not only by the Right but, less expectedly, by the Left. The film consists entirely of still photos, in particular a news photo of Jane Fonda in Hanoi, accompanied by a spoken commentary by Godard and Gorin. In its final effect, *Letter to Jane* is as much an autocritique as it is a criticism of Fonda for not having sufficiently considered what ought to be the relationship between a Western militant and the revolutionary people of Vietnam. But in its local effects, moment by moment, *Letter to Jane* can only be perceived as an attack, however sympathetically launched, on Jane Fonda herself. Godard and Gorin are quite conscious of the problem their film-essay presents as a criticism of a woman by two men. Owning up to their embarrassment, they remark at one point, "Once again, as usual, men are finding ways to attack women."[15] The issue, nevertheless, remains throughout *Letter to Jane*; indeed, by mentioning it, Godard and Gorin assure that it must.

The gender issue is equally evident, if unacknowledged, in right-wing attacks on Fonda. In *Unauthorized Biography*, the narration, spoken by Barbara Howar, condescends magnificently to its subject during the Hanoi segment: "Alone, and without Tom [Hayden] to advise her, Jane allowed her every move to be strategically plotted by the North Vietnamese, who found her an eager accomplice." Poor, dumb woman, in short. In the popular discourse, she was simply referred to as a "Commie Bitch"; the word "bitch," clearly, is meant to be at least as damning as the word "Commie." Barbara Howar sums up the issue precisely: "The girl who as Barbarella wore little more than a silly grin would soon put on army combat boots and march herself to Hanoi. The American G.I.s who'd papered their barracks with pin-up girl posters of a sexy Jane were unprepared for the shock of her in uniform fatigues on an enemy anti-aircraft gun." The female betrayal of male fantasies could not be more complete.

John Wayne's most obvious association with Vietnam was, of course, his production of *The Green Berets* (1968). Although ridiculed from various points of view at the time of its release, Wayne's film, considered some twenty years later, strikes a viewer most forcefully with its unintended surrealism. The mise-en-scène, the casting choices, the narrative strategies, and the characterizations in no way approximate even our imaginative experience of Vietnam. The keynote throughout is a kind of willed innocence and naïveté. A World War II combat film in tone and structure (critics have noted resemblances to *Back to Bataan* [1945], which also starred Wayne), *The Green Berets* is additionally filled with characters and motifs self-consciously borrowed from westerns. Hence, the film seems more than anything else an exercise in nostalgia, albeit one with a bad conscience. Wayne has the courage of his convictions to the extent of depicting, and justifying, the South Vietnamese Army's torture of Vietcong prisoners, but so hysterical do the justifications become that we sense the filmmakers' unease with the material.

Inevitably, *The Green Berets* itself enters the mythos of the Vietnam war. In *The Short-Timers*, Hasford alludes to the film to ridicule it: "This is the funniest movie we have seen in a long time . . . the grunts laugh and whistle and threaten to pee all over themselves. The sun is setting in the South China Sea—in the East—which makes the end of the movie as accurate as the rest of it."[16] Reflecting on the absence of Vietnam-inspired movies, Michael Herr notes parenthetically: "*The Green Berets* doesn't count. That wasn't really about Vietnam, it was about Santa Monica."[17]

What is particularly unsettling about *The Green Berets*, however, is the extent to which the John Wayne persona has been reduced to a simpleminded parody of itself. Wayne's Colonel Mike Kirby (shades of Kirby York) is hardly a character at all; he is, simply, John Wayne as imagined by someone unaware of or insensitive to the previous thirty years of American cinema and Wayne's place therein. Far from the simplistic icon of mindless heroism he enacts in *The Green Berets*, Wayne, from at least *Stagecoach* on, frequently embodied characters either uncertain or unfocused, or, if certain and focused, ultimately shown to be morally "wrong" to a greater or lesser extent. In his best films—*Red River* (1948), *The Searchers* (1956)—he is clearly condemned and even punished for his egotism, arrogance, and single-minded pursuit of dubious goals. But even in lesser, seemingly more straightforward films, Wayne could embody characters who are forced to face unpleasant truths about themselves. The John Wayne film perhaps most frequently alluded to in the Vietnam literature, *Sands of Iwo Jima* (1949), strongly condemns those very qualities—toughness, adherence to a simple code, self-enclosure—that would make for a clear-cut hero. In fact, the film ultimately shows that these character traits are a masquerade, hiding deep emotional wounds. So flawed a character is Wayne's Sergeant Ryker that only death, an unusual though not unprecedented fate for a John Wayne hero, can finally redeem him. Again, the Wayne persona's genuine heroism is not doubted; what is brought into question is the manner in which that heroism is projected and the nature and meaning of the various elements that together constitute the source of its power.

In his earlier sixties films, Wayne had occasionally succumbed to the temptation of being cast (and, in the case of *The Alamo* [1960], casting himself) in roles that fell in line with the simple image we see in *The Green Berets*. But with the right director (Ford or Hawks or Preminger) his characterizations suggest something more complicated or vulnerable. In *The Man Who Shot Liberty Valance* (1962), while Wayne is much more a typical hero than in, say, the earlier *Fort Apache* or *The Quiet Man* (1952), John Ford creates a context that brilliantly complicates at the same time that it acknowledges Wayne's by now near-mythic status. The heroism of Tom Doniphan, the character Wayne portrays, is unquestioned, his virtues are the simple ones of the classic western hero, but, for all of that, he is shown to be an archaic figure, a throwback to an earlier time who ends up a lonely, forgotten man. Without his heroism being in any way diminished, it is shown to be emotionally limiting and, in an increasingly complex world, impractical as well. A world of subtle moral values, of the book instead of the gun, of pacificist impulses and the rule of law, overtakes the western hero. His passing is regretted, but it is also shown to be both necessary and final.

Liberty Valance, and the way it modifies the John Wayne persona, can be seen as a prefiguring of what the later sixties would bring into focus. America's difficult passage through what has come to be known as the "trauma" of Vietnam played itself out very much in the terms laid out in Ford's film. Like the United States in the sixties, *The Man Who Shot Liberty Valance* is movingly schizophrenic in its depiction of the country's history, of progress, of democratic institutions, and of heroism, fame, and violence. And the John Wayne persona stands squarely at the center of these warring impulses. For the Tom Doniphans of the world, the war was a Manichaean struggle between good and evil, with "Communism" an unalloyed, uncomplex villain much like the demonic Liberty Valance. For most Americans, however, the Vietnam War was a morass of conflicting feelings and ambiguous moral questions. Facing the meaning of the war required sudden shifts of thought and feeling, "agonizing reappraisals," radical restructurings of long-held views. Much like Ransom Stoddard, the character played by Jimmy Stewart in the film, Americans tried, as best they could, to work through questions of personal and national honor, the uses of violence, the myth of America's destiny. That the villain could be, not the enemy, but one's own government, was perhaps the harshest lesson that many were forced to learn. At the same time, it was also clear that much of what was "right," as well as "wrong," in American history had depended on the heroics that John Wayne, in the primary mythic version of his persona, especially as presented in *Liberty Valance*, embodied.

Wayne's public activities in the 1960s suggest his own confusion over his identity, as well as his difficulty in keeping clear the distinction between art and life, movies and politics. That, for example, Wayne could be both patriotic and self-serving—without, presumably, experiencing any conflict between these impulses— became evident during his notorious press campaign for *The Alamo*, a film that he produced, directed, and, in part, financed. The main thrust of the advertisements was that it would be unpatriotic not to see *The Alamo*. Although Wayne may have believed sincerely in the moral force of his film, he could hardly have been unaware that the desired effect of such advertising and promotion was to sell tickets and make money for himself and his company. (It took actor Chill Wills, nominated for a best-supporting-role Oscar, to press things well beyond parody by taking an ad in the *Hollywood Reporter* that read, in part: "We of *The Alamo* cast are praying harder—than the real Texans prayed for their lives at the Alamo—for Chill Wills to win the Oscar.")[18] A vociferous advertising campaign, a patriotic subject, and Wayne's box-office appeal were not enough, in any case, to prevent the film, and Wayne himself, from losing a great deal of money.

That John Wayne should have become a spokesman for the more martial elements of the political Right at the same time that he was remembered as the primary cinematic icon of World War II, especially for the young people of the Vietnam era, suggests a striking irony: Wayne starred in combat films throughout the forties in part because he was one of the few major actors of his generation not fighting in the real war overseas. A family man (the father of four children), Wayne received a hardship deferment. While Henry Fonda and James Stewart and Clark Gable, along with many other Hollywood actors, joined up, putting their careers on hold for the duration, Wayne stayed in Hollywood. (An extra irony, of course, is that whereas John Wayne stayed home from World War II, Jane Fonda went to Vietnam.) One can argue, with considerable justice—and it was so argued, at least indirectly, at the time—that Wayne contributed more to the war effort by making morale-boosting films than he would have at Guadalcanal or the Remagen Bridge. The fact remains that other family men, many older than Wayne (who was thirty-four in 1941), both in and out of Hollywood, did enlist. My purpose here is not to judge Wayne for his choice, but simply to suggest that his *image* as the soldier-hero of World War II was precisely that, an image, pure fantasy.[19] It may in part be a vague awareness of Wayne's ambivalent status as an icon of martial heroism that lends such ambiguity to the Wayne allusions that inform so many Vietnam texts. "John Wayne" seems simultaneously a potent symbol of toughness and bravery and a grim joke. The point about John Wayne as hero is the impossibility, the sheer fantasy of his heroic image; to be like John Wayne, to mimic his words, his mannerisms, his actions, is to imitate an imitation, and to reenact as a simplicity something that was always undeniably complex.

Jane Fonda, too, as we have seen, in many ways contradicts the image that popularly defines her in this discourse. The controversy surrounding her name, image, and activities has served to disguise the quintessential Americanness that is at the core of her personality, public as well as, one supposes, private. Fonda's antiwar activities stemmed from the very same kind of naïve, apolitical, and unideological impulses that propelled and supported America's involvement in Southeast Asia in the first place. Her responses to public issues have been more or less improvisational, her energies aimed not at root causes but at surface effects. When she first read Tom Hayden's essays in *Ramparts*, she told an interviewer for *Vanity Fair*, she was impressed primarily because "his analysis was not intellectual, doctrinaire, ideological. It was just *sensible*. I liked the sensibleness of it."[20] In this, she is very much a product of mainstream America. Her film personas and her continuing popularity (in spite of the flack she takes as "Hanoi Jane") both attest to her fundamentally centrist identity. The United States itself, or at least significant elements within it, has, in the last forty or so years, moved with remarkable ease from fifties complacency to sixties "activism" to seventies narcissism to the eighties retreat to "family values" and the insularity that phrase evokes. What many people admire about Fonda is precisely her ability to anticipate, critique, and at the same time benefit from the shifting tides of American life.

In any event, neither John Wayne nor Jane Fonda suffered unduly for their Vietnam activities even from those who might be expected to be the most unforgiving. In Fonda's case, of course, bitter memories undeniably lingered, lying dormant for a time and then, unexpectedly, coming alive with explosive force. While her career in the seventies and eighties suffered no diminution and, indeed, flourished, the Reagan-era revisionist interpretation of the Vietnam War eventually reignited hostility toward "Hanoi Jane." What had been virtually forgotten by the end of the seventies came back with a vengeance by the end of the eighties. Vietnam films intent on justifying the war—*Rambo* (1985), *Hamburger Hill* (1987), *Hanoi Hilton* (1987), and the like—portrayed antiwar protest of any kind as little more than collaboration with the enemy. In such an atmosphere, Fonda's trip to Hanoi becomes a particularly heinous act. *Hanoi Hilton* specifically includes a character based on Fonda without mentioning her by name; the portrait is in every way bitterly unflattering. In real life, Fonda faced much the same kind of villification when she attempted to make a film in Waterbury, Connecticut, and Holyoke, Massachusetts, during the summer of 1988. Her subsequent televised "apology" for going to Hanoi, carefully worded ("That was a thoughtless and careless thing to have done"), did not entirely calm the troubled waters. In spite of all of this, however, her popular appeal and fame have only increased over the years. Her exercise videos, which sell millions of copies at $39.95 each, have made her "a cultural icon of the fitness movement and the unifying figure of its mythology";[21] they demonstrate as well as anything the power of her image, at least among upper-middle-class and upper-class consumers. John Wayne, in his final years, was recognized for the complex performer and sometime consummate actor he was. Even intellectual film critics and reviewers of a liberal or a progressive bent came to regard him with a mixture of awe, respect, and even affection.

Jane Fonda remains a potent cultural icon in part because she seems to hold together, however tenuously, a bundle of contradictory or at least incompatible social and cultural symbols. Like John Wayne but unlike, say, her own father, Jane Fonda presents an image at once hard and soft, concrete and fuzzy, clear-cut and ambiguous. In *Letter to Jane*, Godard and Gorin at one point juxtapose the news photo of Fonda in Hanoi with a still of John Wayne. Their point is that the facial expression in each case is the same. "Formed and deformed by the Hollywood school of Stanislavskian show-biz," it is an expression of an expression, an "expression that says it knows a lot about things, but says no more and no less." As images for the Vietnam era, Wayne and Fonda ironically end up signifying the same thing: an Americanness made up partly of strength and courage and partly of self-indulgence, partly of deep-seated ethical and moral values and partly of surface decoration, partly of an impulse to do good and partly of a desire for self-aggrandizement. America's daughter and America's father—Molly Haskell's "gentle patriarch"[22]—ultimately merge their differences in the mythopoetic melting pot of American popular culture. Just as, to paraphrase Michael Herr, we've all been to Vietnam, so we all carry Jane Fonda and John Wayne within us, twin symbols of a conflict that, impossible either to resolve or to forget, continues to haunt our collective imagination.

Notes

1. Philip Caputo, *A Rumor of War* (New York: Ballantine, 1977) 100.
2. Ibid. 14.
3. Michael Herr, *Dispatches* (New York: Alfred A. Knopf, 1977) 67–68.
4. Ibid. 200–201.
5. Thomas Doherty discusses some aspects of this intertextuality, and

in particular the way John Wayne figures in *Full Metal Jacket* and other texts, in his essay "Full Metal Genre: Kubrick's Vietnam Combat Movie," *Film Quarterly* 42.2 (1988–89): 24–30.

6. Gustav Hasford, *The Short-Timers* (New York: Bantam, 1980) 4.

7. Herr, *Dispatches* 48.

8. See Tobey C. Herzog's "John Wayne in a Modern Heart of Darkness: The American Soldier in Vietnam" in *Search and Clear: Critical Responses to Selected Literature and Films of the Vietnam War*, ed. William J. Searle (Bowling Green, Ohio: Bowling Green State University Popular Press, 1988). Herzog's essay, which came to my attention after my argument was in its near-final form, parallels and supports my discussion of the function of Wayne's persona in Vietnam literature and films.

9. Caputo, *A Rumor of War* 8.

10. Ron Kovic, *Born on the Fourth of July* (New York: McGraw-Hill, 1976) 44.

11. Herr, *Dispatches* 19.

12. For a powerful and generally negative assessment of Fonda as a feminist, see Barbara Seidman, " 'The Lady Doth Protest Too Much, Methinks': Jane Fonda, Feminism, and Hollywood," *Women and Film* 4 (1988): 186–230.

13. Quoted in Fred Lawrence Guiles, *Jane Fonda: The Actress in Her Time* (Garden City, N.Y.: Doubleday, 1982) 208.

14. *Unauthorized Biography: Jane Fonda*, prod. and narr. Barbara Howar (WWOR-TV, New York, 24 October 1988).

15. So Colin MacCabe notes: "*Letter to Jane* is both a very interesting and, often, a very objectionable film. Its greatest problem, which it attempts to avoid by mentioning, is that it is a criticism by two men of the way that a woman has chosen to use her image politically" (*Godard: Images, Sounds, Politics* [Bloomington: Indiana University Press, 1980] 72–73).

16. Hasford, *The Short-Timers* 38.

17. Herr, *Dispatches* 200.

18. Quoted in Donald Shepherd and Robert Slatzer, with Dave Grayson, *Duke: The Life and Times of John Wayne* (Garden City, N.Y.: Doubleday, 1985) 230.

19. According to Shepherd et al., it has sometimes been claimed that Wayne tried to enlist but was rejected (so James Arness reports in a recent PBS documentary); they note, however, that Wayne himself never made such a claim. Even during World War II, Wayne's cinematic heroism could be an object of derision. William Manchester, who was gravely wounded

during the Okinawa landing, recalls an incident that took place while he was recuperating at the Aiea Heights Naval Hospital in Hawaii. One evening, a personal appearance by a special guest was announced, and all of the wounded men who could move or be carried went to the hospital theater. The "special guest" turned out to be John Wayne, dressed in a cowboy outfit. He was roundly booed off the stage by the wounded GIs ("The Bloodiest Battle of All," *New York Times Magazine*, 14 June 1987: 84).

20. Ron Rosenbaum, "Dangerous Jane," *Vanity Fair* 51.11 (1988): 208.

21. Elizabeth Kagan and Margaret Morse, "The Body Electronic: Aerobic Exercise on Video—Women's Search for Empowerment and Self-Transformation," *Drama Review* 32.4 (1988): 167.

22. Molly Haskell, "Comments on John Wayne," *Film Heritage* 10.4 (1975): 34.

Cynthia J. Fuchs

"All the Animals Come Out at Night"
Vietnam Meets *Noir* in *Taxi Driver*

The night of madness is thus limitless; what might have
been supposed to be man's violent nature was only the infinity of non-nature.
— MICHEL FOUCAULT

Yes, it's a nightmare. Yes.
— MARTIN SCORSESE

It was really neat, though. It was red sugary stuff. And they
used Styrofoam for bones. And a pump to make the blood
gush out of a man's arm after his hand was shot off.
— JODIE FOSTER

CHAPTER 2 Vietnam, as Michael Herr notes in the
closing lines of *Dispatches*, has become an inescapable traumatic
experience for all Americans, no matter where they were during the
war. "And no moves left for me at all," he writes, "but to write down
some few last words and make the dispersion, Vietnam, Vietnam,
Vietnam, we've all been there."[1] This lyrical paean brings the war
home in the form of simultaneous lament and indictment: those who
have "been there" share in the suffering and bear responsibility for
the continuing experience called Vietnam.

Throughout *Dispatches*, Herr emphasizes the war's elusiveness,
the massive emotional, political, and ideological shock waves that
Vietnam sent coursing through the moral ground on which America
had erected its righteous self-image. Today this ground remains in
continual "dispersion," as the war and the texts it continues to
produce are reread and rewritten. The unrepresentable "otherness"
of the experience, the pain of war that has, in Elaine Scarry's words,
resisted "objectification in language," has become part of a reevaluation of this country's relation to its recent history.[2]

Paul Schrader and Martin Scorsese's *Taxi Driver,* released in 1976, the year after the American withdrawal from Saigon, explores these complex relations by "bringing the war home," specifically by engaging the war's unrepresentability.[3] Unlike subsequent cinematic representations of the war—*First Blood* (1982) and *Rambo* (1985), which refight a would-have-been war, or *Apocalypse Now* (1979), *The Deer Hunter* (1978), and *Platoon* (1986), which represent and mythologize the "real" war—*Taxi Driver* reveals the disordering effects and the disordered foundations of Vietnam, representing not the war, but its dispersion. And unlike *Casualties of War* (1989) or *Born on the Fourth of July* (1989), which cast returning American veterans as repentant victims, struggling to make peace with themselves at last, *Taxi Driver* is at once politically astute and locked in its own overdetermined time warp. It takes aim not at specific targets (an administration or a policy) but at a cycle of madness based in self-involvement. Travis Bickle is a product of his time.[4]

At first glance, *Taxi Driver's* reference to the Vietnam War appears slight and neatly classifiable. Indeed, as Robert Ray points out, "In many ways, *Taxi Driver* allegorized the American experience in Vietnam: detached isolationism followed by violent, and ultimately ineffective, intervention."[5] I suggest that beyond this, the film examines ideological, emotional, and moral conflicts, concurrent with the broad political situation Ray delineates, specifically by locating the experience of the war—the violence, the frustration, the madness—within an American context. *Taxi Driver's* revisionary use of *film noir* stylistics (such as shadows, neon, and the voice-over narration) and thematic concerns (the duplicitous woman, the inadvertent hero, the confusion of a world out of balance) complements its Vietnam context. For Travis Bickle (Robert De Niro), former member of the King Kong Company, the World he has come back to is indescribably out of balance, but it also exists in a continuum of betrayal and violence. The correlation between the war and this essentially American style[6] underlines the cultural mechanisms that made Vietnam possible, unwinnable, and even inevitable.[7]

These mechanisms are explored through the film's form and narrative, which establish connections among violence, difference, and representation, and which simultaneously and constantly unravel those connections. That is, the film relates difference to violence (how violence determines difference and vice versa) and at the same time exposes the cultural construction of the relation by and in representation.[8] Representational violence, or the assault on audience expectations, becomes a pervasive metaphor for the violence by which Travis orders his world.

Travis's contempt for those whom he perceives as different from himself (figured by gender and race) leads to a paradox: while immersed in the nightscape he reviles ("I'll go anytime, anywhere"), he insists on its absolute "otherness." Conflating *noir*'s stylistic disorientations with the moral chaos of the Vietnam era, the film probes the unrepresentability of difference within Travis's skewed vision. Travis defines himself by opposition to the Other as enemy (through his use of derogatory obscenities, for example), and we are limited to his perceptions; hence, his increasing similarity to that corrupt Other becomes the film's inability to contain its difference from itself.

Specifically, Travis's obsession with the "filth" represented by prostitution as a sign of "otherness" leads to the text's formal and narrative rupture. The relation between sex and violence is based in the violation of the commodified body in a degenerate cultural market. Whether sold for cash (to a john) or for ideology (to the military), the body is betrayed and defiled. Paralleling the film's narrative concern with such transgression is the continual rupture of the textual body (through nondiegetic voice-over, jump cuts, and time lapses), leading to what several viewers have identified as a violent "sexual" climax.[9] This disruption in character and text figures both "man's violent nature" and its dispersion as the "infinity of non-nature": Travis's vision reshapes New York as a war zone, a tumult of Otherness.

This Otherness, however, shifts. During the Vietnam era, unstable terms of difference subverted any simple opposition between "us" and "them," or "us" and "gooks." In *Taxi Driver*, this inconstant Other is recuperated in the cityscape as mindscape, where gender and race delineate boundaries of self. Whether he describes his enemies using sexual language ("you fuckers, you screwheads") or by race ("Some won't even take spooks," he says, "but it don't make no difference to me"), Travis underlines the difference it *does* make. But slowly that difference is made indistinct from external madness. As the "New Guy," rookie cabbie Travis keeps his distance, observing the night; but increasingly he is absorbed into the chaos of the streets, integrating the violence he observes.

Taxi Driver opens with a shot that simultaneously establishes and dislocates its time and place: a taxicab drifts through the hellish steam of New York at night. We recognize the city and the mood of foreboding, but, as Robert Kolker notes, this "credits sequence [is] outside the narrative proper—out of time, a kind of perpetual state of mind that diffuses itself over the film."[10] This state of mind (reinscribed through the diary entries/voice-over and subjective camerawork) remains unfixed and deconstructs the film's linear narrative by referring obsessively to itself out of time.

The continual textual disruption (of cause and effect, of character motivation) led many of *Taxi Driver*'s reviewers to criticize its incoherence and that of its protagonist.[11] But what Andrew Sarris calls the "disorder in the narrative" seems to me crucial to the film's relationship to its era. Sarris's list of possible origins is precisely the cultural expanse from which the character has emerged: "*Taxi Driver* made very little sense to me. Robert De Niro's Travis Bickle baffles me. Where does he come from? He is part Arthur Bremer, part Manson, part Lancelot, part street slob, part cornball, part gun-freak, part Middle America, part alienated Amerika, and all along he is Robert De Niro."[12] Similarly, Vincent Canby calls Travis a "Vietnam vet who displays for us all of the classic symptoms of a first-class psychotic."[13] Denying that the film's subjective viewpoint is connected in any way to its representation of its social milieu, Canby asserts that "where Scorsese and Schrader go wrong in *Taxi Driver* is in attempting to make Travis Bickle in some way politically and socially significant. But he's not. He's an aberration."[14]

An "aberration" adrift in an aberrant environment, Travis's

"significance" lies in his internalized collapse of political, social, moral, and representational boundaries. His confusion mirrors the external world, where language does not signify, where representations float without referents. One of the film's critical metaphors is Palantine's campaign slogan. The candidate's eyes look down from his presidential campaign poster onto the quotation beneath, which reads, "We *are* the people." The ambiguous pronoun "we" (as opposed to the exclusive group named by the defective campaign buttons that say "*We* are the people") allows a play of meaning, a signifier determined by its speaker (or listener). The campaign aims, of course, to capitalize on this representative transience: the reader/viewer assumes membership and pledges a vote for "us." But how are "we" defined? Against those who *are not* the people? As language disperses, meaning becomes unfixed and binary determinations of difference also dissolve.

In part, as Herr demonstrates, the loss of faith in representation is a function of the overwhelming disparity between the war's surreal violence and its too-real results.

After a year I felt so plugged in to all the stories and the images and the fear that even the dead started telling stories, you'd hear them out of a remote but accessible space where there were no ideas, no emotions, no facts, no proper language, only clean information.[15]

A similar kind of unmediated information bombards Travis as he drives his taxi. But this information is not "real clean" (as Travis describes his conscience and his driving record to the cab-company owner), but confusing filth. He does not absorb the information; he defines himself against it, whatever it is. "All the animals come out at night," he says, "whores, scum, pussies, buggers, queens, fairies, dopers, junkies." Deviance is in effect created in his choice of words, in representation: while we watch from behind the windshield with Travis, the lighting lurid and the camera roving, his list of corruption refers to no one in particular, yet to everyone we see.

The ferocious ambiguity of Travis's language—general obscenities and broad abstractions—coincides with the unrepresentability of the war, which Travis never mentions.[16] "I don't know," he tells Wizard (Peter Boyle), "I got some bad ideas in my head." These "ideas" are not in themselves indicative of Travis's specific emotional state (except that they are "bad"); his stumbling language does not refer to the world nor does it express his pain's "felt-characteristics."[17] Caught in a limbo of unrepresentability, Travis cannot name the action: "I just wanna go out and really . . . really do something." Ironically, Wizard's response insinuates the disintegration of self that Travis fears: to "do something," even if undefined, defines one: "You do a thing and that's what you are. You got no choice anyway. We're all fucked, more or less, y'know."

"More or less," Travis understands this: ready for the assassination, he writes, "Now I see clearly my whole life has pointed in one direction. I see that now. There never has been any choice for me." Paradoxically, his "clear" vision determines his lack of choice; his self-definition depends on his relation to an external Other. Travis names himself in opposition to his enemies, but this same representational gesture links him to them.[18] Increasingly trapped in a relentlessly self-referential subjectivity, Travis's difference from the Other becomes unrepresentable as that Other is internal(ized). Sleepless, he prowls his own relentless nightmare.

The depiction of that nightmare both depends on and subverts its Otherness. The textual construction of Travis's madness is based on his voice-over, which recuperates what Foucault calls the "language of unreason," which is not a language.[19] Examining the social and linguistic construction of insanity by its opposition to sanity, Foucault suggests that madness is itself unspeakable. And if madness is silence or absence, then "the paradox of this *nothing* is to manifest itself, to explode in signs, in words, in gestures. For madness, if it is nothing, can manifest itself only by departing from itself, by assuming an appearance in the order of reason and thus become the contrary of itself."[20] Travis's Otherness is made manifest specifically by his inability to articulate it; his rampant metaphorical "silence" is the text's representation of madness. The voice-over structure both organizes and undermines our understanding of his madness, much as the language of the war mediated its (mis)representation.[21] The unspeakable is paradoxically made coherent as spoken incoherence.

In *Taxi Driver* the war's silence (its unrepresentability) emerges in the film's self-disruptive structure.[22] Offering no certain explanations for Travis's vision, no wartime memories, the film locates the crisis in *the World* as Travis perceives and absorbs it: New York seethes with heat and chaos. As Lenny Rubenstein observes, "We do not know how long Travis has been on the verge of lunacy. We learn nothing of his experience in Vietnam with the King Kong Company whose emblem adorns the military jacket he wears."[23] Instead, we only see Travis see himself—surrounded by the enemy. Here, as in other *films noirs*, the brutal night reigns supreme.

Travis's New York night still belongs to an objectified Charlie. And here, as in Vietnam, sex and violence are continuous.[24] Travis writes, "Each night when I return the cab to the garage I have to clean the come off the back seat. Some nights I clean off the blood." Yet while he condemns the couples he sees on the street or in the back of his cab, Travis yearns to "become a person like other people." His radical decentering into violence begins with his attempt to derail his "morbid self-attention" through association with the self-threatening Other, named and mastered, as it was in Vietnam, through the mythology of mission.[25]

The desire for meaning—a mission—proves Travis's undoing. His sense of control is rampantly false, constructed by media and language ("We *are* the people"). "All my life needed," he says, "was a sense of someplace to go." And then we see Betsy, as she "appear[s] like an angel," walking in slow motion above the crowd, dressed in white. Imagining that "they cannot touch her," Travis insulates Betsy; he defines her by her Otherness, her whiteness, her purity. Yet the paradox he establishes here cannot be sustained, even within the logic of his madness. Even as he describes her, she shuts the door, disappearing from view.

When he declares "them" Other, Travis erects a "we" ("we *are* the people"). Separating Betsy from the "filth," Travis tries to make her difference his. He assumes that Betsy is followed by the same dark night that plagues him. "You're a lonely person," he tells her, "and all this [his hand passes over her desk at the Palantine head-quarters] means nothing." In reading Betsy's desk as an indication of her loneliness, as meaning "nothing," of course Travis imbues it with his meaning, denies her difference. He interprets Betsy according to his need for a rescue mission, making her an objective of his subjective search for meaning by her similarity to himself.[26] The film's construction of this quest as both noble and debased, altruistic and self-centered, renders Travis's motive obscure and our relation to it problematic.[27] We perceive his social awkwardness (as when they talk at cross-purposes in the coffee shop, separated by single shots) and his madness (when he storms her office after her rejection, the camera moves with him), but she is represented according to his vision.[28] She remains a cipher by which to interpret Travis.

As such, she is rendered an object: the woman as "penetrable body," vulnerable to violation.[29] The act of doing "something," the mission, becomes its own means and end (a sense of mission not unlike the war of attrition in Vietnam).[30] The correlation between Betsy and Iris (Jodie Foster), based in their analogous roles as victims/prostitutes, makes them interchangeable as Travis's objects-in-distress.[31] Originally, Travis identifies Betsy and Iris differently (the angel and the whore), establishing a typically *noir* distinction between chaste and corrupt objects in a male subjective text.[32] But the film subverts these conventions, not by inverting them or by creating another "whore with a heart of gold," but by exposing the construction of the opposition as Travis's own. The women are both part of the expansive Otherness that terrifies Travis. Both are, at last, untouchable and unfathomable objectives. Both are, at last, two more impossible missions.[33]

The key to the connection Travis draws between these missions is the commodified and (thus) violated body. His decision to assassinate Palantine is simultaneously his extreme retaliation against Betsy's rejection and the fulfillment of his self-assigned mission to save her. Experienced in playing the pimp for his fares (he drives his cab "anytime, anywhere," providing the means for a variety of sexual encounters), Travis now reimagines himself as commando-rescuer.

The film underlines the irony of his sense of control over circumstances by demonstrating Travis's growing lack of self-control. Escalating the (self-)expressionist stakes of conventional *noir*, Travis's condition accentuates the absolute loss of self in a postmodern world, one in which balance is irrecoverable. The madness around him mirrors and shapes his own. Travis resembles the protagonist of what Schrader calls *noir*'s "third phase," when "the *noir* hero, seemingly under the weight of ten years of despair, started to go bananas." While the films of this phase are "painfully self-aware," their characters remain, for the most part, in the dark.[34]

Much like the psychologically disintegrating detective Dave Bannion (Glenn Ford) of *The Big Heat* (1953), Travis resorts to unlawful violence to battle corruption. But unlike Bannion, Travis is less motivated by self-righteous vengeance than by a compulsion toward self-destruction. Colin Westerbeck suggests that "Travis achieves the moral authority of the good [*noir*] hero not in spite of having been the bad hero, but *because* of having been him. Far from depriving one of such authority, turning into a psychopath now becomes a way to attain it."[35] But Travis has no moral grounding; it is perhaps part of the legacy of Vietnam that his suicidal mission can be reclaimed in the media as heroism. Language subsumes meaning; cultural constructions subvert intention.

Yet the film makes Travis's self-destructive impulses clear. The third encounters with Betsy and Iris parallel each other: the movie date with Betsy and the "rescue" of Iris are both versions of Travis's drive to suicidal redemption, hinging on violations of women's bodies. Going to the pornographic theater (a cultural sign of such violation) seals the difference between Travis and Betsy, even as he attempts to locate them on the same side of a scopic economy (as voyeurs). But the episode only exposes their essential gender- and class-based differences. Despite Travis's protest that "all kinds of couples" go to see the films, Betsy's self-righteous departure allows no excuses (though the evening is punctuated with Travis's confessions of cultural ignorance as he tries to keep up with her: "I don't really follow music . . . I don't know much about movies").[36]

Because his world is built on objectification, Travis has no resources to understand Betsy's extremely subjective anger. He cannot imagine her place. His violent reaction to Betsy's betrayal is a reaction to all betrayals of his faith in binary order—by his government, his language, and his military training.[37] So, he redefines her difference from himself by her sameness with the world: "I realize now how much she is just like all the others, cold and distant. Many people are like that. Women, for sure. It's like a union." That Travis attempts to bust this union with violence indicates his return to self, a self he can contain by rote training, a body he can condition into obedience. Yet, as he disciplines his body, Travis's diary entries become more obsessive, more incoherent and fragmented ("You're . . . only . . . as . . . healthy . . . as . . . you . . . feel"). His return to self is in fact figured in physical pain associated with bankrupt sexuality; while his apartment fills with the stench of flowers rejected by Betsy, he notes in his diary, "I think I've got stomach cancer."[38]

Travis's self-imposed exile from "all the others" is marked by a violent break in the text. The scene immediately following Betsy's abandonment features Martin Scorsese's appearance as the "pretty sick" fare who watches his wife from Travis's cab. This is the longest sequence devoted to any of Travis's fares. As the film's turning point (prior to Travis's late recognition of the transition: "Then suddenly, there is a change"), the scene is remarkable for its representation of violence in language and for its specific reference to the intersection of race and gender as the ultimate focus of Travis's physical violence; here the female body coincides with the black body as representation of the visible site of difference.

The location of debased Otherness is "a nigger's" apartment. The wife Travis watches is doubly damned. From the dark back seat of the taxi, Scorsese directs the action—"Don't write. Put the thing down. Just sit"—and describes his violent plan.

> I'm gonna kill her. I'm gonna kill her with a .44 Magnum pistol. . . . Did you ever see what a .44 Magnum pistol could do to a woman's face? It'd fucking destroy it. It'd just blow it right apart. That's what it would do to her face. Did you ever see what it can do to a woman's pussy? That's what you should see.

During this part of Scorsese's speech, the camera remains focused on Travis, who watches the woman in the window, transfixed. After the repetitive rhythms of body parts as isolated targets degrade the female Other to nonhuman status by dismemberment, the camera angle changes to show the woman's body in silhouette, segmented by the window panes. The image is potent: that is what we should see.

Travis's gaze becomes more and more violent, yet turned more toward himself. He shoots into the camera at the firing range; then the film cuts to show him pointing his finger, as if it were a gun, at the screen of a porn theater. While the movie's soundtrack builds to its climax ("It's getting harder and harder. It's throbbing now"), Travis points his gun at the screen.[39] Lest this allusion be missed, his voice-over overlaps ("The idea had been growing in my brain for some time"), linking his increasing madness not simply to sexual frustration but to his growing sense of difference from the world he watches, a world defined by visibly Other and penetrable bodies.[40] The next scene shows Travis firing at the Palantine poster in his room, then turning to fire at the mirror. His own body is becoming part of the Otherness of the world. In reconstructing his body to destroy the corrupt social body, he erects a boundary between himself and the Other, even as that definition collapses internally.

This collapse is reflected in the breakdown of the body of the film, which occurs simultaneously with his physical buildup: the training is represented in short, abrupt scenes and images become even more limited to Travis's enclosed world. We see him alone in his room, made small in an internal frame at the shooting gallery, more and more resembling the diseased world he despises. His body becomes his vehicle of alienation; he appears less often in the cab and more often immobile. "Too much abuse has gone on for too long. . . . No more destroyers of my body," he intones, as we watch him do pull-ups and push-ups, polish his boots, practice shooting his multiple guns. Travis's anger is directed at himself as Other, and we, in league with his thoughts throughout, represent that Other/self: we see the words, "Here is," and then he fires a pistol at the camera.

He tests himself by holding his hand, like G. Gordon Liddy,

over a flame—he embraces pain. This conditioning of the body is accompanied by his decreasing attention to the diary. As he descends deeper into his mission, his narration drops off. As Scarry notes, "Physical pain—to invoke what is at this moment its single most familiar attribute—is language-destroying."[41] Breaking off communication, he no longer appears watching fares in the rearview mirror; now he imposes a watchful distance from himself. Facing off with the mirror in his apartment, weapons at hand, he questions himself (which is us; we are that mirror image and he reflects us). "You talkin' to me?" he asks. "Well I'm the only one here." Threatening and threatened by himself, Travis here demonstrates the breakdown of the visible difference that once defined him. He now looks at the enemy who is the same.

This collapse into self is reflected in the film's metaphorical play of cowboys and Indians and the representation of African Americans; both representations reach a kind of climax in Travis's final encounter with Iris. Our look at African Americans throughout the film is filtered through Travis's acculturated distrust: sitting with the other cabbies discussing Harlem as "fuckin' Mau-Mau Land," the camera reveals his look at ominous black pimps in the next booth; just after he first sees Iris in his cab, a group of black youths assault his cab with garbage. As Travis feels his life closing in on him, the blacks appear more frequently, and in more violent circumstances. While Travis follows Iris down the street a black man walks by her in the opposite direction, yelling, "I'll kill her. I'll kill her." The violence is also directed at blacks. When Travis shoots the stickup man at a neighborhood grocery store, the owner's vicious beating of the sprawled and bloody body (whether alive or not) seems almost more brutal than the shooting itself.

The conflation of the visibly different body with the paradoxical violation and recovery of self becomes most acute with the introduction of Sport (Harvey Keitel), Iris's pimp and Travis's enemy as alter ego. The difference between the two men is established using conventional "us" and "them" iconography, based in a culturally prescribed racism (again, a primary cause and referent for the Vietnam War). Travis is the inarticulate cowboy and Sport is the fast-bargaining Indian (an apparatus of difference that is especially pertinent to the description of Vietnam as "Indian Country"). Seeing that Travis's boots are genuine (he hides no gun in his sock), Sport scoffs at the apparently harmless john, "Shit, you're a real cowboy. That's nice, man." Their difference seems apparent by their appearances: Sport is a mass of uncontainable energy; Travis seems nearly inert. For Travis, their difference is overdetermined by Sport's sales pitch: "She'll suck your cock so hard she'll make it explode, man. But no rough stuff. . . . Catch ya later, copper."

In Travis's view, this denigration of Iris to "a little piece of chicken" (his recollection, curiously not said by Sport as we hear him), marks him as the moral "copper" to Sport's corruption, according to Travis's binary ethical structure. But even this distinction collapses with Travis's representation of what Schrader calls the *noir* hero's "personal disintegration" within a mad world. As Schrader observes of late (1950s) *noir*, "The inhumanity and meaninglessness of the hero are small matters in a world in which The Bomb has the final say";[42] after Vietnam, the obvious fact that the power to drop that Bomb is granted to dishonest, insincere world leaders is almost too much to bear.[43]

For Travis, to annihilate the self seems an appropriate recourse. He conceives his mission as restorative: to clean the "sewer" of New York, to flush all the filth "right down the fucking toilet" (at whatever cost, as in, "We had to destroy the village in order to save it"). Clearly, the ideological pimp Palantine is unable to effect those "radical changes" he mentions while riding in Travis's cab. At an early political rally, we watch Travis in dark glasses, sitting motionless in his cab, while we hear Palantine's speech dispersing the ubiquitous, self-referential "we" over all potential voters: "We are the people. We suffered. We were there. We the people suffered in Vietnam. We still suffer."

The location of suffering has ostensibly changed (to New York), but in *Taxi Driver*, as Palantine's offscreen voice describes Columbus Circle, "We meet at a crossroads in history." The camera, which has been slowly panning the dais and audience, finds Travis's lower body and abruptly moves up to reveal him in his Mohawk haircut, the visual sign of his madness and consummate difference from the crowd around him. And indeed, Sport and Travis will meet at this self-reflexive crossroads-as-mirror, where the cowboys look like Indians, where Americans were killing themselves as well as others in Vietnam, where difference is made similarity. The sudden vision of Travis thus reincarnated is intended to shock us, to indicate his complete depravity in an instant. As well, Ray observes that at this point *"Taxi Driver* has implicated the audience in any resulting violence, for the audience has willed this hero and trusted his impulses."[44]

The heroic rescue becomes Travis's mission only when the assassination fails, yet the two actions share the same objective: to purify polluted streets, to exorcise "bad ideas."[45] Travis's need for redemptive duty is left over from the marines; he needs a mission to make existence tolerable (just so, without a sense of mission, Vietnam was impossible for even the U.S. government to sustain). Again undertaking a combat mission, Travis is able at last to embrace the full deployment and destruction of his body. Scarry describes the soldier's dissociation of self from (Other) body during war.

> What in killing he does is to wrench around his most fundamental sanctions about how within civilization (and his particular civilization, his country) another embodied person can be touched; he divests himself of civilization, decivilizes himself, reverses not just an "idea" or "belief" but a learned and deeply embodied set of physical impulses and gestures regarding his relation to any other person's body.[46]

So "divested," Travis annihilates the external enemy (Sport, the john, the building owner) and confronts himself as enemy, reversing as well his relation to his own body (which by the end of the shooting resembles the bloody bodies around him). With his final gesture (pointing his bloody finger at his head) Travis disembodies himself. His failure is finally his inability to kill himself, his inability to rid himself of the "bad ideas in [his] head."[47]

But, as Herr reminds us:

> A lot of what people called courage was only undifferentiated
> energy cut loose by the intensity of the moment, mind loss
> that sent the actor on an incredible run; if he survived it he
> had the chance later to decide whether he'd really been brave
> or just overcome with life, even ecstasy.[48]

The horrific final irony is the city's reward for Travis's madness, his
"ecstasy" of survival, renamed "courage." Travis is reclaimed by
the very culture he has rejected, made the same as what he has
called different. (Even Betsy's interest is renewed after the shoot-
out: reappearing as a disembodied head in Travis's rearview mirror,
she says, "I read about you in the papers.") But just as the headlines
designate Travis's madness as heroism, so the film explodes the
myth of heroism by contextualizing it within cultural madness.[49]
But how does context (re)create moral boundaries? "War is excep-
tional in human experience," writes Scarry, "for sanctioning the act
of killing, the act that all nations regard in peacetime as 'criminal.'"[50] Clearly, madness is relative. The film's resolution implicates us along with the diegetic tabloid readers for voyeuristically
participating in Travis's obscene violation of bodies (including his
own).[51]

The sexual charge associated with watching violence is not
news. But *Taxi Driver* simultaneously makes this correlation more
immediate and more remote. Madness may be relative, but so is
representation. The violence here is filtered through the media.
When Scorsese insists on the similarity between the film's representation of the shoot-out and "real life," his explanation suggests the
distance between "reality" and what Herr would call "information."

> Right, the violence has got to be plain, straight, and fast, and
> awkward, awkward and stupid-looking, just the way it would
> happen in real life. It's got to be just as if the Daily News
> photographer went there and shot the whole thing. It's gotta
> be just like a tabloid.[52]

"Real life" is really representation: the *Daily News* version of "real
life" transforms it specifically by representing it. As *films noirs* have

taught us, style defines content. And as the television images of Vietnam remind us, representation shapes meaning.

Appropriately, then, *Taxi Driver* turns back on itself. The images at film's end reflect its beginning. The wounds Travis receives are quickly elided by the text. Within minutes of the shoot-out we see him with a full head of hair, back with his community of cabbies. The wounding, which "is able to open up a source of reality that can give the issue force and holding power," is thus rendered immaterial by the self-conscious text.[53] After the film's extended display of the violent rending of bodies, Travis's wounds are made alarmingly "unreal" by their immediate erasure.

This unreality is precisely the point. For the film absorbs and repels the legacy of Vietnam by its representation of violence and the very violence of that representation. Instead of attempting to represent the extreme violence of experience, the film presents its Otherness as same. And here, finally, is *Taxi Driver*'s most profound understanding of Vietnam: to represent the body is to violate it, and the embodiment of the war can only be its dispersion.

Notes

1. Michael Herr, *Dispatches* (New York: Alfred A. Knopf, 1977) 278.

2. Elaine Scarry, *The Body in Pain: The Making and Unmaking of the World* (New York: Oxford University Press, 1985) 5.

3. All references to dialogue are from the soundtrack of *Taxi Driver* (Columbia Pictures, 1976): produced by Michael Phillips and Julia Phillips; written by Paul Schrader; directed by Martin Scorsese. As Schrader has made clear, the script was written in 1972, emerging out of his personal experience and feelings of alienation at the time.

4. When *Taxi Driver* opened in 1976 (after the publication of the Pentagon Papers and after Watergate), faith in the media and in political rhetoric was at a new low. New York theaters were running *The Story of O*, *Inserts*, *One Flew Over the Cuckoo's Nest*, *Hester Street*, *The Man Who Would Be King*, *Dog Day Afternoon*, *Seven Beauties*, *The Story of Adele H.*, *Barry Lyndon*, and *Snuff* (in which a woman was reputedly dismembered on screen). Alongside a brief interview with Jodie Foster, the *Times* ran "*Snuff* Is Pure Poison," in which *Times* film critic Richard Eder related his experience of walking out of the film: "By the time I'd buttoned my coat,

they were applying a chainsaw to her leg" (*New York Times*, 7 March 1976: B13, B24).

5. Robert B. Ray, *A Certain Tendency of the Hollywood Cinema, 1930–1980* (Princeton, N.J.: Princeton University Press, 1985) 360. Ray reads *Taxi Driver* as a "corrected Right film," revising the formal and narrative strategies of a *Death Wish* or a *Walking Tall* through "stylistic defamiliarizations" and through repudiating the myth of "regeneration through violence" (the phrase is Richard Slotkin's) (ibid. 349–60).

6. Paul Schrader has been one among many to identify *noir* as a style (not a genre), and a particularly American one at that, emerging from a specific time (after World War II) and ethos. See Schrader, "Notes on *Film Noir*," *Film Comment* 8.1 (Spring 1972): 8. See also Foster Hirsch, Film Noir: *The Dark Side of the Screen* (New York: Da Capo, 1983), and E. Ann Kaplan, ed., *Women in* Film Noir (London: British Film Institute, 1980).

7. In considering *Taxi Driver*'s cultural milieu, I do not propose to posit the filmmakers' intentions or to draw direct connections between the film's social and political circumstances and its "inherent" meaning. "Cultural history is too diffuse to allow of clear causal relationships," writes Richard Maltby; "the most it can do is to establish a chain of plausibility, to suggest that one explanation for a particular representation is the existence of a particular set of circumstances." However, Maltby's conclusion that the "relationship between movies and their historical moments . . . remains essentially metaphorical" seems to me to understate the critical and cultural value of this relationship. Rather, I suggest that *Taxi Driver*'s emergence from its "historical moment" both reflects and shapes that moment, and that reading the film as in part a product of the early seventies illuminates its representation of Travis's "madness" (Maltby, "*Film Noir*: The Politics of the Maladjusted Text," *Journal of American Studies* 18.1 [1984]: 50–51).

8. See, for example, Teresa de Lauretis, *Technologies of Gender: Essays on Theory, Film, and Fiction* (Bloomington: Indiana University Press, 1987); Jacques Derrida, *Writing and Difference*, tr. Alan Bass (Chicago: University of Chicago Press, 1978); Hal Foster, ed., *The Anti-Aesthetic: Essays on Postmodern Culture* (Port Townsend, Wash.: Bay Press, 1983); Alice A. Jardine, *Gynesis: Configurations of Women and Modernity* (Ithaca, N.Y.: Cornell University Press, 1985); and Jean-François Lyotard, *The Differend: Phrases in Dispute*, tr. Georges Van Den Abbeele (Minneapolis: University of Minnesota Press, 1988).

9. Pauline Kael writes that it has "an erotic aura. There is practically no sex in it, but no sex can be as disturbing as sex. And that's what it's about: the absence of sex—bottled-up, impacted energy and emotion, with a blood-spattering release. The fact that we experience Travis's need for an explosion viscerally, and that the explosion has the quality of consummation, makes *Taxi Driver* one of the few truly modern horror films. . . . And, given his ascetic loneliness, it's the only real orgasm he can have" (Kael, "Underground Man," *New Yorker*, 9 February 1976: 85–86). See also Frank Rich: "The slaughter sequence of *Taxi Driver* rocks the screen and the audience as an orgasm might—and Scorsese has given the entire film the shape of a sexual act" (Rich, *New York Post*; quoted in *Taxi Driver* advertisement in *New York Times*, 7 March 1976: 15); and Jack Kroll, who describes the film's "positively erotic sense of guilt" (Kroll, "Hackie in Hell," *Newsweek*, 1 March 1976: 82).

10. Robert Phillip Kolker, *A Cinema of Loneliness: Penn, Kubrick, Scorsese, Spielberg, Altman*, 2d ed. (New York: Oxford University Press, 1988) 188. Kolker argues that by this "act of visual displacement . . . the viewer is permitted neither proximity to the central character, sympathy for him, nor comfortable distance" (ibid. 191).

11. Walter Goodman, for example, writes that the film indulges in "the psychopathetic fallacy: if a character is presented as cracked in the first scene of a movie, then anything he does thereafter, no matter how peculiar, is permissible, since, after all, he *is* cracked and cracked people do peculiar things" (Goodman, "On Making Movies about Madness," *New York Times*, 14 March 1976: 13). And John Simon laments: "Even more problematic [than the unexplained cruelty of the city] is the implicit connection: the City is so wicked, so seductively diabolical, this poor bastard becomes unhinged" (Simon, "Hack Work," *New York*, 23 February 1976: 68).

12. Andrew Sarris, "Confessions of a Wishy-Washy Critic," *Village Voice*, 16 February 1976: 146. See also Charles Michener: "Reduced to its baldest terms, this is topical pulp, compounded not simply of the Bremer saga, Vietnam fallout, junior psychology of sexual frustration, and lurid confirmation of Johnny Carson jokes about Fun City, but other recent movies like *Death Wish* and *Nashville*" (Michener, "Review: *Taxi Driver*," *Film Comment* [March–April 1976]: 4). And Kolker: the film is a "portrait of an obsessive, a passive obsessive . . . no analysis of, no reasons given for, his behavior—none, at least, that make a great deal of rational sense" (Kolker, *A Cinema of Loneliness* 194).

13. Vincent Canby, "Scorsese's Disturbing *Taxi Driver*," *New York Times*, 15 February 1976: B15.

14. Ibid.

15. Herr, *Dispatches* 31.

16. Scorsese affirms Travis's combat experience: "He was in the Special Forces, in the marines. You only get that by watching the kind of knife Travis is using at the end. It's called a K-bar. Only Special Forces use it. . . . The haircut, that's very important at the end—because the Special Forces, before they went out on patrol in North Vietnam, they would shave their hair like that" (Richard Goldstein and Mark Jacobson, "'Blood and Guts Turn Me On!': Interview with Martin Scorsese," *Village Voice*, 5 April 1976: 69).

17. Scarry, *The Body in Pain* 17. Schrader describes his own "bad ideas": "An interesting thing about guns, which my shrink pointed out to me and which pertains to *Taxi Driver*, is that all of my suicide fantasies are exactly the same: they all involve shooting myself in the head . . . they're all about blowing those evil thoughts out of my head, and then I'll be all right" (Richard Thompson, "Screen Writer: Interview with Paul Schrader," *Film Comment* [March–April 1976]: 19).

18. Schrader says, "Travis's problem is the same as the existential hero's, that is, should I exist? But Travis doesn't understand that this is his problem, so he focuses it elsewhere: and I think this is a mark of the immaturity and the youngness of our country" (Thompson, "Screen Writer": 10).

19. Michel Foucault, *Madness and Civilization: A History of Insanity in the Age of Reason*, tr. Richard Howard (New York: Vintage, 1988) 262.

20. Ibid. 107.

21. Ibid. 97. See Herr, *Dispatches*, or Gustav Hasford, *The Short-Timers* (New York: Bantam, 1980), for references to "the propaganda machine": "History may be written with blood and iron, but it's printed with ink" (Hasford, *The Short-Timers* 61–62).

22. Derrida argues that Foucault's project collapses in on itself, that the silence of madness is unspeakable from outside itself, can only be stated metaphorically (Derrida, *Writing and Difference* 31–63).

23. Lenny Rubenstein, "Review of *Taxi Driver*," *Cineaste* 17 (1976): 35.

24. See Adrienne Rich, "Vietnam and Sexual Violence," *On Lies, Secrets, and Silence* (New York: W. W. Norton, 1979) 108–16.

25. See also *Apocalypse Now* (Omni Zoetrope, 1979): directed by Fran-

cis Ford Coppola; written by Coppola, John Milius, and Michael Herr. Feeling trapped in Saigon, out of the jungle, Willard says: "I wanted a mission and for my sins they gave me one. Brought it up to me like room service. It was a real choice mission. And when it was over, I'd never want another one."

26. According to Schrader, Travis himself is "not intelligent enough to give [his condition] any real meaning; it only has meaning as we look at it. It has no meaning for him" (Thompson, "Screen Writer": 14).

27. Scorsese has cited the influence of Ford's *The Searchers* (1956), another version of a captivity narrative, in which the female object of the male search is simultaneously reviled and desired. See Kolker, *A Cinema of Loneliness* (especially 198), for a discussion of the specific parodic parallels between *Taxi Driver* and *The Searchers*, including the relations between Sport and Chief Scar (Henry Brandon), Iris and Debbie Edwards (Natalie Wood), and Travis and Ethan Edwards (John Wayne).

28. The film's single privileged moment with Betsy (that Travis cannot hear) parallels and parodies a similar moment with Iris. Betsy and Tom (Albert Brooks) debate the possible (violent) causes for a black newsie's lost fingers, revealing Betsy's perverse interest in violence. Iris, on the other hand, craving affection, is nonetheless similarly linked to violation and exploitation. Despite Michael Bliss's suggestion that Sport "is not detaining [Iris] against her will," the power of this scene lies in its clear, unnerving representation of "seductive" emotional violation—Iris is twelve years old (Bliss, *Michael Cimino and Martin Scorsese* [Metuchen, N.J.: Scarecrow Press, 1985] 93). See also Michael Dempsey: "The movie flirts with the possibility that Iris prefers her street hustler's existence" (Dempsey, "Review," *Film Quarterly* 29.4 [1976]: 38).

29. Foucault, *Madness and Civilization* 150.

30. Schrader says, "It's a purely suicidal mission he's on, so to give greater meaning he fixes on the surrogate father—Betsy's boss, the candidate—then on the other surrogate father—Iris' pimp; he has to destroy that image to break free" (Thompson, "Screen Writer": 14).

31. See, for instance, Colin L. Westerbeck, Jr.: "In the person of Iris' pimp there is even a counterpart for the candidate whom Betsy serves with such devotion" (Westerbeck, "Beauties and the Beast: *Seven Beauties/Taxi Driver*," *Sight and Sound* 45 [1976]: 138). For a reading of prostitution as metaphor, see Jack Kroll: "For Travis, the city is a whore, its streets rankling with pimps, pushers, hookers, and weirdos" (Kroll, "Hackie in Hell": 82). Kolker sees the women as extensions of Travis himself: "each is

not a character as much as a further creation of his aberrant sensibility" (Kolker, *A Cinema of Loneliness* 195).

32. I would hardly agree that Iris is "a demonic reincarnation of the untouchable Betsy" (Westerbeck, "Beauties and the Beast": 137).

33. Iris appears from the first as Travis's self-designated opposite—one of the "animals" that come out at night. He sees her in the street at night; she invades his cab, seemingly desperate to escape and very unlike the aloof Betsy. But the developing relationship with Iris essentially replays the plot with Betsy: Travis meets each at her "office" (Betsy at the campaign headquarters, Iris in her room), then makes a date to go to an innocuous coffee shop. While Travis narrates the details of his date with Betsy ("I had black coffee and apple pie with a slice of melted yellow cheese"), the date with Iris is presented to us directly, signaling Travis's diminishing control over his narrative. Still, the similar structures of the meetings indicate the equivalence of these female objects for Travis. Informing both that he can save them from their respective existences (Betsy's boredom, Iris's corruption), Travis posits himself as mythic hero. Both women remark his unusual intensity: Betsy is intrigued by its strangeness ("I don't believe I've ever met anyone quite like you"), and Iris identifies with it ("I don't know who's weirder, you or me"). And both encounters are filmed as a series of alternating single shots (the one of the woman is over Travis's shoulder), with opening, middle, and closing two-shots, suggesting the distances between Travis and his objectives.

34. Schrader, "Notes on *Film Noir*": 12.

35. Westerbeck, "Beauties and the Beast": 139.

36. Oblivious of social conventions, Travis tentatively calculates his distances by watching what others do. With reference to Wizard's speech on being defined by what you "do," the fact of Travis's watching pornography would seem to distance him from it. The question becomes, when is the voyeur the violator as well?

37. This is contrary to Walter Goodman's comment that "we are thus led to believe that Travis Bickle is driven to murder because he has been rejected in love" (Goodman, "On Making Movies about Madness": 13).

38. This line's reference to Robert Bresson's *Diary of a Country Priest* has been noted by others, including Schrader (Thompson, "Screen Writer": 11).

39. "The movie's pretty damn cunning *mise-en-scène* is a mystical genuflection to The Gun" (Patricia Patterson and Manny Farber, "The Power and the Gory," *Film Comment* [May–June 1976]: 28).

40. Westerbeck sees the change in Travis as definitive rather than continuous: "This substitution of one woman for another is accompanied by a substitution of violence for sex" (Westerbeck, "Beauties and the Beast": 138).

41. Scarry, *The Body in Pain* 19.

42. Schrader, "Notes on *Film Noir*": 12.

43. Kolker writes, "*Taxi Driver* defines its central character not in terms of social problems (though it does suggest these) nor by any *a priori* ideas of noble suffering and transcendent madness, but by the ways the character is perceived and perceives himself and his surroundings. He is the climactic *noir* figure, much more isolated and very much madder than his forbears. No cause is given for him, no understanding allowed; he stands formed by his own loneliness and his own isolation, his actions and reactions explicable only through those actions and reactions" (Kolker, *A Cinema of Loneliness* 186).

44. Ray, *A Certain Tendency* 357.

45. Michael Ryan and Douglas Kellner argue that "the narrative displacement [of targets] suggests that liberal permissiveness and hypocrisy allow crime and vice to flourish" and that "the representational rhetoric of the film . . . is as fragmentary and fetishistic as Travis's moral vision. It touches on surfaces and immediate street-level experiences, but it does not indicate the interconnections of the system that gives rise to the things that repulse Travis and motivate his actions" (Ryan and Kellner, *Camera Politica* [Bloomington: Indiana University Press, 1988] 89). On the contrary, I would suggest that far from being a moral indictment (of whatever ideology), the change in Travis's objective indicates the complete infertility of any ethical ground at this point in history. The film's "fragmentary" vision in fact speaks indirectly but explicitly to the systemic causes for Travis's actions.

46. Scarry, *The Body in Pain* 122.

47. Scorsese says, "He wants to sacrifice himself. . . . Travis goes through every detail, and the only thing is that he blows it, because he doesn't get killed" (Goldstein and Jacobson, " 'Blood and Guts' ": 69).

48. Herr, *Dispatches* 69.

49. Foucault writes, "Madmen remained monsters, that is, etymologically, beings or things to be shown" (Foucault, *Madness and Civilization* 70). Travis is recontained in social text by making him a spectacle on the front page of a newspaper.

50. Scarry, *The Body in Pain* 121.

51. Scarry mentions the "referential instability of the hurt body," by which it is capable of assuming various meanings (ibid.). Many readers have objected to the final violence; Kolker, for example, writes, "Unfortunately, no matter how much is revealed by such analysis, it remains an excrescence, a moment of grotesque excess in an otherwise controlled work" (Kolker, *A Cinema of Loneliness* 203).

52. Goldstein and Jacobson, "'Blood and Guts'": 70. "I like the idea of spurting blood," says Scorsese, "it's really a purification, you know, the fountains of blood" (ibid.: 71).

53. Scarry, *The Body in Pain* 124.

John Hellmann

Vietnam and the Hollywood Genre Film
Inversions of American Mythology in *The Deer Hunter* and *Apocalypse Now*

CHAPTER 3 Since their respective releases in 1978 and 1979, Michael Cimino's *Deer Hunter* and Francis Coppola's *Apocalypse Now* have enjoyed remarkable popular and critical success. But their wide recognition as contemporary cinematic masterpieces has been accompanied by a corresponding controversy regarding their thematic significance and coherence. In addition, none of the commentaries on either of these two epic-scale films about the Vietnam War has searched for possible connections between them. My first purpose in this chapter is to show that each film draws its design from a popular American narrative formula, with the separate formulas providing the basis for the differences between *The Deer Hunter* and *Apocalypse Now* as interpretations of the Vietnam War. I further wish to demonstrate that a link between those formulas establishes an underlying relation between the two films, embodying their essential aesthetic strategy. The allusion of *The Deer Hunter* to *The Deerslayer* signals the presentation of the Viet-

Reprinted, by permission, from *American Quarterly* 34 (Fall 1982): 418–39. Copyright 1982, American Studies Association.

nam War through the popular genre for which Cooper's Leather-stocking Tales are the prototype: the western. Similarly, the opening scenes of *Apocalypse Now* establish the presentation of the symbolic journey of *Heart of Darkness*, itself an adventure/mystery tale, through the specific conventions of the hard-boiled detective formula. This use of popular genres that are related to central American myths of the nineteenth and twentieth centuries connects the two films.

A popular genre, as Stanley Solomon succinctly defines it, is "a certain mythic structure, formed on a core of narrative meaning found in those works that are readily discernible as related and belonging to a group."[1] As the two most enduring genres of American pulp literature, Hollywood movies, and television series up to the time of the Vietnam War, the western and hard-boiled detective formulas provide *The Deer Hunter* and *Apocalypse Now* with a culturally resonant means for interpreting a national experience. And because both formulas are genres of romance, they provide the directors with the "mythic, allegorical, and symbolistic forms" that Richard Chase has traced as the main strategy of the American literary tradition for encountering the contradictions and extreme ranges of American culture and experience, of which Vietnam is a recent and particularly traumatic example.[2]

Despite its decline in recent years, the western has been the major formula story of American popular culture over the last century and a half, establishing its central significance as American myth. Rather than a single pattern of action, the western is defined instead by the influence of its symbolic landscape, a frontier between civilization and wilderness, upon a lonely hero.[3] The confrontation of these basic forces creates a sharply delineated conflict resulting in a variety of stock characters and plot configurations. With its emphasis on the relation of the hero to a frontier landscape, the western deals with the conflict created by the dominant direction of American experience, the flight from community (Europe, the east, restraint, the conscious) into a wilderness (America, the west, freedom, the unconscious).

With *The Deer Hunter*, Cimino, who in the subsequent *Heaven's*

Gate (1980) turned with notorious ambition directly to the genre, presents America's experience in Vietnam through the conventions of the western. While virtually every commentary on the film has pointed out the connection between the protagonists of *The Deerslayer* and *The Deer Hunter,* to my knowledge only David Axeen and Colin Westerbeck, in separate articles, have gone beyond this to the perception that the film is presented in the terms of the form Cooper invented. But instead of exploring the specific elements involved, both use the observation to dismiss the film for being, as Axeen phrases it, "fatally oversimplified."

> The problem with the Cooper-Cimino Western is that it asks us to suspend our knowledge of history, and ignore the realities of social structure. . . . Neither Cooper nor Cimino wants to consider the people and forces really in control. They want us to identify with their heroes as natural aristocrats in still unspoiled wilderness domains.[4]

This familiar criticism leveled at the romantic tradition of American literature identifies the link between that tradition and Cimino's use of the western in *The Deer Hunter.* As Leslie Fiedler has shown, the "low" forms of fantasy literature, particularly those emphasizing violence and terror, have provided symbolic vehicles for the exploration of basic conflicts within the American consciousness.[5] Although the function of the popular western, as John Cawelti has observed, is "to resolve some of the unresolvable contradictions of American values that our major writers have laid bare," the genre has, in the hands of literary practitioners such as Owen Wister and filmmakers such as John Ford, served as a vehicle for sophisticated popular art.[6] In addition, it has also provided an important influence and impetus for the more disturbing explorations of American culture found in Hawthorne, Melville, Twain, Hemingway, and Faulkner. The western formula affords Cimino the strengths of the central national myth in dealing with Vietnam as a collective American trauma. At the same time, *The Deer Hunter* achieves more than a perpetuation of past myth by its understanding of the essence of the myth and its critical examination of it. Unlike *The Green Berets*

(1968), an unthinking use of the western formula, *The Deer Hunter* is a western affected by the shift in landscape. *The Deer Hunter* is an important artistic interpretation of the war precisely because it so fully comprehends the essence of its source and self-consciously explores its meaning in reference to recent American experience.

In *The Deer Hunter* the notions and character of a lonely hero, Michael Vronsky (Robert De Niro), are closely associated with wilderness landscapes, the basis for a structure of violent conflicts and sharp oppositions. The film turns on such characteristic devices of the western as male bonding, the repressed love of the hero for a "good woman," the terror of confrontation with savage denizens of a hostile landscape, dancehall girls, even a "shoot-out" across a table in a crowded gambling room. But even as Cimino thus sets the Vietnam experience squarely in the context of the dominant American historical/mythic tradition, he stands the genre on its head. Assimilating the Vietnam experience into the American consciousness by embodying it in the western formula, Cimino substitutes for its traditional plot motifs (implying the inevitable triumph of white consciousness) a story of traumatic captivity. The accusations of racism made against *The Deer Hunter* are not correct in a political or social sense; Vietnamese are shown among the victims of the Vietcong in the Russian roulette captivity scenes, a black American soldier without arms in the military hospital is one of the most vivid statements against war in the film, and white Americans are prominently shown placing bets in the final Russian roulette scene. But the film does employ the imagery that has obsessed the romantic tradition of American literature from its beginnings with a violent confrontation between the conscious and unconscious, civilization and wilderness, played out in the white imagination as a struggle between light and dark. *The Deer Hunter*, through the western formula, presents Vietnam as yet another historic projection of an internal struggle of white American consciousness, but one where the dream of mastery over nature and the unconscious, or alternatively of benign communion with them, is turned upside down into a nightmare of captivity.

The defining elements of the western are first presented in *The*

Deer Hunter in a timelessly mythic configuration: the hero, Michael, lives on an edge between civilization and nature. The Pennsylvania steel town named Clairton where he was raised represents both European tradition and modern industrialization, and the surrounding mountain forest embodies the original American wilderness. Cimino has written that he explained to his director of photography "at the beginning my feelings about location, my feelings about the importance of size and presence of landscape in a film—and the statement that landscape makes, without anyone realizing it."[7] His mythic intentions are asserted by his representation of a Pennsylvania steel town with a composite of eight separate locations from Cleveland to Pittsburgh, of the Alleghenies with the Cascade Mountains of Washington state, and of the deer with a stag imported from a wildlife preserve in New Jersey—representations that sacrifice authentic setting for a more powerfully symbolic landscape.[8]

The deer hunter himself has the salient traits embodied in his Cooper prototype and in virtually every western hero to follow. Living on the outer edge of the town in a trailer, he is a part of the community, and yet is clearly separated from it by his alienation from its corruption and by his strict adherence to a personal code closely associated with the uncorrupted wilderness and its original inhabitants. For example, he despises all of his friends except Nick (Christopher Walken) for their inability to understand the ritualistic importance of killing a deer with "one shot." And at the wedding reception he responds to whispers from Stanley (John Cazale) about the actual father of the pregnant bride's unborn child by running down the street stripping off his clothes, a compulsive flight from social corruption. Finding little relevance in the old European traditions of the community, Michael has, like his literary ancestor, turned to nature. In the opening sequence he perplexes his companions by insisting that they go on a hunt that night because the "sun dogs" he sees in the sky are an old Indian sign of "a blessing on the hunters sent by the Great Wolf to his children."[9] And in strong contrast to his detachment from the elaborate rituals of the Russian Orthodox wedding, which he knows are mocked by the pregnancy of the bride, he is intensely involved in the proper preparation, practice, and culmination of the hunt. Finally, the taunts of Stanley that Michael does not take advantage of opportunities with women clearly set Michael in the tradition of the celibate western hero.

Michael is also characterized as separated from his community by the more disturbing traits of the western hero. Suggestively, the characters regard Michael with both respectful awe and uneasy perplexity, finding his omen reading crazy and his hunting prowess extraordinary. From the viewer's perspective also, Michael's characteristics have contradictory significance. His need to prove self-reliant results in reckless activity, as in the scene in which he risks his own and his friends' lives by passing a truck on the inside merely on a casual bet. And his deer hunting, attractive for its skill and sense of value, results in the image of a gutted deer sprawled across his old Cadillac's hood as it speeds down the mountain road to drunken singing. Even Michael's distaste for the practice and consequences of sexual promiscuity is set off against his repressed passion for Nick's girlfriend (Meryl Streep), revealed in his chivalrous courting of her during the wedding reception. Indeed, the narcissistic, promiscuous, and pistol-flashing Stanley, who is Michael's antagonist, is also the dark reflection of Michael's repressed self, just as the outlaw is the mirror image of the western hero. When Michael derides Stanley's obsession with womanizing and carrying a pistol by holding up a bullet and saying "*this* is *this*, this isn't something else," his insistence on the bullet's lack of symbolic significance, while he himself cradles his deer-slaying rifle, must be ironic for the viewer. Michael, like the western hero, is a man of extraordinary virtues and resources, which are dangerous unless properly channeled into a role protective of the community.

While the defining elements of the western, the influence of a frontier landscape upon the character and actions of a lonely hero, are those of *The Deer Hunter*, they are conceived in more complex psychosymbolic terms. The western has conventionally projected the conflicts of the American consciousness in black-and-white characters representing good and evil (hero versus outlaw, lawmen versus rustlers, cavalry versus Indians, noble Indian tribes versus threatening tribes) in a single landscape. Cimino uses the same psychosymbolic method and terms, but dramatizes the conflicts within the consciousness of the hero and projects them in a division of both characters *and* landscape. The film develops through the stock oppositions and melodramatic confrontations of the western, but they are presented more explicitly as external images of the protagonist's consciousness, projections of his impulses and thus of the national consciousness he represents as mythic hero. As a result, Vietnam functions in the film as a mirror image of America, a dark landscape turning upside down the benign landscape of Cimino's mythic Alleghenies.

This relation of Michael as western hero to the landscapes and secondary characters of *The Deer Hunter* is brilliantly embodied in the remarkable cut with which Cimino abruptly moves the film from America to Vietnam. One moment Michael, after returning to the bar from the mountain hunt, is in a quiet reverie as he listens with his male friends to melodic piano; the next, surrounded by dead American soldiers, he lies unconscious amid the exploding horrors of Vietnam. The effect of the cut is to have Michael wake up from his dream of the deer hunt to a nightmare inversion of the landscape and its relation to the hero and community. The first third of the film shows Michael in flight to nature and away from a strained, corrupt, but strongly bonded community. But, as Michael recovers consciousness, that flight has taken the viewer into hell. The camera shoots Michael from a downward-looking angle showing him struggling to lift himself from the jungle grass, a sharp contrast to the upward-looking angles of Michael against the sky during the deer hunt. The community, a small Vietnamese village, is surrounded not by snow-capped, pine-forested mountain peaks but by dark jungle foliage. In contrast to the opening shots of the film showing Michael and his friends at the mill harnessing fire to make steel, now helicopters destroy the village with incendiary bombs. Steven's pregnant bride metaphorically and his mother literally dragged him from the male haven of the bar; now a grinning North Vietnamese cadre tosses a grenade into a shelter full of women and children. Michael and his friends found satisfaction in hunting and gutting a deer; now pigs fight over the entrails of dead American soldiers.

Nature and civilization are the dominant terms of both the American and Vietnamese settings, but in Vietnam the asylum of nature has become an invading hell.

Yet Michael is revealed as in his element here, for his influence and impulses have been unleashed in this frontier landscape. His countenance immediately verifies this, for the hunter who guided himself by Indian lore now wears a cloth headband and has war paint (for camouflage) streaked on his face. He is, in fact, an airborne ranger, and both his appearance and the term "ranger" link him to the tradition of Indian fighters who used Indian skills, became like Indians, to protect the community from Indians. Michael, who like the Deerslayer and other western heroes could only flee the internal threat of corruption inherent in social relations, responds to the external threat of a darker-skinned man firing on a woman and child by literally purging him from the earth with fire. Michael's intense compulsions in the first third of the film were manifested in reckless driving, excessive drinking, flight from women, and a hunt resulting in the image of a gutted deer. Michael, like the western hero, finds a place for his violent impulses only in a threatened community. This scene classically parallels the image of the frontier hero protecting innocent settlers by killing the savage Indian. But Michael's method, a furious blast from a flamethrower, visually asserts the deeper ambiguity of the scene—it opened with the village being blown apart by American napalm. The North Vietnamese soldier is only an undisguised version of the evil that Michael's "good" forces bring to the community. And both the "evil" North Vietnamese and "good" American helicopters act out the repressed hatreds against community found in the male culture of Clairton's bars and hunts.

This ambiguity, based in a visual presentation of the "good" and "evil" elements of the western in clear mirror relation to each other, is brought to its fullest implications in the central sequence of the film, the forced Russian roulette scenes. This scene has been the focus of the most outraged attacks on the film, for it has to many critics seemed to present white America as innocent victim of the savage Vietcong.[10] And, indeed, it is a portrayal of America's experience in Vietnam out of that earliest source of the western, the

Indian captivity narrative in which innocent whites are subjected to hideous tortures. But there are deep ambiguities within this apparent confrontation between innocent whites and dark savages. The Vietcong, as they grin, drink beer, and bet money while forcing their captives to play Russian roulette, display the same impulse and even the same iconography as did Michael and his friends in the bar in Clairton when they drank and bet on televised football. And the one-shot nature of Russian roulette is a parallel to the one-shot value of Michael's hunt. Finally, just as Michael has been the restrained, intense leader of loutish companions, the Vietcong have the look of grinning, stupid brutes except for the impassive, controlled visage of the leader.

The effect is that the Vietcong function as demonic images of the latent impulses of the American culture, particularly as embodied in the western hero, Michael. The Indians and other darker races, closely associated with the wilderness landscape in which the white culture confronts them, have functioned in the myth and literature of American culture as symbols of forces in the unconscious. The larger symbolic design and implications of the film are a continuation of those elements of the western: the Vietnam jungle and its savage Vietcong denizens are the nightmare inversion of the American forests and beautiful deer. Nightmare and dream, both landscapes and their inhabitants are projected aspects of the unconscious, a region beyond the confines, restraints, and limits of the conscious mind embodied in the community. The captivity scene, as did the Puritan narratives of Indian captivity, embodies a nightmare journey into the darker implications of wilderness. If the wilderness landscape (the unconscious) is a place to which the hero goes in order to dominate his passions without external restraints, it can also be the place where he may find himself captive to those same passions. The hunter becomes the hunted, the one shot of complete control an emblem of self-destruction.

By making a captivity narrative the central episode of the film, Cimino inverts the terms of the western formula. While the captivity narrative was a major nonfiction genre of early American writing, the western employs its horrors only to set the revenge/quest plot in motion: in effect, the western substitutes a fantasy emphasizing the eventual assertion of white power and value for a genre of historical narrative that had emphasized the dilemma posed by the experience of complete passivity before an alien culture. Conceiving of the Vietnam War as a western in which the captivity experience is the pivotal episode, Cimino makes *The Deer Hunter* deeply disturbing on the most resonant level of cultural myth.

The final third of the film develops the consequences of the captivity experience. *The Deer Hunter* presents Vietnam as a frontier landscape so hostile that America, having come as hunter with dreams of omnipotence, is held captive in it and forced to confront the full implications of its own impulses. There is no revenge/quest in *The Deer Hunter* because it would be beside the point; the point is to determine how a culture proceeds once it has experienced the inversion of its central assumptions about itself. Michael's resourcefulness as western hero enables him and Nick to kill their captors, but not before they have suffered the experience of being held captive to unrestrained violence. Nick, who called Michael a "control freak" and resisted his obsession with killing the deer with "one shot" in favor of "thinking about the deer" and "the way the trees are in the mountains," is psychologically destroyed. In the Puritan narratives of Indian captivity, as Richard Slotkin has pointed out, "captivity psychology left only two responses open to the Puritans, passive submission or violent retribution."[11] Nick in effect follows both courses. He first has to be restrained by Michael from repeatedly beating a Vietcong corpse, but then turns the unleashed impulse to destroy back upon himself. Unable to call Linda, then lured into the Russian roulette of Saigon, fading into dope and finally death, Nick embodies an innocent acceptance of nature that cannot survive the dark revelations of Vietnam. Michael, the hunter who dominates nature (his unconscious) through controlled violence (repression), discovers in captivity that he cannot be omnipotent.

For both of these Adamic characters Vietnam is a "fall," but for Michael it is a fortunate one. In the second deer hunt of the film, which follows the Vietnam captivity experience, he does not shoot the deer, despite his increasingly frantic pursuit of it. Instead, when the deer faces him, he shoots into the air and says "okay," then sits by a stream and angrily shouts the word, which is this time echoed back by the mountains. "Okay" is of course an expression of acceptance, and Leo Marx identifies the echo as a standard device of pastoral literature representing the establishment of a reciprocal relationship with nature, the "pastoral ideal" of locating a "middle ground somewhere 'between,' yet in a transcendent relation to, the opposing forces of civilization and [primitive] nature."[12] When at the climax of the film Michael once again faces Nick across a table at a Russian roulette game, he is desperately attempting to bring Nick back from his captivity in the violent compulsions once latent but "controlled" in Michael and subsequently transferred to Nick in the first Russian roulette scene. While Michael has responded to the trauma by moving toward a cautious version of the acceptance of nature that Nick had, Nick has become the alienated nihilist Michael had seemed potentially. Nick had abandoned the "one-shot" obsession of Michael for simple primitivist communion with his benign ideal of nature, but the traumatic experience of captivity has turned his innocence into the opposite extreme of an obsession with a "one-shot" submission to passivity. The same experience has led Michael to abandon his "one-shot" obsession with control, instead accepting a balance, or "middle ground," between the conscious and the unconscious.

A common device in such Hollywood westerns as *The Searchers* (1956) and *The Magnificent Seven* (1960), perhaps originating in Cooper's use of Natty Bumppo and Duncan Heyward in *The Last of the Mohicans*, is the "doubling" of the hero.[13] Typically, the experienced hero rides off at the end, free but alone, and the "novice hero" settles down with a woman, domesticated but "happy." This gives both forces of American consciousness mythic affirmation and thus avoids a cultural choice. Cimino has reversed the usual fates of the two heroes, with the experienced hero giving up his freedom in order to "settle down" in the community and the novice hero now finding himself unable to return to it. In addition, he has substituted for the ambiguous image of riding off into the sunset a clear image of self-destruction in an alien landscape.

In settling down, Michael does not abandon the personal code of the western hero based on the hunter myth. [14] He instead brings it to the preservation of the community. After accepting the freedom of the deer, a recurring symbol for the feminine principle of the unconscious, [15] he returns to his male companions that night to find Stanley, in response to sexual taunts, pointing his pistol at their friend Axel. In a rage at this mirror image of the compulsion he has just thrown off, Michael purges Stanley through Russian roulette of his dark obsession with male sexual power. With this purgation of his darker self, Michael is able to overcome his initial confusion and passivity upon his return to go back down into town and join Linda, who embodies the feminine values of love and compassion and the possibility of a stable relationship. He also brings the crippled Steven home from the machine-like institution at the veterans' hospital, and then returns to Vietnam in an attempt to bring back Nick. Michael's return is set against the background of America's flight from Vietnam during the fall of Saigon. His agonized failure is nevertheless a crucial journey *The Deer Hunter* suggests America must make, a return to its Vietnam experience to face the fact of its destroyed innocence. When he holds Nick's blood-soaked head Michael faces, and thus can fully recognize, the result of his prior obsession.

The controversial ending of the film is thus neither jingoistic absolution for America's Vietnam involvement nor an ironic commentary. All the surviving characters, male and female, have been brought together by the hero to a table in the former male haven of the bar. Close shots of the table being set, chairs lifted, and characters squeezing in around the table emphasize the daily heroism involved in preserving a community. Accepting loss and trauma, the western hero has taken a place in the community. In joining in the spontaneous singing of a tearful "God Bless America," finished by a smiling toast to Nick, Michael also joins it in asserting the continuing value of the ideal embodied in a simple love for America, for the dream of a benignly magnificent landscape, but with a full awareness both of the dangers of chaotic nature and of a person's, or society's, obsession with control. The basic impulse of the western has been the concept of regeneration through violence. In *The Deer Hunter* this concept is stood on its head, for the regeneration results from the response of the hero to violence turned back on him. Purgation is replaced by shock, and then acceptance. Vietnam is viewed as the self-projected historical nightmare through which America can awaken from its dream of innocence into a mature consciousness.

The opening scenes of *Apocalypse Now* quickly disabuse the viewer of any expectations that the film will attempt a faithful adaptation of *Heart of Darkness*. Instead, they signal the development of the broad symbolic outline of Conrad's classic novella through the specific ethos, imagery, and pattern of the hard-boiled detective formula. Many commentators have noted a similarity between the voice-over narration spoken by Captain Willard (Martin Sheen) and the narration of Raymond Chandler's detective Philip Marlowe, but Veronica Geng, while not perceiving the full use of the formula, has identified the most explicit particulars of this source in the film.

> Willard talks in the easy ironies, the sin-city similes, the weary, laconic, why-am-I-even-bothering-to-tell-you language of the pulp private eye. . . . Our first look at Willard is the classic opening of the private-eye movie: his face seen upside down, a cigarette stuck to his lip, under a rotating ceiling fan . . . , and then the camera moving in a tight closeup over his books, snapshots, bottle of brandy, cigarettes, Zippo, and, finally, obligatory revolver on the rumpled bedsheets. This guy is not Marlow. He is a parody—maybe a self-created one—of Philip Marlowe, Raymond Chandler's L.A. private eye.[16]

Geng sees these private-eye elements as vaguely functioning to transform the film into a black comedy with overtones of pulp literature and comic books, but they more specifically signal the use of the hard-boiled detective formula as the structural, stylistic, and thematic center of the film, the specific source by which Coppola presents the Vietnam subject through the broad symbolic vision of

Heart of Darkness. Once this is perceived, elements of *Apocalypse Now* that formerly appeared confused or at least puzzling and gratuitous become apparent as aspects of a complex presentation of one source in the terms of another.

The hard-boiled detective genre, originating in the *Black Mask* pulp magazine in the 1920s, is a distinctly American version of the classic detective story, raised to a high artistic level by Dashiell Hammett and Raymond Chandler in fiction, and by John Huston and Howard Hawks in film. The private eye, rather than the brilliant mind of the classic detective, is a twentieth-century urban, and thus more sophisticated and cynical, descendent of the western hero, combining the tough attributes necessary for survival in his environment with a strict integrity based on a personal code of ethics. The setting is a modern American city, most often in southern California, embodying an urban wilderness or "neon jungle" that is geographically, historically, and mythically correct for the genre, because the hard-boiled detective moves through a corrupt society that has replaced the frontier.

There are important similarities, reflecting their common source in quest myths, between *Heart of Darkness* and the hard-boiled detective formula. Both have isolated protagonists on a mystery/adventure who are in the employ of others while actually preserving their personal autonomy of judgment. In both works the protagonist encounters revelatory scenes of the depravity of his society in the course of his journey. And the final apprehension of the criminal, while on the surface restoring moral order, actually ends in dissolution, with the protagonist more cynical about his world than before. Thematically, both Conrad's novella and the hard-boiled detective genre are generally understood to be journeys through a symbolic underworld, or hell, with an ultimate horror at the end providing a terrible illumination. In method both combine the classic quest motif of a search for a grail with a modern, geographically recognizable locale. And while the clipped, slangy style of the hard-boiled genre has on the surface little in common with the obscure, evocative style of *Heart of Darkness*, they pursue similar purposes in the dreamlike (or nightmarish) effect with which they render reportorial detail. The one crucial distinction between *Heart of Darkness* and the hard-boiled genre lies in the relation of the protagonist to the criminal. The detective, despite his similarity to the underworld in speech and appearance, remains sharply distinct from the murderer, for in not only exposing but also judging the murderer he embodies the moral order of the ideals of his society not found in its reality; Marlow, in contrast, comes to identify with Kurtz, finally admiring him as much as he is repelled by him, thus making *Heart of Darkness* ultimately a psychosymbolic journey within to the unconscious. As a result, while the hard-boiled formula posits an individual integrity as an alternative to a corrupt society, Joseph Conrad's novella implies a universal darkness in man.

In *Apocalypse Now* Coppola uses the hard-boiled detective formula as a means for transforming the river journey of *Heart of Darkness* into an investigation of both American society (represented by the army) and American idealism (represented by Colonel Kurtz [Marlon Brando]) in Vietnam. The river journey in *Apocalypse Now* is full of allusions to southern California, the usual setting of the hard-boiled genre, with the major episodes of this trip through Vietnam centering around the surfing, rock music, go-go dancing, and drug taking associated with the west coast culture of the time. As a result, the river journey drawn from *Heart of Darkness* takes the detective and viewer, not through Vietnam as a separate culture, but through Vietnam as the resisting object of a hallucinatory self-projection of the American culture. Captain Willard's river journey is both external investigation of that culture and internal pursuit of his idealism. Willard is a hard-boiled detective hero who in the Vietnam setting becomes traumatized by the apparent decadence of his society and so searches for the grail of its lost purposeful idealism. Kurtz represents that idealism and finally the horrific self-awareness of its hollowness. If the hard-boiled detective, denied by his pervasive society even the refuges of nature and friendship with a "natural man" available to the western hero, is forced by his investigation of a corrupt society to retreat into his own ruthlessly strict moral idealism, *Apocalypse Now* forces the detective into a quest for that idealism itself.

From the beginning of the film it is clear that Willard lacks the genre detective's certainty of his own moral position. Willard has already been to Vietnam, and upon leaving has found that home "just didn't exist anymore." Further, his return to Vietnam is without clear purpose: "When I was here I wanted to be there, when I was there all I could think of was getting back into the jungle." While the opening imagery establishes Willard's identity as hard-boiled detective, it also asserts his diminished version of that figure. The close-up shots of a photograph of his ex-wife and of letters from home represent what he has had to abandon. His drunken practice of Oriental martial arts, as opposed to the controlled drinking and solitary chess playing of Philip Marlowe, represents a shift from tormented purpose to self-destruction. And Sheen's taut characterization generally embodies this deterioration of the detective's cynical armor for his personal idealism into the explosive alienation of a James Dean. Similarly, the narration written by *Dispatches* author Michael Herr and spoken by Sheen in voice-over, widely derided as a banal parody of Raymond Chandler, evokes the sardonic perspective of a Philip Marlowe without the strong sense of personal identity conveyed by Marlowe's penetrating wit. Willard takes the mission to assassinate Kurtz as a murderer despite his feeling that "charging a man with murder in this place was like handing out speeding tickets at the Indy 500." Willard could also be called a murderer, for he has a record of unofficial assassinations. When the soldiers come with his orders he responds drunkenly with "What are the charges?" And in the voice-over narration he says of Kurtz, "There is no way to tell his story without telling my own, and if his story is really a confession, then so is mine." Willard's quest, as that of a hero figure of a central American mythic formula, becomes an investigation of not just corrupted American reality but of the American view of its ideal self.

In melding *Heart of Darkness* and the hard-boiled detective formula, *Apocalypse Now* owes more of its particulars to the latter. Willard, having been summoned from his Saigon quarters, an equivalent to the private eye's seedy downtown office, receives his assignment from a general who clearly evokes the manager in *Heart of*

Darkness by speaking of "unsound" methods while engaging in the brutal exploitation of a country. The specific development of the scene, however (as the general tells Willard that Kurtz disappeared with his Montagnard army into Cambodia when he "was about to be arrested for murder"), is made in the terms of a conventional episode of the hard-boiled formula. Sitting over an elegant lunch in the elaborately furnished trailer serving as his headquarters, and with a melancholy expression listening to Willard's record as an assassin before having him assigned to "terminate" Kurtz, the general is, in the context of the Vietnam War, a military version of the powerful client who receives the detective with palpable distaste in his impressive mansion. Marlow's private aloofness from his employers in *Heart of Darkness* is portrayed in *Apocalypse Now* as the hard-boiled detective's retention of his self-reliance and judgment while ostensibly working for his client: "I took the mission. What the hell else was I gonna do? But I really didn't know what I'd do when I found him."

Likewise, while the journey upriver in *Apocalypse Now* adopts the parallel development in *Heart of Darkness* of the protagonist's growing repulsion from his society and increasing attraction to Kurtz, this pattern is once again specifically presented according to the hard-boiled formula. In that formula the detective, while pursuing the murderer, uncovers such pervasive corruption in the society that his final isolation and judgment of the criminal is undercut. George Grella identifies the portrayal of the official representatives of society, the police, in the detective genre as "brutal, corrupt and incompetent."[17] These traits are consecutively the point of the three major discoveries Willard makes on his journey about how the army is "legitimately" fighting the war. Witnessing Colonel Kilgore's use of overpowering technology to decimate a Vietcong village full of women and children in order to capture briefly a surfing beach, Willard is shown with expressions of puzzlement and disgust, saying: "If that's how Kilgore fought the war, I began to wonder what they really had against Kurtz. It wasn't just insanity and murder. There was enough of that to go around for everyone." After leaving the USO show where he has seen profiteering and dehumanized sex, the glamorous corruption typical of the detective novel, he comments in voice-over: "The war was being run by a bunch of four-star clowns who were going to end up giving the whole circus away." And his reaction to the futile and apparently endless battle of the Do Lung bridge, fought merely so the generals can say the bridge is open, is a disgusted "There's no fuckin' CO here." These scenes develop vague parallels from *Heart of Darkness* through the specific terms of the detective formula.

Similarly, Marlow's attraction in *Heart of Darkness* to the hearsay he encounters concerning Kurtz is developed in *Apocalypse Now* through a stock device of thrillers: a dossier full of fragments of evidence that the detective must study and interpret. Willard, repelled like Marlow and the hard-boiled detective by the depravity of his society, recognizes in his "investigation" of Kurtz that this "murderer" is the embodiment, in vastly larger scale, of his own inner ideals. Kurtz has openly asserted the purposeful action, unhypocritical ruthlessness, autonomy from considerations of personal gain, and adherence to a personal code that are the hard-boiled characteristics of Willard. As a result Willard, like Marlow, finds himself attracted to the murderer. In the voice-over narration, as he looks through Kurtz's dossier, Willard speaks of how the more he learns of Kurtz the "more I admired him," how Kurtz made a report to the Joint Chiefs and Lyndon Johnson that was kept classified because he apparently saw the developing failure of the American approach to the war, and how Kurtz ignored his lack of official clearance to order effective operations and assassinations. Here again Coppola follows the hard-boiled formula while altering its plane to the symbolic investigation of the self adapted from *Heart of Darkness*. The detective often has a friend or is attracted to a woman who turns out to be the murderer, but he discovers this later and is only then confronted with the dilemma; Willard is attracted to Kurtz *after* society has identified him as a murderer. Like Marlow, he consciously moves away from a corrupt, inefficient society toward an idealistic, efficient outlaw. By the time he approaches Kurtz's compound Willard has made Marlow's "choice of nightmares":[18] "Kurtz was turning from a target into a goal."

This identification of the detective figure with the murderer, never allowed in the hard-boiled formula, is brought to its disorienting climax in the scene that Coppola has called the most important in the film,[19] the shooting by Willard of the wounded Vietnamese woman, followed with Willard's explicit explanation: "We'd cut'em in half with a machine gun and give'em a Band-Aid. It was a lie. And the more I saw of them, the more I hated lies." Just before Willard later kills Kurtz, Kurtz says that there is nothing he "detests more than the stench of lies." By developing *Apocalypse Now* according to the defining elements of the hard-boiled formula, but extending the investigation into the self, Coppola shocks the audience from a moral witnessing through the detective figure of the external horror of his society into a questioning of the formula's normal source of order: the moral idealism, the uncorrupted honesty, the purposeful efficiency of the detective himself. This scene prepares the viewer to experience the confrontation between Willard and Kurtz as a meeting of the detective figure with the final implications of his moral idealism. Thus *Apocalypse Now* shows Vietnam forcing the hard-boiled detective hero into the investigation of his unconscious provided by the symbolic motif of *Heart of Darkness*.

The final scenes of the film, set at Kurtz's compound in Cambodia, represent the most visible use in the film of Conrad's novella. Here again, however, the particulars owe considerably more to the hard-boiled detective formula. In many works of the genre the murderer turns out to be what Grella calls a "magical quack," a charlatan doctor or mystic presiding over a cult or temple.[20] Free of social restraint, Colonel Kurtz has, like his literary namesake, set himself up as a god among primitive tribesmen, becoming a ghastly figure of evil. The Russian "fool" in *Heart of Darkness*, now a countercultural American photojournalist (Dennis Hopper), still praises Kurtz mindlessly in mystic terms. But these elements are presented within a more detailed portrayal of Kurtz as the "magical quack" the hard-boiled detective tracks down to his southern California headquarters, a significance first suggested by allusions to Charles Manson in a newspaper story about the Sharon Tate slayings and in the similarity of the "Apocalypse Now" graffiti to the "Helter Skelter" scrawled at the LaBianca home. This portrayal is even clearer in the plot development, for whereas Marlow confronts a pathetic Kurtz crawling away in the grass, this Kurtz, if psychologically "ripped apart," is nevertheless still a powerful, controlling figure who has Willard brought to him. Like the magical quack in the hard-boiled detective formula, he sneeringly taunts, tempts, and intimidates Willard. The murderer often scorns the detective for his low socioeconomic position and quixotic quest (Kurtz tells Willard, "you're an errand boy sent by grocery clerks to collect the bill") and has him held captive and drugged or beaten (Kurtz has Willard caged, brutalizes him by leaving him exposed to the elements, and drives him into hysteria by dropping the severed head of a boat crewman into his lap). Grella identifies one function of the "magical quack" device in the hard-boiled formula to be an emblem of the desperate search of the faithless for significance in a dispirited world (the worshipping photojournalist and Willard's converted predecessor on the assassination mission, the zombie-like Captain Colby, embody this trait). Even more important in Grella's view:

> The bizarre cults and temples lend a quasi-magical element of the Grail romance to the hard-boiled thriller—the detective-knight must journey to a Perilous Chapel where an ambivalent Merlin figure, a mad or evil priest, presides. His eventual triumph over the charlatan becomes a ritual feat, a besting of the powers of the darkness.[21]

The explicit use of Weston's *From Ritual to Romance* (shown by the camera as one of Kurtz's books) in the final confrontation between Willard and Kurtz involves precisely the ritualistic pattern described above, though once again with the implications of a confrontation with the self brought from *Heart of Darkness*.

While the hard-boiled formula is completed by Willard's rejection of his attraction to Kurtz when he sees that Kurtz is indeed a murderer without "any method at all," and by his resistance to Kurtz's intimidation and brainwashing in order to fulfill his mission, he himself knows that his slaying of Kurtz is at the latter's direction: "Everyone wanted me to do it, him most of all." The ritualized confrontation further suggests that the detective figure is in fact killing not an external evil, but his unconscious self. [22] Willard's discovery of the moral chaos that has resulted from Kurtz's pursuit of a moral ideal has led him to see the darkness that pervades not only the hypocrisy of the army, but also the darkness at the heart of his own pursuit of an honest war. The indulgence in death and depravity, of total power, that Willard finds in Colonel Kurtz's display of severed heads, his reading of selected lines from Eliot, and his parable of a Vietcong atrocity is a devastating illumination of the same hollowness, the darkness, that in *Heart of Darkness* Marlow finds in the figure of Kurtz. Here the Vietnam context and hardboiled detective persona of the protagonist give it a specific commentary on the American identity: not just the corrupted American reality, but the American self-concept of a unique national idealism is itself a fraud, a cover for the brute drives for power that dominate Americans as much as any people. Just as Marlow discovers in Kurtz the essential lie of European imperialism, Willard as hardboiled detective finds in Colonel Kurtz the essential lie of his own and his nation's Vietnam venture.

Both Willard and Kurtz, discovering the inherent weakness and corruption of their society, have turned mentally to the enemy. Willard speaks admiringly during the film of "Charlie's" purity and strength, observing that the Vietcong soldier "squats in the bush" and does not "get much USO." Kurtz tells Willard that his illumination came when he realized "like I was shot with a diamond . . . bullet right through my forehead" that the Vietcong's cutting off the children's arms he had inoculated was a stronger act: "If I had ten divisions of those men then our problems here would be over very quickly." This motif has been mistakenly interpreted as the film's view that America was defeated by its reliance on technology and by its conscience. [23] Viewed in the context of the detective formula, it is properly understood as a critique of the hollowness of a "mission" that is based on an illusory abstraction as much as is the redeeming "idea" of Conrad's imperialism. The pure pursuit of an ideal, the obsession with efficient method, becomes the lack of "any method at all," the moral chaos Willard finds at Kurtz's compound, and that dark illumination causes him to draw back from his grail.

In the river journey Willard uncovered the corruption of the actual American mission: in Kurtz Willard finds the emptiness even of the ideal. This is the significance, a virtually explicit reference to the role of the genre detective, of Kurtz's telling Willard "you have a right to kill me . . . but you have no right to judge me." Willard acts out the reassuring action of an agent of moral order, but in doing so realizes that he is judging himself, taking a moral stance toward his own unconscious self. When Willard leaves with Kurtz's book (a report on which Kurtz has scrawled "Drop the bomb" and "Exterminate them all!") and Lance, the surfing innocent traumatized into acid-dropping acceptance of the surrounding madness, he duplicates Marlow's lie to Kurtz's "Intended." Willard at last sees, like Marlow, that the only possible response to the utter dissolution of his moral assumptions is to preserve innocence and the false ideal. Willard departs a hard-boiled detective who has made an investigation down the ultimate mean streets, his soul: "I wanted a mission, and for my sins they gave me one. Brought it up to me like room service. It was a real choice mission, and when it was over, I'd never want another."

The different interpretations of the Vietnam War provided by *The Deer Hunter* and *Apocalypse Now* result logically from the different meanings of the western and hard-boiled detective genres. Since the western is a nineteenth-century myth looking forward to a new civilization, and the detective formula a twentieth-century myth looking around at a failed society, the visions that *The Deer Hunter* and *Apocalypse Now* bring to the Vietnam experience are literally a century apart. In *The Deer Hunter* Cimino transforms Vietnam into a regenerative myth that makes the traumatic experience a conceivably fortunate fall for the American Adam; in *Apocalypse Now* Coppola presents Vietnam as a nightmare extension of American society where only a marginal individual may preserve the American ideal. Beyond the implications of the separate use of the two formulas is the different relation of each film to its formula. *The Deer Hunter* stands the western myth on its head, retaining its central elements while showing that the Vietnam landscape inverts its meaning; *Apocalypse Now* follows the pattern of action of the detective formula but extends the area of investigation to the self, merging the genre with the theme of *Heart of Darkness*. The result is that *The Deer Hunter* insists that Vietnam can be encountered in strictly American terms, while *Apocalypse Now* undermines the one dependable source of American order, the idealistic self-concept embodied in the "pure" motivation of the formula hero. Cimino sees the Vietnam involvement as a projected mirror where Americans can recognize their darkest impulses, but in response return once again to the original promise Cooper had recognized in the precolonial days of the young Deerslayer. Coppola views Vietnam as the projection of southern California into an alien landscape where even American idealism stands at last exposed.

The *Deer Hunter* and *Apocalypse Now*, while presenting distinctly different interpretations of the Vietnam War based on the separate formulas shaping their structures, also have an underlying relation resulting from their common use of major formulas of American popular romance that are themselves linked by the relation between their central heroes. The major criticisms leveled at the two films, their implausibility and ambiguity, are essential aspects of the romance mode by which the major American narrative tradition has dealt with extreme experience revealing basic cultural contradictions and conflicts. Both *The Deer Hunter* and *Apocalypse Now* avoid the limits of naturalistic, fragmented, or personal approaches to the war (found respectively in James Webb's novel *Fields of Fire*, Michael Herr's memoir *Dispatches*, and the film *Coming Home* [1978]) by couching the terror of Vietnam in American myths. Each of these two films takes a hero who is a version of the national archetype, thus embodying the essential longings and anxieties of the American psyche, and sends him on a quest conveying the aberrant, fragmented, hallucinatory Vietnam experience while giving it a familiar, meaningful structure. Within the generic confines of the western and hard-boiled detective formulas, Vietnam may be contemplated, the terror reenacted, and the meaning probed. These formulaic genres, comprising central moral fantasies of American culture, provide collective dreams through which the trauma of the Vietnam War may be reexperienced, assimilated, and interpreted. Further, since these films significantly invert or undercut the implications of their mythic sources, they suggest the significance of Vietnam as a pivotal experience for American consciousness.

Notes

Acknowledgments: I thank Stephen Tatum, James Machor, and Robert Schulzinger for helpful suggestions.

1. Stanley Solomon, *Beyond Formula: American Film Genres* (New York: Harcourt, 1976) 3.

2. Richard Chase, *The American Novel and Its Tradition* (Baltimore, Md.: Johns Hopkins University Press, 1957) 13.

3. For my definitions and discussions of the characteristic elements of the western and hard-boiled detective genres, I draw largely on Solomon's *Beyond Formula* and John G. Cawelti's *Adventure, Mystery, and Romance: Formula Stories as Art and Popular Culture* (Chicago: University of Chicago Press, 1976). My discussion of the hard-boiled detective genre also draws on George Grella's fine essay, "Murder and Mean Streets: The Hard-Boiled Detective Novel," in *Detective Fiction: Crime and Compromise*, ed. Richard Stanley Allen and David Chacko (New York: Harcourt, 1974) 411–29.

4. David Axeen, "Eastern Western," *Film Quarterly* 32.4 (1979): 17. Colin L. Westerbeck, Jr., calls the film a western, but only to attack it as a simplistic and "sickening" cowboys-and-Indians melodrama. See his "Peace with Honor: Cowboys and Viet Cong," *Commonweal*, 2 March 1979: 115–17.

5. Leslie Fiedler, *Love and Death in the American Novel*, rev. ed. (New York: Stein and Day, 1975) 142–82.

6. Cawelti, *Adventure, Mystery, and Romance* 194.

7. Michael Cimino, "Ordeal by Fire and Ice," *American Cinematographer*, October 1978: 1031.

8. Ibid.: 965, 1006–7.

9. Dialogue has been transcribed from the films.

10. See, for instance, Marsha Kinder's "Political Game," *Film Quarterly* 32.4 (1979): 13–17, and comments in "Vietnam Comes Home," *Time*, 23 April 1979: 23.

11. Richard Slotkin, *Regeneration through Violence: The Mythology of the American Frontier, 1600–1860* (Middletown, Conn.: Wesleyan University Press, 1973) 145.

12. Leo Marx, *The Machine in the Garden: Technology and the Pastoral Ideal in America* (New York: Oxford University Press, 1964) 23.

13. See Michael D. Butler's "Narrative Structure and Historical Process in *The Last of the Mohicans*," *American Literature* 48 (1976): 117–39.

14. For a discussion of the relation of the hunter myth to the code of the western hero, see "Book Two: The Sons of Leatherstocking," in Henry Nash Smith, *Virgin Land: The American West as Symbol and Myth* (New York: Vintage, 1950) 49–120, and "Man without a Cross: The Leatherstocking Myth (1823–1841)" in Slotkin, *Regeneration through Violence* 466–516.

15. See Slotkin, *Regeneration through Violence* 429, 490.

16. Veronica Geng, "Mistuh Kurtz—He Dead," *New Yorker*, 3 September 1979: 70.

17. Grella, "Murder and Mean Streets": 414.

18. Joseph Conrad, *Heart of Darkness*, ed. Robert Kimbrough, rev. ed. (New York: W. W. Norton, 1971) 63.

19. Greil Marcus, "Journey Up the River: An Interview with Francis Coppola," *Rolling Stone*, 1 November 1979: 55.

20. Grella, "Murder and Mean Streets": 422–23.

21. Ibid.: 423.

22. See Garrett Stewart, "Coppola's Conrad: The Repetitions of Complicity," *Critical Inquiry* 7 (1981): 455–74.

23. See David Bromwich, "Bad Faith of *Apocalypse Now*," *Dissent* 27 (1980): 207–10, 213.

David Desser

"Charlie Don't Surf"
Race and Culture in the Vietnam War Films

If it wasn't for the people, [Vietnam] was very pretty.
—LIEUTENANT COKER in *Hearts and Minds*

CHAPTER 4 Since the late 1970s, Hollywood has made a significant effort to portray America's Vietnam experience. Yet the films produced, beginning in 1978, something of a watershed year for films about the Vietnam War, hardly present a unified, coherent vision. If we take these films as a group, we find contradictions and ambiguities throughout, while many individual works are similarly conflicted in what they are trying to say about the Vietnam War and America's involvement in it. At the same time, all of these films have at least one overriding commonality: a vision of the war as a problem within American culture. The reasons the United States entered the war, the response of American soldiers to the war, and the effects of the war on returning veterans and on the larger American society dominate the discourse of films about or inspired by the Vietnam War.

One of the more memorable sequences in Francis Ford Coppola's *Apocalypse Now* (1979) can be taken as emblematic of the way Hollywood films have seen the war in specifically American terms. Captain Willard, our stand-in for the journey into the heart of darkness that was Vietnam, comes into contact with Colonel Kilgore, the Air Cavalry madman memorably enacted by Robert Duvall. Kilgore determines to take a coastal village less for its strategic value or as a suitable site for Willard's boat to enter the river than because Lance, a champion California surfer, accompanies Willard, and because "Charlie don't surf." It is not so much the absurdity of bringing down the might of American technology on the "primitive" combatants of the North Vietnamese Army (NVA) or the Vietcong (VC, alias Charlie) merely for an opportunity to surf, although that is the operative analysis that Willard undertakes: thinking that Kilgore risks his own men and slaughters the villagers near the shore merely to surf, Willard wonders why Colonel Kurtz is thought mad in the face of psychopaths like Kilgore. It is, rather, as screenwriter John Milius recognized, that America tried to import and impose its own culture into Vietnam and that cultural differences and prejudices underlay many of our government's more outrageous, thoughtless, violent, and tragic actions.[1]

But it goes even deeper than that. America *always* saw the war only in strictly American terms. Even the critiques of the American involvement in the war see it as a flaw in American society, a defect of character, culture, or metaphysics. And, as we shall see, the misguided entry into the war was condemned later for its effect on America, on veterans, and on the American soul. The official discourse justifying our entry into the war, as well as the discourse of many antiwar activists, reveals the cultural blindness that got us into the conflict in the first place—a cultural blindness, revealed especially in the *retrospective* films and television shows, that plagues us still.

That most Americans always saw the Vietnam War as an American war can be recognized, first, in what we might call the "benevolent theory" of United States involvement. This theory is best explicated by Loren Baritz in *Backfire*, where he proclaims that there is a "benevolence of our national motives, the absence of material gain in what we seek, [and] the dedication to principle."[2] It is the notion of the New World, America as the City upon a Hill, a light unto the nations, the new Israel. Thus, in this conception, America's foray into Vietnam was underlaid by essentially idealistic notions, a mythology of America as the leader of the free world, obligated to help others. This obligation may be a heavy burden, may come at a high price, but as Lyndon Johnson is shown saying in *Hearts and Minds* (1974) "there is no one else who can do the job," no one else who can defend the freedom and aspirations of other peoples. Baritz quotes from LBJ's inaugural address: "We aspire to nothing that belongs to others."[3] In this respect, Americans were different from the French, who fought (with U.S. monetary and military help) merely to maintain the remnants of their colonial empire. Or, as LBJ expressed it in April 1965, "We fight for values and we fight for principles, rather than territory or colonies."[4] And there was John F. Kennedy, proclaiming to the world, "We shall pay any price, bear any burden, meet any hardship, support any friend, oppose any foe to assure the survival and the success of liberty. I do not shrink from this responsibility—I welcome it."[5] Or we find Richard Nixon stating that "never in history have men fought for less selfish motives—not for conquest, not for glory, but only for the right of people far away to choose the kind of government they want."[6]

Retrospective critics of the U.S. involvement in Vietnam, like Baritz, see this idealism as mistaken, or as outdated, or as a misunderstanding of the original Puritan myth, whose corollary was that we should *not* involve ourselves in the affairs of others but merely provide an example, a beacon light, for those who choose to follow it. But such critics do not doubt that this idealism was a genuine structural component of America's entry into Vietnam. Moreover, this vision, not only of American uniqueness, but of America as world leader, as moral center, was common to both liberals and conservatives. In fact, anti–Vietnam War rhetoric in the late 1960s as often as not revolved around how America's entry into the Vietnam War was a betrayal of *American* ideals.

A corollary of this idealism, this mission to the world, as Baritz notes, is a belief that the rest of the people of the world want to be like Americans, want to be Americans.[7] As a gung ho colonel tells a bemused Joker in *Full Metal Jacket* (1987): "Inside every gook there is an American trying to get out."[8] That the United States was trying to impose Americanism on another culture, another people, was simply never considered, since Americanism was *a priori* a desirable state to be in.

Of course, there is also a simpler explanation for America's entry into Vietnam: anti-Communism. Vietnam was merely an extension of the Cold War, a fight against Communist aggression. America had fought in Korea to preserve democracy, and America created and defended South Vietnam for the same reason. The anti-Communist crusade (with all the moral and religious overtones implicit in the term) saw South Vietnam as menaced by North Vietnam, which wanted to impose a Communist dictatorship. This dictatorship took its orders from Moscow, and the anti-Communist crusaders knew that the Soviet Union (Russia, really) was the leader of the "evil empire." Cold War rhetoric abounded throughout the Vietnam era, beginning with Eisenhower, who claimed that "the forces of good and evil are massed and armed and opposed as rarely before in history," and that "freedom is pitted against slavery; lightness against the dark."[9] By now in our history, we understand clearly the anti-Communist fears of the Cold War era and can recognize the (seeming) irony of Democratic presidents (Truman, Kennedy, and Johnson) involving us in worldwide anti-Communism in general, and in Vietnam in particular.

On the one hand, we can see this anti-Communism as part of American benevolence and the belief in American chosenness and uniqueness. But we can also see how the Democratic presidents used anti-Communism as a sop against the Republicans and the forces of conservatism. Thus it is no surprise that the illegal and immoral activities of the so-called HUAC hearings began to flourish while Truman was in office. And think how much worse, how much more tragic and venal, the McCarthy hearings would have been had not a Republican former army general been in the White House. Anti-Communism is also sometimes seen as a paranoid response to America's perceived decline as a world power and the need to find a scapegoat for this event. We can point to the first "Red Scare" in the wake of the Bolshevik Revolution and World War I, where our emergence on the world scene was threatened by an economic revolution abroad and increased unionizing activities at home; and then to the post–World War II era, where the mightiest nation on earth was threatened by the second mightiest nation on earth. The Cold War continued throughout the postwar era, justifying our Korean and Vietnam involvements, our Latin American forays, and even some of our Middle East commitments. And then we can even see how the abatement of the "Communist threat" in the Gorbachev era necessitated (necessitates) a new scapegoat for perceived American decline or threats to our power—the shift from the Soviet Union as the "evil empire" to (or back to) Japan, a point to which we shall return.

Juxtaposed to the theory of America's benevolent Vietnam intervention (even allowing paranoid anti-Communism a benevolent side) is a theory in which the United States is guilty. That this explanation for the war is a given among leftists may be indexed by the mere sketch such an explanation receives in Michael Ryan and Douglas Kellner's *Camera Politica*: "Liberals usually avoided the broader implications of the war, its origin in a desire to maintain access to Third World labor, markets, raw materials, etc. and to forestall the rise of noncapitalistic sociopolitical systems."[10] That "etc." is a wonderful rhetorical move, as it elides any real analysis on their part while constructing the reader as a right-thinking person willing and able to fill in details of the party line.[11]

In a more serious challenge to the benevolent view, Marilyn B. Young notes that Loren Baritz's *Backfire* "ratifies the claims of the very war presidents he elsewhere opposes."[12] Although she is speaking about Baritz's views of the NLF (National Liberation Front, the Vietcong as they were called), her critique stands in for the larger problem of accepting the benevolent theory, a problem not simply of the NLF, but of the role of the Vietnamese in the Vietnam War. For what is striking about the rhetoric of the post-Vietnam era across political boundaries is the absence of the Vietnamese as a factor in the Vietnam War. One of the most common litanies heard, in fact, is how *American* culture was responsible for the Vietnam War. That the war had any kind of integrity, so to speak, of its own, that it was part of *Vietnam*'s history of resisting colonialism and imperialism, that Vietnam had a class structure and class warfare of its own, was never considered seriously.

Even more disturbing, perhaps, is the shift in the terms of discussion since 1975. Suddenly, it is not that the U.S. presence in Vietnam was misguided or simply wrong, but that the *character* of how America fought the war was misguided.[13] Thus we find American politicians, soldiers, and critics beating their breasts over American cultural blindness and insensitivity. On this score, Loren Baritz quotes from American generals who state, "we never took into account the cultural differences," or "we erroneously tried to impose the American system on a people who didn't want it [and] couldn't handle it."[14] Is the notion here that if we Americans understood that it was okay for Vietnamese men to hold hands we would have understood them better and hence fought for and with them more effectively?[15] Apparently so: "America fought the wrong war in Vietnam, and almost everyone in Washington knew it."[16] Thus even many well-intentioned critics of the Vietnam War fall into the same trap that, among other things, got America into Vietnam in the first place: the absence of the Vietnamese as factors in the war.

"Let smiles cease," Converse said. "Let laughter flee. This is the place where everybody finds out who they are."

Hicks shook his head.

"What a bummer for the gooks."

— ROBERT STONE, *Dog Soldiers*

The two dozen or so significant films made about the Vietnam War (all of which were made in the postwar era)[17] are by no means unified in their vision of it. Critics have attempted to divide these films broadly into "liberal" and "conservative." Yet no matter how a particular film is categorized, what is apparent is that in virtually all of these films about the war "except as targets, the Vietnamese scarcely exist; they are absent as people."[18] Among the few critics to comment on this absence, Ryan and Kellner praise the documentary *Hearts and Minds* for the way in which "what other films pose as an object [the Vietnamese], this film grants some subjectivity."[19]

Similarly, Terry Christensen faults *The Deer Hunter* (1978) for its obliviousness "to the impact of the war on the Vietnamese."[20] In most Vietnam War films, the enemy is barely seen, only always *out there* in the jungle. They are seen literally as targets in *Apocalypse Now*, targets that occasionally strike back; or in *Platoon* (1986) via a few shots taken from the enemy's point of view, but without any real subjectivity; or in *Hamburger Hill* (1987), where they are acknowledged as fierce fighters but never personalized.

On the one hand, we should not be surprised at this. How many World War II combat films personified the enemy? Or how many personified the enemy in a *positive* way? It was not until after the war that the United States could undertake a reconsideration of its opponents. Thus we find, years later, films that attempt to separate the *Wehrmacht* officer from his Nazi superiors, with such figures as Erwin Rommel emerging as ambiguously tragic heroes. And, although it is significant in terms of how racism found its way into the Vietnam War era, and into Vietnam War films, that we find more portrayals, more personifications, of our European former antagonists than our Asian enemies, we can still point to such films as *Hell in the Pacific* (1968), *Tora! Tora! Tora!* (1970), *Midway* (1976), and even the more recent *Farewell to the King* (1989) as endowing some human subjectivity to the Asian objects of America's aggression and blood-lust.

Even twenty years after the Vietnam War, few films deal with, or even acknowledge, the Vietnamese as subject. The Left automatically condemns films that criticize the enemy, or, as we have just seen, condemns in part those films that do not personalize the enemy. This is, however, extremely revealing, extremely indicative of how we still see the Vietnam War in terms of *American* culture and how critics have not recognized the significance of this view. For instance, Ryan and Kellner condemn liberal vet films that focus on personal issues at the expense of the historical and the global (condemn, that is, such films as *Coming Home* [1978], *Cutter's Way* [1981], *The Deer Hunter*, etc., for being American films) and that criticize the Vietnam War "for what it did to good, white American boys, not for what ruin it brought to innocent Vietnamese."[21] Thus, it is *Americans* who are victimized by the war, an image portrayed most especially in *Coming Home*, among other returning-vet films. Even here, however, in the concept of victimization, we find ambiguity and ambivalence. On the one hand, there is the victimization of the vets who fought *in* the wrong war; but, on the other, there are the vets who fought the wrong war, who were prevented from fighting the war in the *right* way—John Rambo's notorious, overdetermined "Do we get to win this time?"

But seeing the war through how *we* were victimized, that is, how it affected the American soldiers who fought in Vietnam, not how it affected the Vietnamese, as individuals, as a nation, as a culture, is also nothing new, nothing for the Left to be surprised at. Such postwar Japanese films as *Harp of Burma* (1956) and *Fires on the Plain* (1959) use the victimization of the Japanese foot soldier to condemn not Japanese culture for the Pacific war, but the Japanese militarists. Similarly, the West Germans manipulated the Great Communicator, Ronald Reagan, into participating in the "victimization" of German soldiers by the "Madman" theory of Hitler and the Nazis.[22] Ella Shohat seems to be surprised at how new Israeli films examine the theme of that country's occupation of the West Bank from the point of view of its effect on the occupiers themselves.[23]

The absence of the enemy, or the relative absence at least, is indicative of how we still see the war as a function of American culture, how the war was a product of a sickness within American society, or how the war led to a sickness within American society. This is the operating metaphor of *Dog Soldiers*, and the underrated film version of it, *Who'll Stop the Rain* (1978). Albert Auster and Leonard Quart see both book and film as "a metaphor for the war's corruption of American society [and] for America's capacity for violence and self-annihilation."[24] Or, as Oliver Stone's Chris has it in *Platoon*: "We did not fight the enemy, we fought ourselves and the enemy was in us."[25] But of course we did fight the enemy, or fought something, *someone*, and the failure to acknowledge this is indicative of a larger failure to examine the Vietnam foray in the first place and a continued failure to come to terms with it.

The few cinematic portrayals of the enemy, then, are revealing. Sketchy characterizations of the VC and the North Vietnamese, as seen in *The Boys in Company C* (1978), *Apocalypse Now, Good Morning, Vietnam* (1987), and *Off Limits* (1988), among others, and more detailed, highly negative characterizations in such films as *Rambo* (1985), *Hanoi Hilton* (1987), and *Missing in Action* (1985), not to mention the controversial, highly charged, but ultimately ambiguous portrayal in *The Deer Hunter*, tell us much about America's attitude toward its former enemy, an attitude that still prevails. But portrayals of America's allies, the South Vietnamese, are equally shaped by cultural prejudice and racism.

Recent Vietnam War films portray the South Vietnamese as objects of misguided good intentions (*Good Morning, Vietnam*), or as victims of an unintentionally corrupting influence that they justifiably resent (*Off Limits*). Two earlier films betray more ambiguous attitudes toward America's supposed allies. Both *The Boys in Company C* and *Go Tell the Spartans* (1978) indict the corruption of the South Vietnamese officer corps, who seem more interested in preserving their troop strength and ammunition in case of a coup than in defending an embattled group of American Army advisers and South Vietnamese soldiers in the field. The U.S. Army command in Vietnam and, by implication, the politicians in Washington are portrayed as cynical about the South Vietnamese attitude toward the U.S. soldiers—in the climax of *The Boys in Company C* the American platoon is ordered to lose a soccer match to a South Vietnamese team under penalty of returning to the jungle. As Auster and Quart point out, "given a choice between release from a war they don't like and their self respect and pride, the Americans opt to win." For Auster and Quart, the "hardly subtle message here is that whatever the particular realities of the war, GI Joe is still a hero and winner."[26] But why should an American team be ordered to lose to its allies? The implication of the order is that the Oriental team would be embarrassed by a loss; a win would convince them that they are as good (or better) than the Americans. The order proceeds from the assumption that the Americans would otherwise win, and that they must placate their "allies," fool them, treat them like children, and give them a sense of self-respect the Americans know to be false. Baritz notes how in Vietnam it was common for the grunts to respect the enemy, respect Charlie, far more than their own South Vietnamese allies.[27] As we shall see, respect for Charlie did not mean admiration or understanding, nor did it mean a genuine sense of who the enemy actually was. But it did mean that the VC and the NVA were held in more esteem than the ARVN. *Go Tell the Spartans* even more clearly enables us to see the essential ambivalence the United States as a culture felt for Vietnam and the Vietnamese, the dislike of its alleged allies and the grudging respect for its erstwhile enemies.

I also wish to express my thanks and affection to (then) First Sergeant Alva (said to have been a full-blooded Navaho Indian), who called me into his Orderly Room office the day I left for overseas and told me "remember, this is not a white man's war."
— LARRY HEINEMANN, *Close Quarters*

Under the credits of *Go Tell the Spartans* a South Vietnamese Raider, prominently wearing a Stetson, can be seen mistreating a Vietnamese POW. This Vietnamese Raider is nicknamed Cowboy, and he is told by Major Barker, a tall, commanding American Army officer, to stop torturing the prisoner. The major can only shake his head in dismay that an ally can act in this manner. Later, this well-built, multilingual, highly skilled Vietnamese mercenary will behead a captured VC, which will cause the green second lieutenant nominally in command of a unit en route to garrison Muc Wa to throw up. The sympathetic draftee who volunteered to join the Raiders and serve in Vietnam will then be told by the battle-weary Korean War veteran to remember: "It's their war, Courcey." Set in 1964 (although made in 1978), *Go Tell the Spartans* reminds us that, in fact, it was not to be their war, it was to be America's, tragically so for both countries.

Auster and Quart credit the film for its "dark portrait of inept, poorly trained South Vietnamese soldiers; decadent and corrupt French-speaking province chiefs; and vicious, anti-Communist South Vietnamese noncoms"; they praise the way "it succeeds in conveying much of the futility and absurdity of the Vietnam experience."[28] In fact, one must pay tribute also to Daniel Ford, whose novel, *Incident at Muc Wa*, written in 1967, provides the source material for the film.[29] Although in most respects the film is superior to the novel (it wisely eliminates a subplot focusing on Courcey's relationship to a coed turned radical journalist who eventually shows up in Vietnam doing a story, and gives more thematic weight and pathos to Major Barker in the casting of a powerful, commanding Burt Lancaster), the novel sees the American foray into Vietnam as misguided, misdirected, and mistaken. It is the novel that recalls the French experience in Vietnam and the reference to Herodotus's account of the Battle of Thermopylae (from whence the film takes its title), and it is the novel that provides many prophecies of the tragedies to come, mainly the sentiments by General Hardnetz that the "only way we're going to win this war is to get American ground troops in here." But it is the film that best reveals America's ambivalence toward the Vietnamese.

The emotional center of the film is Courcey, the draftee corporal played by Craig Wasson, and his attitudes toward the Vietnamese and the war stand in for ours. As Rob Edelman notes in a short article written some years after the film's release, "Unlike all the other Americans, who constantly refer to the Vietnamese as 'goddamn gooks' and 'stinking dinks,' Courcey sees them as human beings."[30] Even before Courcey's arrival, we have seen Cowboy hanging a prisoner upside down in a water barrel, and we are repelled with Courcey by the beheading (although fans of the Japanese samurai film must take note of Cowboy's skill); the portrayal of other, more overtly sympathetic allies is no less problematic.[31] A telling scene, for instance, finds a Vietnamese Ranger wounded during a VC attack, lying just outside the perimeter of the defended camp. None of the ARVN Rangers or mercenaries will go to get him. But the American lieutenant, diarrhea and all, goes out. The ARVN soldier is dead already, and the lieutenant only gets himself killed in discovering that. We take away from this highly charged scene not necessarily the fact that the ARVN soldiers are cowards (although we could think we are asked to conclude that), but rather that it illustrates General William Westmoreland's sentiment, expressed ingenuously in *Hearts and Minds*, that "the oriental doesn't put the same high price on life as the Westerner." Or, in the South Vietnamese soldiers' apparent callousness toward death in combat, we might recall the "insane" admiration expressed by the renegade Colonel Kurtz in *Apocalypse Now*, who marvels at how the VC hacked off the newly inoculated arms of South Vietnamese children. Even if we recognize the lieutenant's actions as sentimental, amateurish, foolish, and wasteful, we are still asked to sympathize with the American—his ideals and essential good-heartedness.

A scene shortly after the lieutenant's death must also be read in light of American in contrast to Vietnamese attitudes. The battle-hardened, battle-weary, burnt-out Sergeant Oleonowski (called "Ski" in the novel but, in deference to Polish-American sentiments no doubt, called "Oleo" in the film) does not want to hold a burial service for the lieutenant. But Courcey angrily insists. As the still-idealistic corporal leaves the sarge's tent, a gunshot rings out—Oleo has shot himself. It is a puzzling scene in that Oleo's reaction is, shall we say, highly theatrical and overdetermined. It can be understood to have multiple root causes. Oleo is already an alcoholic by the time he joins Major Barker's command. This Korean War hero has obviously been battered by Vietnam, which is interesting in itself, considering the ubiquity of comparisons, in this film and in numerous other films and novels, to World War II. Even Korea, we are to take it, had a purpose, made some sense, which Vietnam clearly lacks.[32] But why does it lack a purpose? Of course, it lacks a purpose to us, to the viewers, because we know that the Vietnam War lacked a purpose. But to Oleo, *in this film*, the purposelessness is the sacrifice of U.S. soldiers to defend an unworthy ally. Oleo's refusal to hold a burial service was his implicit acceptance of the Vietnamese code; realizing that he had lost his essential Americanness, his idealism, his respect for life, and his honor as a soldier, he had no choice but to kill himself.

But if the film sees America's allies as, in many ways, unworthy of American support, undeserving of American deaths, it is also cognizant of how America betrayed them. In a scene that clearly alludes to the famous network television news shots of the fall of Saigon, with Vietnamese frantically and desperately trying to grab onto the skids of departing helicopters, the U.S. Raiders bug out of Muc Wa, denying the Vietnamese Raiders transport, the helicopter pilot and gunner even threatening to shoot any Vietnamese who try to get on board. Both Major Barker and Corporal Courcey stay behind to try and "exfiltrate" through the jungle with the Vietnamese Raiders. Thus, official U.S. policy cynically betrayed America's allies (who were never especially worthy of support in the first place), but there is still something decent and noble in the American soldier, who dies for his nobility. (At least Major Barker dies— the World War II veteran who did not play by the army's rules in the postwar period, and who tragically sacrificed himself in "the wrong war.")

Images of the South Vietnamese also slip over into images of the enemy. The VC here are called "Charlie," as they typically are in other films, and as they were by the grunts in the field. (In the novel, the VC and the North Vietnamese Army are called "Charlie Romeo," reflecting the military argot of the period.) Oleo early on exclaims that "any place we turn up, Charlie turns up"; the Americans complain that whereas "Charlie always knows what we're going to do, we never know what Charlie is going to do." Charlie thus has almost magical powers (or a network of spies, which is also a possibility, as we shall see). This near-mystical ability is most evident in the mysterious figure "One-Eyed Charlie," who turns up on three separate occasions in the film, a VC soldier who materializes out of the jungle and silently, effortlessly disappears into it.

Such characterizations of Charlie are common elsewhere. In *Dispatches*, for instance, we are told that "Vietnam was a dark room full of deadly objects, the VC were everywhere all at once like spider cancer."[33] Or in *A Rumor of War* by Philip Caputo we learn that "there was no enemy to fire at, there was nothing to retaliate against. . . . Phantoms, I thought, we're fighting phantoms." Or the complaint rendered in Mark Baker's *Nam*: "I could deal with a man.

That meant my talent against his for survival, but how do you deal with him when he ain't even there?" Or as neatly, paranoically, summed up in James Webb's *Fields of Fire*: "They were nowhere. They were everywhere."[34]

Another aspect to Charlie, however, is even more sinister: the way in which in *Go Tell the Spartans* Courcey is duped by a group of VC posing as refugees. Again, the film is ambivalent on the score— perhaps "balanced" is a better word. For while Courcey rescues them, and insists on treating them as refugees against Cowboy's initial willingness to kill them and in the face of his continued insistence that the family, including an attractive adolescent girl, are "Communist people," the family does betray Courcey and the garrison. On the one hand, this reflects what Lloyd Lewis calls the "VC's remarkable success at infiltration." It was this tactic, he claims, that made the Vietnam War "cognitively insufferable to the Americans."[35] This is the simple but painful refrain heard time and again from veterans, in novels and in films: that they could not distinguish ally from enemy, friend from foe. The Occidental, racist cavil that all Orientals look alike became painfully all too true in Vietnam. In *Go Tell the Spartans*, the VC are condemned, for the warfare they wage is a betrayal of common standards of decency. Courcey saved their lives and offered them American hospitality. They repaid him with their betrayal.

We are to be outraged at this, a reflection of American cultural insistence (molded by the media) that there is something in warfare called "fair play." Time and again, American soldiers complained at the way the VC constantly did not play by the rules.[36] On the other hand, Courcey himself is apparently spared by the VC—he is left alive at the end, his fellow combatants, Major Barker and the South Vietnamese Rangers, dead and stripped naked on the battlefield. We saw the adolescent girl among the VC company that attacked the Rangers, and we might conclude that she spared Courcey's life, although he is wounded. On the other hand, we might conclude that Courcey was well hidden from view, as he was helped into the jungle by Corporal Old Man, who then returned to the fighting to die. Or we might believe that he is apparently mortally wounded.[37] In Ford's novel, Courcey is wounded after the fierce fight to bug out; he then returns to Muc Wa, only to be shot dead by the novel's equivalent of One-Eyed Charlie. In the film, however, upon returning to Muc Wa Courcey is spared by this character, leaving his fate ambiguous.

Yet for all of the ambiguity, including the possibility of seeing a kind of backhanded gratitude on Charlie's part, we are left with the sensation of moral confusion and bitterness. Courcey is never able "to penetrate the protective masks of the Vietnamese or comprehend the implacability of the Vietcong."[38] Moreover, the use of an adolescent girl, replete with the veneer of Oriental sexuality, to characterize the perfidy of the VC represents an imposition on the film's part. Earlier (before we learn that the refugees are really "Communist people") Courcey leads a platoon against a mortar nest. He grenades it and is then surprised to see a woman's body among the dead. This represents merely the manner in which, we are told by memoirs, novels, and films, the VC recruited anyone, regardless of age or gender, to fight. (We might recall Kilgore's assault on the village in *Apocalypse Now*, when a young woman tosses a hat that contains a grenade into a grounded chopper.) But the character of the young woman, named Butterfly in Ford's novel, but unnamed except for the end credits in the film, who is attracted to Courcey (but whom he resists sexually) is *not* a VC spy or sympathizer in the book. In fact, she becomes Ski's (Oleo's) wife, and she is pregnant by him and rescued by the chopper when Muc Wa is exfiltrated (Courcey gives her his place, as in the novel the South Vietnamese are similarly not permitted the ride out). The film's transformation of Butterfly from refugee into VC thus participates in a common literary and cinematic image of the enemy-as-woman. "There was no reliable criterion by which to distinguish a pretty Vietnamese girl from a deadly enemy; often they were one and the same person."[39] Yet we should acknowledge not only the recurrence of female VC, here and in *Full Metal Jacket* most spectacularly, but also the rhetoric surrounding both enemy and ally as "feminized." This motif is taken up again in a powerful way in *Casualties of War* (1989), where the twisted logic of Sergeant Meserve allows him to kidnap, rape, and murder a Vietnamese village girl to avenge what the VC did to his platoon.

In fact, the image of the VC-as-woman, the ubiquity of women who are VC, is a near-hysterical reaction to the shock to the (masculine) American psyche that this physically smaller, technologically inferior race could defeat the hypermasculinized, hypertechnologized American soldier.[40] And while it is of primary significance to acknowledge that the enemy-as-woman also easily translates into, or is reflective of, rather, the woman-as-enemy, the best we can do in the present context is to acknowledge that misogyny also underlay America's Vietnam foray, as well as the manner in which the war was fought. One condensation of misogyny and anti-Vietnamese sentiments can be found in the psychopathic actions of the murderer in *Off Limits* (1988). Although this film is a structural and generic mess, it does detail the corruption that America wrought on urban Vietnam (Saigon) and the way in which sexism and racism were important undercurrents of American attitudes toward the Vietnamese.

Even without the image of the enemy as feminized, and the hysterical sexism that it implicates, we do find a disturbing racist undertone to much of the unconscious rhetoric of many (most) of the Vietnam films, as I have indicated above. But these attitudes extend beyond Vietnam, and reveal more deep-seated hostilities and ambiguities in American culture. Consider the following characterizations of our enemy: "universally cruel and ruthless" and "tough but devoid of scruples." Or that we fought "a war against an enemy whom Americans at first underrated," a fighting force perceived as "scrawny, near-sighted, and poorly trained and equipped," people whom Americans regarded "as not quite human, endowed with a strange mixture of animal cunning and ability to live in the jungle, and [a] superhuman devotion" that rendered them fearless in battle with a willingness to commit suicide for the cause.[41] Accurate descriptions of American sentiments about the VC and the NVA, to be sure, except in this case all drawn from the anti-Japanese rhetoric of World War II. As John Dower notes, in an analysis equally applicable to our conceptions of the VC, America was torn between two opposed images of the Japanese: "From subhuman to superhuman, lesser men to supermen. There was, however, a common point throughout, in that the Japanese were rarely perceived as human beings of a generally comparable and equal sort."[42] Sheila Johnson notes the manner in which stereotypes of Asians "can be pasted like labels onto either the Japanese or the Chinese (or the Koreans or Vietnamese) as the occasion warrants" and how "during the Korean War and again during the Vietnam War, all the old World War II epithets applied to the Japanese resurfaced: gooks, slopeheads, slant-eyes, yellow devils, and so on."[43] That there was an element of race and racism in the U.S. entry into and combat strategies in Vietnam is undeniable and crucial.

Further, all of America's combat forays since World War II have been essentially against non-Europeans and nonwhites (Korea and Vietnam, obviously, but also our various Caribbean and Central American expeditions, not to mention the Middle Eastern disasters of the marine barracks in Lebanon, the muscle flexing of the Libyan bombing, and the massive troop presence in Saudi Arabia following Iraq's invasion of Kuwait and culminating in Operation Desert Storm). But it is the utter lack of recognition of "others"—that there are people not like us, who do not want to be like us, who do not, in fact, like us, and a moral and ethical blindness masquerading as moral certitude (Americans as missionaries of the one true way)— that involved us tragically in Vietnam. And even the retrospective dramatic analyses of the Vietnam War focus on *us*, on what the war did to us, on how we entered Vietnam with either good or bad intentions, but never on Vietnam as a historical site, never on the Vietnamese as genuine subjects, as people with a culture, a heritage, a political agenda, even a cultural and political confusion all their own.[44] We need to come to terms with not simply how race and culture colored America's Vietnam excursion, and led to the entirely preventable tragedies of the war, but as well with how an essential cultural myopia got America into the war in the first place and clouds Americans' vision still.

Notes

1. I deliberately attribute this insight to John Milius, as the surfing sequence appears in his original screenplay (written in 1969). Many of the

ambiguities of *Apocalypse Now* can be credited to the three "authors" involved in the film: Milius, Coppola, and Conrad. The importance of surfing, as life and as metaphor, appears prominently in Milius's *Big Wednesday* (1978—the watershed year for Vietnam films). And while it is fashionable to condemn Milius for his neofascist leanings, with some justification in light of *Red Dawn* (1984), we should not overlook the progressive, critical elements that he is also capable of communicating.

2. Loren Baritz, *Backfire: A History of How American Culture Led Us into Vietnam and Made Us Fight the Way We Did* (New York: William Morrow, 1985) 29.

3. Ibid. 37.

4. Quoted in ibid. 38.

5. Quoted in ibid. 42.

6. Quoted in ibid. 43.

7. Ibid. 30.

8. Also quoted, in another context, in James A. Stevenson, "Beyond Stephen Crane: *Full Metal Jacket*," *Literature/Film Quarterly* 16 (1988): 242.

9. Quoted in Baritz, *Backfire* 42–43.

10. Michael Ryan and Douglas Kellner, *Camera Politica: The Politics and Ideology of Contemporary Hollywood Film* (Bloomington: Indiana University Press, 1988) 199.

11. A more complex vision of how the United States entered the Vietnam War through a series of gradual steps, seen primarily (but not exclusively) in economic terms, may be found in Andrew J. Rotter, *The Path to Vietnam: Origins of the American Commitment to Southeast Asia* (Ithaca, N.Y.: Cornell University Press, 1987). Rotter does, in part, support the benevolent theory of our Indochina intrusion, when he notes some of the key features of "the ideology of American diplomacy . . . : (1) the belief that people have the right of self-determination; (2) the belief that no people truly exercising self-determination will choose communism or authoritarianism because all people desire representative political institutions; (3) the belief that economic progress and political freedom can exist only where the means of production are, for the most part, privately owned . . . [and that] behind these ideas is a faith that America's moral rectitude is absolute and a confidence that American power is sufficient to persuade the unconvinced" (3). Unfortunately, these ideals, especially the economic components of them, had by the late 1940s "been hopelessly compromised" (4).

12. Marilyn B. Young, "Review of *Backfire*," *Bulletin of Concerned Asian Scholars* 8.3 (1986): 61.

13. In an article cowritten with Gaylyn Studlar, "Never Having to Say You're Sorry: *Rambo*'s Rewriting of the Vietnam War," *Film Quarterly* 42.1 (1988): 9–16, we make the point that the question "Were we right to fight in Vietnam" has shifted to "What is our responsibility to the veterans of the war" as a means of rewriting our initial involvement. We might take such a shift toward questioning *how* we fought the war, instead of *why* we did so, as a variation on this mythic process.

14. Quoted in Baritz, *Backfire* 40.

15. Ibid. 22.

16. Ibid. 233.

17. I am here eliminating *The Green Berets* (1968) from "significance" primarily because what significance it has is a perverse one—the only film actually made in *favor* of the war.

18. Michael Pursell, "*Full Metal Jacket*: The Unraveling of Patriarchy," *Literature/Film Quarterly* 16 (1988): 222. Pursell is speaking primarily of *Platoon*, but the quote can stand for many Vietnam War films.

19. Ryan and Kellner, *Camera Politica* 197.

20. Terry Christensen, *Reel Politics: American Political Movies from Birth of a Nation to Platoon* (New York: Basil Blackwell, 1987) 152.

21. Ryan and Kellner, *Camera Politica* 198.

22. For this whole question of victimization, see Studlar and Desser, "Never Having to Say."

23. Ella Shohat, *Israeli Cinema: East/West and the Politics of Representation* (Austin: University of Texas Press, 1989) 241. Even much of the political discourse in Israel and the United States among Jews condemns the occupation of "Palestinian" territory for its effects on the nature of Zionism and the soul of Israel.

24. Albert Auster and Leonard Quart, *How the War Was Remembered: Hollywood and Vietnam* (New York: Praeger, 1988) 57–58. I would say, however, that Stone's novel sees America as *already* corrupted, as indicated by the shift in the character portrayed by Tuesday Weld. In the novel, she works in a pornographic movie theater; in the film she works with her father in a Berkeley bookstore. This fact, combined with the *deserted* former hippie commune of the climax, gives the film a "death of the sixties" flavor—Vietnam as the end of innocence and utopia—that the more cynical novel does not possess.

25. Also quoted in Christensen, *Reel Politics* 208.

26. Auster and Quart, *How the War Was Remembered* 56.

27. Baritz, *Backfire* 30.

28. Auster and Quart, *How the War Was Remembered* 54, 54–55.

29. Daniel Ford, *Incident at Muc Wa* (Garden City, N.Y.: Doubleday, 1967).

30. Rob Edelman, "A Second Look: *Go Tell the Spartans*," *Cineaste* 13 (1983): 18.

31. Edelman claims that "Cowboy is no freedom fighter, just a sadist who relishes torturing and murdering his countrymen. It is poetic justice that he is nicknamed Cowboy, a symbolic token of America's presence in Vietnam" (ibid. 19). But this gloss on the name strikes me as insufficient. First of all, why do we need a "symbolic token of America's presence" when the American presence is overt, there in the flesh, in the form of U.S. advisers (who are, in fact, combat troops). It overlooks the sense of American perceptions of the cruelty of the Oriental, the links between this Vietnamese soldier and the Japanese samurai. But most significantly, his analysis underrates the influence of American culture on Vietnam—that Cowboy has reformulated an image of himself based on American cinema.

32. The use of references to World War II is virtually ubiquitous in all of the discourses surrounding the Vietnam War, including, and especially, novels, films, and television, and is too complex to go into here. In *Go Tell the Spartans*, Major Barker experiences World War II nostalgia—the longing for the sense of a clearly defined right and wrong, and for the (European) landscape on which the war was fought, interestingly enough. In addition to the obvious references U.S. soldiers make to John Wayne movies (as in *Full Metal Jacket*), we should also note how World War II *movies* functioned as a kind of myth for arriving American soldiers in Vietnam, the shattering of which myth is alleged to be the root cause of so much of the disillusionment and alienation of the U.S. grunt. For an in-depth discussion of how the "John Wayne Wet Dream" created by World War II movies "served to initiate young American males into the mysteries of war, the purposes that war is intended to accomplish, and the role one is expected to adopt within that war," see Lloyd B. Lewis, *The Tainted War: Culture and Identity in Vietnam War Narratives* (Westport, Conn.: Greenwood Press, 1985) 22, and 19–37 generally.

33. Michael Herr, *Dispatches* (New York: Alfred A. Knopf, 1977) 74.

34. Excerpts from *A Rumor of War*, *Nam*, and *Fields of Fire*, quoted in Lewis, *The Tainted War* 91.

35. Ibid.

36. Ibid. 31.

37. Auster and Quart, *How the War Was Remembered* 54.

38. Ibid.

39. Tim O'Brien, *If I Die in a Combat Zone* 119, quoted in Lewis, *The Tainted War* 93.

40. Susan Jeffords, in "Women, Gender, and the War," *Critical Studies in Mass Communications* 6 (1989): 87, makes the point that "dominant representations of the Vietnam War should . . . be read as cultural responses to changing gender relations in the United States." She challengingly accuses not only what we have above termed as "right-wing" Vietnam films, like *Rambo* and *Uncommon Valor,* but also those more typically thought of as "leftist" films, including *Platoon* and *Full Metal Jacket,* of participating in "efforts to reestablish the social value of masculinity and restabilize the patriarchal system of which it is a part."

41. Sheila K. Johnson, *The Japanese through American Eyes* (Stanford, Calif.: Stanford University Press, 1988) 19–20. The idea that the Japanese were poorly equipped was a constant in the early phase of the Pacific war. We simply did not believe that their technology was as good as ours, even in the case of the Zero fighter plane, generally accepted now as the finest of World War II. This notion that Japanese technology was inferior to ours found a resonance in the Vietnam War, except our enemies were devalued for their (alleged) total *lack* of technology. Thus we still shake our heads in wonderment at how we lost the war in Vietnam to a nation without technology.

42. John Dower, *War without Mercy: Race and Power in the Pacific War* (New York: Pantheon, 1986) 99.

43. Johnson, *The Japanese through American Eyes* 8–9.

44. Although it was fashionable among some members of the counterculture and the New Left to side with the North Vietnamese, to praise Ho Chi Minh at the expense of LBJ or Richard Nixon, the antiwar forces never had much knowledge of the North Vietnamese; for instance, comparing their situation, albeit in a sympathetic way, with that of Native Americans. I do not think you can find a genocidal imperative in the American involvement in Vietnam, as you can, of course, within Manifest Destiny and the European response to native peoples. (Michael Pursell, in the article "*Full Metal Jacket,*" cited above, does think there was a genocidal undercurrent, and he links it to a "gynocidal" impulse within patriarchy; see especially 221.) Moreover, even acknowledging that the governmental and social system of contemporary Vietnam (the unified Vietnam since

1975) is hardly the model of democracy one might wish for does not negate the anticolonialist imperative of North Vietnam and the VC, or the attempt to establish nationhood and national identity. One is reminded of some right-wing discourse in the wake of the revelations of the horrors committed by the Khmer Rouge in Cambodia (the killing fields)—that their actions retrospectively justified our Indochina involvement. That is the equivalent of saying a major European power would have been justified in occupying the U.S. during our Civil War on the basis of what the North did to the South in the Reconstruction period!

Ellen Draper

Finding a Language for Vietnam in the Action-Adventure Genre

CHAPTER 5 In *Swimming to Cambodia*, Spalding Gray reworks two maxims concerning the American involvement in Southeast Asia:

> How does a country like America, or rather how does America, because certainly there's no country like it, begin to find a language to negotiate or talk with a country like Russia or Libya if I can't even *begin* to get it with my people on the corner of Broadway and John Street?

> It was a kind of visitation of hell on earth. Who needs metaphors for hell, or poetry about hell? This actually happened here on this earth. Pregnant mother disemboweled. Eyes gouged out. Kids, children torn apart like fresh bread in front of their mothers. And this went on for years until two million people were either systematically killed or starved to death by the same people. And no one can really figure out how something like that could have happened.[1]

Our perception of what happened is limited by our subjectivity even now; and our systems of signification are exposed as meaningless in the face of the war's violence. Perhaps while it was being fought, and certainly now that it is being mythologized by the cinema, Vietnam has been the postmodern war par excellence. The United States did not lose the war: we withdrew, but we lost ourselves in the process. Beginning with *The Deer Hunter* in 1978, movies about Vietnam have documented the loss with more and more sophisticated confessions of failure, culminating in *Full Metal Jacket* a decade later in 1987. In an essay on the Kubrick film, Thomas Doherty implies that our retelling of what happened in Vietnam has become tantamount to cinematic suicide.

> It is in the barracks lavatory that [Leonard] freaks out, that the violent rite of passage comes to a head. For this sequence, Kubrick's set design bears comment because it is reportedly his only liberty with authentic Marine interior decor. Stark white, two rows of open toilets face each other, with Leonard, himself in white underwear and astride a john, smack dab in this literal world of shit. On fire watch, Joker enters and Leonard explains that his M-14 is indeed being loaded with live rounds ("7.62 mm, full metal jacket"). Hartman bursts in on the commotion, totally unintimidated by the live weapon, and bellows, "What is your major malfunction, numbnuts?" A patented slo-mo impact shot records Leonard's high-velocity answer: Hartman's chest explodes and he falls lifeless to the immaculate floor. After a tense consideration of Joker, Leonard sits down, turns the barrel into his mouth, and blows himself against the bathroom wall. His red blood splatters against the pure white tile. After this, Vietnam is redundant.[2]

What the movies mean when they say "Vietnam" is the collapse of American culture on every level: institutionally, interpersonally, and semiotically. To say this meaningfully through the collapsed, failed medium of a Hollywood film is no simple feat. Films about the American experience in Vietnam are at the disadvantage of having to represent this failure within their diegesis; and by and large they have not found the means of qualifying their own power of representation enough to realize the bitter potential of Vietnam as a cinematic trope. A curious sentimentality pervades such films as *Platoon* (1986), the sentimentality of believing that movies about Vietnam can signify something within the culture. Only in isolated instances have films about Vietnam managed enough cynicism to realize the cinematic myth of Vietnam: Kubrick demonstrates his singular power of detachment and analysis in *Full Metal Jacket*; and Jonathan Demme and Spalding Gray successfully approach the futility of Vietnam via the marginality of performance art in *Swimming to Cambodia*. In both cases an individual questions the conventions of Hollywood filmmaking to show us how inadequate all American institutions have become since Vietnam corroded our culture.

Sustained generic deconstruction of the American experience in Southeast Asia is more than we can expect of films about Vietnam: precisely insofar as they constitute a genre, a set of conventions, Vietnam films will have traded critique for consensus. Instead of looking to the genre of Vietnam combat films for an account of the American experience in Southeast Asia, we would do better to look at another genre—action movies, in which the displaced trauma of Vietnam recurs as the failure of American culture.

Action films are uniquely qualified to take up the critique of American institutions, including Hollywood, for in order to revel in the mechanical violence of an action film a viewer must accept the film's proposition that traditional Hollywood processes of cinematic signification have collapsed in upon themselves and failed. The American cinema, these movies assume, is a semiotic wasteland, and the films figure that wasteland in their settings. A few action films name the wasteland Vietnam—I am thinking of *Rambo* (1985), which seems to me much more an action film than a Vietnam film— while others allude to the American involvement in Vietnam or Cambodia as the source of moral and semiotic failure. In this chapter I concentrate on two action films that recognize the failure of American culture and cinema and attempt to overcome it: *Aliens* (1986) and *Predator* (1987). These films are not literally Vietnam films, but that lack of cultural self-consciousness makes them all the more successful accounts of the suicidal legacy of Vietnam.

Despite its sci-fi overtones, *Aliens* is first and foremost an action film. Its production history alone would entitle it to consideration as an action picture: it has become Hollywood lore that James Cameron wrote *Rambo* and *The Terminator* (1984) and *Aliens* at the same time, at three separate desks in the same apartment, before going on to direct the latter films. Production history aside, one has only to watch *Aliens* to recognize its commitment to violent and repetitive action. After a quiet opening section the film explodes into a prolonged battle sequence that rarely lets up. For the last hundred minutes of the film the protagonists fire guns, flamethrowers, grenades, and rockets at the alien life force they encounter on a distant planet, and if the body count stays relatively low by action-film standards it is only because the monsters are so amorphous that it is difficult to tell when they die on screen.

What all the action in *Aliens* may distract one from noticing is that the plot of the film is very basic. A spacecraft lands on a small planet where a colony of settlers has disappeared. On board are Ellen Ripley (Sigourney Weaver), sole survivor of the original film *Alien* (1979), a Company man named Burke, a squad of marines, and a "synthetic person" who is a sophisticated robot. Searching the abandoned colony for alien life, they encounter the monstrous aliens in an area directly beneath the cooling system for the colony's central nuclear reactor. In the firefight that ensues, the marines rupture the cooling system and it begins to fail, leaving the protagonists only a few hours to regroup, get back to their spaceship, and get off the planet before a nuclear explosion engulfs them together with the aliens.

This sounds like the plot of at least half a dozen episodes of *Star Trek*, not to mention several fifties' sci-fi films, but not to worry: in *Aliens* this plot is given scant attention. It has nothing to do with character development, thematic unity, or even the film's subplots, such as Ripley and Burke's struggle for control of the troops. What gives *Aliens* its aesthetic integrity and its structural coherence is not its plot but its participation in the genre of action films. In other words, *Aliens* is such a quintessential action film that it sacrifices plot to action on a grand scale, and that is why the film interests me.

In placing action in opposition to plot I am implicitly differentiating contemporary action films from such predecessor genres as the war film and the western, genres that devote considerable narrative attention to plotting action that will be undertaken against the enemy or the bad guys in the black hats. To some degree, of course, action sequences always disrupt plot development. In traditional Hollywood genres, however, the plot projects meaning onto the significatory chaos of a battle or chase scene. In action films the plot of the film defers to the insignificance of the action. Action sequences stand as self-contained segments of the film, rather like the dance numbers in Hollywood musicals: they do not advance the plot except in an indirect manner, and they depend upon the audience suspending its expectations of cinematic realism if they are to succeed. Instead of characterizing the incoherence of fighting as the threat wielded by the enemy Other, and celebrating victory as the restoration of social and narrative order, an action film defers to the meaninglessness of fight scenes and is liable to conclude that the violence we are party to is just what we should expect of our culture.

The idea that as serious filmgoers we have been reduced to merely suspending the rules of narrative logic and dramatic unity to watch bodies and vehicles explode by the dozens during an action film is not an attractive proposal. During a Christmas visit in 1987 I had a long argument with a sister who had been to see *Lethal Weapon* (1987) and was appalled that a pair of thirteen-year-old boys behind her were cheering at the violence in the film. The boys found the scene in which a house explodes with its resident within it especially satisfying. I suppose my sister could have been sitting in front of thirteen-year-old sadists so hardened to pain, and at the same time so naïve to the conventions of Hollywood films, that they believed that the violence they saw was real and enjoyed it as much as they would have enjoyed such atrocities in everyday life. However, I like to think that the boys recognized the violence as artificial and orchestrated—as we all do when we watch these films.

The best argument I have for the knowingness with which we watch the violence in action films is the way in which the films themselves recognize the failure of cinematic signification. *Predator*, the Arnold Schwarzenegger vehicle of 1987, develops this failure of cinematic signification as its primary plot. In *Predator*, Arnold plays Dutch, a mercenary who leads a crew of former Marines on international rescue missions. At the beginning of the film, Dutch and his men are recruited by the U.S. government to rescue diplomats from rebel forces in an unspecified Central American country. This plot turns out to be bogus: the diplomats are CIA agents with blood on their hands, and as Dutch and his men approach the rebel stronghold to free them the "diplomats" are executed by the rebels. The Americans prepare to attack: "Showtime!" one of them announces cheerfully. A battle ensues in which several dozen Central American nationals and their Russian military advisers are killed. After a four-minute battle montage that includes dozens of explosions, half a dozen burning bodysuits, several slow-motion machine-gun deaths, one impalement, and a signature bad pun ("Stick around"), Dutch discovers that the violence was anticipated: the entire mission has been a hoax. Dutch is bitter about this. He resents having been lured into Central America on false pretenses, but by this point all he can do is gather his men and start toward a location where U.S. helicopters can pick them up.

At this point, when the plot of the film has been exposed as pointless and all that remains is an exit from the jungle, the real threat in the film makes an appearance. Not coincidentally, the joking about violence stops. The Predator initially appears as a Rick Greenberg special effect, a distortion of the image of the jungle in the shape of a humanoid. It looks as if the filmstrip itself is being stretched and moved by a human shape beneath it. Later the Predator doffs this disguise and reveals himself to be a Stan Winston monster, a sort of cross between a space alien and the Terminator, with mandibles instead of a mouth but sophisticated prosthetic armor and equipment. In his latter incarnation the Predator is disappointing: it is in his disguise that he is genuinely frightening, because he disguises himself not as a part of the jungle but as the *image* of the jungle.

If we know that the violent battle sequences in action films are elaborately staged set pieces, we still cannot be sure of their meaning. Do action films give us a representation of some real struggle between good and evil, or are they merely formal exercises in cinematic montage and special effects? And what would count as a definitive answer to the question, one way or the other? The real tension in action films comes, not from the montages of explosions and falling bodies, but from our inability to evaluate such violence, except in terms of its formal accomplishment. When the Predator first appears he literally brings to life the threat of meaningless formalism. An alien life force capable of disguising itself as a cinematic image threatens the process of cinematic signification at the most basic level. Exploding buildings and simulated shootings are child's play compared to this threat of violence, which exposes the inadequacy of the cinema as a repository of narrative meaning and culture.

This is the point at which a Vietnam film would have to stop, leaving us with its more or less successful deconstruction of Hollywood filmmaking as a metaphor for/misrepresentation of Vietnam. When Kubrick's marines march off into the night singing the Mickey Mouse Club theme song in the last shot of *Full Metal Jacket,* the Marines and the film are recognizing that their struggle admits no rational rhetoric. The enemy has become indistinguishable from the act of fighting. *Full Metal Jacket* has chronicled the collapse of the distance between cinematic signifier and signified, and it is over. Action films being the children of melodrama, however, they do not end at an impasse. They proceed to redeem the cinematic process of signification at the expense of all plot credibility.

In *Predator* Dutch's men are killed by the monster in short order. The sexist dies first, the brute second, and then the merely macho falls victim to the jungle monster. The blacks die heroically, and finally the Native American turns to meet the Predator: guided by what the film assumes are his cultural traditions, he ritually cuts himself to hasten the approach of the monster. Dutch sends the female revolutionary his squad has taken prisoner ahead to meet the American helicopters,[3] and he and the Predator prepare for hand-to-hand combat.

In order to fight the Predator, Dutch discovers that he must cover himself with native soil. Once he has become a part of the earth he becomes invisible to his enemy, whom he can now counter-attack in an elaborate ambush using such natural materials as vines, sticks, and rocks. Covered with native soil he can fight the Predator on the monster's terms, using the jungle as a disguise, as it does.

Predator is not the only action film in which the hero covers himself with native soil: in *Rambo* the conclusive action sequence begins when John Rambo literally bursts from the side of a hill, where he has buried himself, and attacks the Russians who are stalking him. Both of these sequences, in *Rambo* and in *Predator*, mark the films' recognition of the impossibility of reconciling American interests and native interests at the level of human interaction. In *Rambo* the union of Rambo and the land comes immediately after the Vietnamese woman with whom he has fought and fallen in love has been killed by the Russians. In *Predator* Dutch's discovery of his camouflage occurs after the mission to save American diplomacy in Central America has been aborted on every level. In these literal back-to-the-earth scenes the action-film genre recognizes that foreign territories are so hostile to American colonization that it is meaningless to posit foreign nationals as the enemy. We are the problem, and when we fully confront the horror that threatens us we find that the monster is a dark reflection of ourselves. Only by burying himself in native slime can the protagonist address the monster within.[4]

At the end of *Predator*, when Dutch has defeated the monster by springing one of the traps he rigged from vines and logs, the following confrontation takes place. Dutch is standing over the wounded alien with a large boulder, ready to smash the monster, when the creature removes his Darth Vader mask and reveals his insect face. The sight gives Dutch pause. He lowers the boulder and exclaims "What the hell are you?" Unexpectedly, he receives a reply. In a guttural, mechanical voice the alien repeats the question back to him: "What the hell are you?" Devoid of intonation, the alien's response mirrors Dutch's question on two levels. It literally turns the protagonist's question back on himself and asks Dutch to ponder who he is and what he is doing. At the same time the alien's question repeats the protagonist's words with such mechanical exactness that it questions the whole process of cinematic signification. What does it mean to ask this question? The flat, mechanical repetition of the monster not only asks Dutch to consider what he is doing fighting for the United States; it also asks us to ponder what the actor Arnold Schwarzenegger is doing standing in the jungle holding a rock while we watch him from a theater seat.

Having attained a moment of deconstruction so pervasive that it amounts to cinematic suicide, the film plays out the scenario in its narrative. The Predator punches a detonation code into a wristband and laughs in anticipation of his impending explosion. Dutch realizes what is happening and starts running. A few seconds later a climactic fireball rips through the jungle. From the helicopter on its way to rescue Dutch a mushroom cloud is visible above the rain forest. The confrontation between man and monster double—and the configuration between film and monster double—is finally figured as a suicide by nuclear explosion.[5]

Where does this leave us with *Aliens*—or, to be more precise, where does it leave Ripley with the alien monster? When in *Aliens* the marines track the bodies of the colonists to the central cooling station they discover a landscape that looks like nothing so much as the inside of a human body. Ripley's final frightening discovery is the egg chamber of the queen monster: as numerous critics of the film have noted, the ultimate threat to Ripley in *Aliens* is a vision of feminine sexuality writ large. What it means to let a female protagonist remain the protagonist of an action film is, according to *Aliens*, to shift the battleground of the film from geographical locations like Vietnam or Central America to the female body. When Ripley turns her flamethrower on the egg cases and backs away with Newt, the orphan she has adopted, the violence of the image is horrifying; and yet it is consonant with a woman's need to control her own body. Like the monsters in *Rambo* and *Predator*, the alien in *Aliens* is indistinguishable from the landscape, but in this case the landscape turns out to look like the inside of Ripley herself. The alien is not a double for Ripley but a part of her, and the foreign territory she must negotiate to defeat it is some part of herself.

This is ultimately the point of the Vietnam films, that the alien we engaged with in that war was not foreign but familiar. We were, and as the movies go, still are, fighting a part of ourselves in the rice paddies of Southeast Asia. Without directly addressing the issue of the U.S. involvement in Vietnam, such action films as *Aliens* and *Predator* offer a critique of American culture and of Hollywood moviemaking that speaks eloquently of the American loss in Southeast Asia.

Hollywood being an institution that in its very nature as an institution condones racism, sexism, capitalistic exploitation, and artistic compromise, it is the last place we should look for sincere and moving representations of what happened to the U.S. cultural consciousness in Vietnam. Spalding Gray notes in *Swimming to Cambodia* the exploitation of Asians, now not in the name of a battle for democracy but in the name of filmmaking. During the production of the film *The Killing Fields* (1984), Gray reports working among

> Thai peasants lying for twelve hours with chicken giblets and fake blood all over them . . . they're getting paid $5.00 for a twelve-hour day smiling back at you; if they're real amputees they get $7.50 for the day. You don't have to act. It's very much like the real event.[6]

Gray sardonically proposed that next time we should just do a movie and skip the military invasion.

Where Vietnam movies are hampered by the very corrosion of culture that they would document, action films are free to remark the failure of the cinema, and so in an important sense they are truest to the American experience in Vietnam. Their critique of American institutions, including Hollywood, effectively marginalizes most mainstream Vietnam films by showing us that the real legacy of the American involvement in Southeast Asia, a pervasive mistrust of cultural institutions, prevents film from being able to talk about anything in a straightforward manner. Finding a cinematic language in which we can talk about Vietnam, the action films remind us, may well require not mentioning Vietnam as a subject.

Notes

1. Spalding Gray in *Swimming to Cambodia* (Cinecom Pictures, 1987): directed by Jonathan Demme.

2. Tom Doherty, "Full Metal Genre: Kubrick's Vietnam Combat Movie," *Film Quarterly* 42.2 (1988–89): 24–30.

3. Why she completes this rendezvous remains entirely unexplained: given what we have seen of the military in this film, we have every reason to object to the credibility of her "rescue" by American choppers. Although the implication that Dutch's impending combat with the Predator could not be undertaken by a woman is disturbing, relegating a woman to the role of helpmate would be even more unsettling. One can only be consoled that *Predator* has not worked through the generic problems of women in action films; and be heartened by the fact that in Schwarzenegger's *Total Recall* (1990) there is a woman-to-woman fight scene that redresses this shortcoming in *Predator*.

4. This image of immersion in native slime is so central to the action-film genre that it occurs with minimal plot justification. Consider, for example, the mud-wrestling and hand-to-hand combat finale in *Lethal Weapon*.

5. If we accept this image of self-destruction, we may as well accept the film's conclusion, which is hardly upbeat but which defies plot credibility so completely that it qualifies as melodramatic happy ending: Dutch inexplicably survives the nuclear explosion, and he and Anna, the Central American revolutionary, fly off in a helicopter with U.S. government agents.

6. Spalding Gray, in *Swimming to Cambodia*.

Tony Williams

Narrative Patterns
and Mythic Trajectories
in Mid-1980s Vietnam Movies

CHAPTER 6 Since the 1983 release of *Uncommon Valor*, critical opinion has discerned considerable differences between recently released Vietnam films and those of the seventies. While nearly all Vietnam films present the conflict as a personal American tragedy and avoid any complexities of political reinterpretations (with the honorable exception of *Twilight's Last Gleaming* [1977]), eighties products have a more conservative bias contrasting with their more venturesome predecessors.[1]

One explanation for this tendency lies in the contemporary political climate. The elections of Reagan and Bush, with their ideologically conservative simplistic dreamworlds, had an undeniable appeal to a nation that has safely distanced itself from past historical humiliations.[2] As in the final years of the Weimar Republic and in post–World War I Italy, leaders emerge promising a return to former greatness and reversal of a previous decade's negative experiences. This nostalgic clarion call ignores continuing past and present historical complexities. It actively attempts to deny them any avenues of contemporary expression. Similarly, conservative ideological-communication mechanisms actively engage in new linguistic structures. Vietnam becomes a "noble crusade." Fantastic invocations of American unity emerge by negatively reworking semantic significations of such terms as "liberal" and the oppositional associations of previous decades, such as the sixties.

The Hollywood industry also reflects this social and political climate. As well as illustrating eighties cultural impoverishment, contemporary American cinema engages in an attempt to refurbish discredited concepts of previous decades. The cult of patriarchal masculinity in the emergence of Chuck Norris, Arnold Schwarzenegger, and Sylvester Stallone is one example. A second is the comfortable "yuppie" conclusion of sixties radicalism in *The Big Chill* (1983) and the incorporation of a new youth generation within the dominant ideological norms of *St. Elmo's Fire* (1985). Another tendency is an attempt to restore the fictional World War II *master narrative* to Vietnam reinterpretations. As Steve Fore has ably demonstrated in his doctoral dissertation, the generic World War II movie formula suffered from the Korean War.[3] It eventually collapsed (seemingly beyond repair) as a result of the Vietnam experience, which could not comfortably fit into any previous formula providing identifiable interpretative keys to either participants or spectators.

Uncommon Valor unexpectedly struck a chord by providing a mythical fantastic reinterpretation of the Vietnam experience in codes familiar to its audience.[4] Chief among these were the restoration of patriarchal heroic leadership, reversal of national humiliation, and the reinvocation of the Puritan Captivity Narrative mastercode that often provided a convenient answer in times of emergency. It is a key product of the eighties, providing both the necessary mythic undertones and linear narrative trajectory to a conflict that historically refused both. Mid-1980s Vietnam movies have emerged in a Presidential realm whose "dream factory" aura appears to confirm post-1968 critical suspicions about the worst aspects of narrative cinema.

The "obvious" reaction is to write off eighties Vietnam movies as pathological expressions of an era's dominant tendencies in contrast to their seventies predecessors. However, closer examination reveals a much more complex process in operation, blurring any conveniently clear lines of demarcation. Indeed, there are actually more continuities than radical differences in both narrative content and mythic trajectories. Divisions between *Apocalypse Now* (1979) and *Uncommon Valor* may be more apparent than real. While allowing for each decade's historical influence on any given text, it is a mistake to view eighties Vietnam films as *entirely* ideological productions of Reaganite entertainment.[5]

Seventies and eighties Vietnam films have very specific connections and belong to a developing genre. Each work reflects and modifies its predecessor in certain ways, but the alteration may not be as radical as it seems. All Vietnam films attempt to impose some form of narrative order upon a conflict that refuses, both historically and fictionally, any form of convenient definition. In the seventies and eighties there are parallel cultural significations in terms of myth and narrative. While a film might articulate a one-dimensional monologic meaning—Coppola's Vietnam "Heart of Darkness" or Stallone's "noble crusade"—the text's very nature might reflect mixed images refusing a seamless suture. It can do this by revealing the hysterical violence of narrative superimposition, as in *Rambo* (1985) and *Missing in Action* (1984). Conversely, it can reflect the dialogic[6] tensions of earlier generic narratives in opposing eighties sacrificial heroism to bureaucratic bunglings and misadministration. Here *Hamburger Hill* (1987) has an undeniable relationship to both *Pork Chop Hill* (1959) and *Attack!* (1956) despite its ideological emphasis on grunt heroism. Also, though Vietnam War films appear exclusively male oriented, we must not forget the crucial role of sexual difference. The war film "also almost incorporates the direct representation of women, no matter how 'contrived' or 'clumsy' this may seem in terms of the logic of a given narrative."[7]

Influenced by the war-movie genre, Vietnam literature, historical awareness, and personal experience, all Vietnam films employ their version of "the truth."[8] It is a practice similar to previous war representations. However, no film has yet depicted the broad historical complexities of the entire conflict. The films usually concentrate on a limited area, both historically and geographically, as if realizing Vietnam literature's similar dilemma of creating any absolute truth about the conflict.[9] This is a common factor of seventies and eighties films and of the one Vietnam movie made during the time of the actual conflict. *The Green Berets* (1968) deals with the period before heavy military commitment, as does *Go Tell the Spartans* (1978). *Apocalypse Now* is set sometime after the Tet offensive, while the MIA subgenre avoids the past to achieve a mythical victory years after the conflict's historical resolution. Most eighties Vietnam movies resemble those literary narrative structures where several genres frequently recombine rather than permanently fuse in any established prose pattern.[10] Contemporary generic mixtures occur with *film noir* and *film policier* (*Off Limits* [1988]), comedy (*Good Morning, Vietnam* [1987]), and westerns (*Uncommon Valor, Missing in Action, Missing in Action II: The Beginning* [1985], and *Braddock* [1988]). The badly distributed *Riders of the Storm* (1986) merges Vietnam's historical lessons with an anarchic attack on contemporary political and media manipulations against politicians seeking to fight the War again in Latin America. These generic fusions have their antecedents in earlier films with explicit (*The Green Berets*) or implicit (*Soldier Blue* [1970], *Dark Star* [1974], *Ulzana's Raid* [1972], *The Missouri Breaks* [1976], *Dead of Night* [1972], *Southern Comfort* [1981]) associations.[11] The Vietnam motif is influential in works far removed from the war genre, such as *Aliens* (1986) and *Predator* (1987), which equally warn against bringing technological faith to inhospitable terrains.[12]

Although all are rich in Vietnam associations, they reflect a tendency to use selected motifs for fictional reconstructions rather than deal with the entire sociohistorical complexity. Hanoi's eventual 1975 victory dealt a devastating blow to America's belief in twentieth-century extensions of Manifest Destiny. Even today its consequences are disavowed. Instead, "Vietnam" is a dominant phantom whose historically complex presence still awaits demystified recognition. So far, this affront to the chosen race's beliefs in historical invulnerability can only be displaced to other generic structures, where it functions as an important background submotif.

Although the heroic figures of *Aliens* and *Predator* eventually succeed, it is by qualities of human initiative rather than faith in technological superiority that failed in Vietnam's "Indian Country." Similarly, the western/Vietnam displacements in *Ulzana's Raid* and *Southern Comfort* contain the negative messages of ignominious defeat.

Thus all films attempt the impossible task of making sense of or imposing some order upon representations of the conflict. Toby G. Herzog's comments about Vietnam literature have an undeniable application to filmic depictions.

> Critics of American fiction emerging from the Vietnam War often note the novelist's difficulties in getting a handle on the war experiences and shaping them into a tightly fused work similar to novels emerging from previous wars. Vietnam with its fragmentation, complexity and illogic presents special problems for an author attempting to order the chaos in a meaningful way. The novelist's disadvantage is that this was a war with no center, no decisive battles; it was all circumference and it is therefore difficult to filter the thing through unified plot and point of view. [13]

Such is the dilemma of the Vietnam film genre. Many films tend conveniently to focus upon a predominantly individualized personal tragedy or adolescent bildungsroman. *Platoon* (1986) illustrates Bakhtin's recognition of this motif's antihistorical tendencies. [14] If any attempt at historical-realistic excavation is impossible, there is always escape into wish-fulfillment fantasy, a path taken by Tim O'Brien in *Going after Cacciato*. [15] This is the predominant strain in the majority of Vietnam movies. Ignoring any accurate depictions of the broad social and historical picture, they focus instead on fantastic displacements. These involve familiar patterns of anachronistic cultural myths and narratives. Removed from the dusty cabinets of American historical consciousness, dry-cleaned, and stitched together again after the successful ravages of contradictory arguments, old fantasies become cosmetically reworked to fit the circumstances of an era far removed from their original applicability.

Hollywood's delay in coming to terms with the war was no accident. Far beyond the necessary distancing perspective needed to focus on the conflict, the delay allowed conservative ideological forces, in disarray since *The Green Berets*, to regroup successfully and counterattack. Filmic representations of Vietnam occupy a mythic ideological position similar to that of Custer's Last Stand. Both use mythic and narrative themes to counter the schizophrenic tensions of anti–status quo issues that may or may not be satisfactorily resolved. Nineteenth-century newspaper reinterpretations of the Little Big Horn disaster, juxtaposed with attacks on feminism and on ethnic and working-class movements,[16] bear an uncanny resemblance to those eighties attacks on the media and antiwar demonstrators seen in *Hamburger Hill* and *The Hanoi Hilton* (1987). Feminization of "the enemy" in mid-1980s Vietnam films parallels nineteenth-century interpretations that equated liberalism with softness and sentimentality.[17]

Similar gendered misrepresentations are common to seventies and eighties Vietnam movies. Cimino's Vietcong in *The Deer Hunter* (1978) bear close similarities to the male-hysteria tendencies observed in the Hollywood melodrama, while Coppola's Cambodians in *Apocalypse Now* are virtually savage little children needing a big white father. Both Kurtz and Willard disavow their wives to reinforce a primal sense of patriarchal leadership necessary to win the war. *Rolling Thunder's* (1977) climax represents the power of brutal masculinity over the depicted weakness of feminized family life. Craig Wasson's liberal in *Go Tell the Spartans* soon learns the error of his ways, as does his counterpart in *The Boys in Company C* (1978). *Uncommon Valor* is explicit about the negative female influence on Jason Rhodes's "A-Team," who need his masculine presence to restore their male roles. In *Rambo*, Murdock has undoubted feminine traits.[18] He represents a government bureaucracy that has denied Vietnam's emasculating significance on American powers of male leadership. Thus eighties versions of the Puritan Captivity Narrative logically now have males, instead of females, as victims.[19] This has drastically affected the western and war movies' patriarchal male trajectory, forcing it to adapt to new circumstances.

Government impotence results in MIA feminization. The only recourse is to revive the old hunter-warrior in the guise of Chuck Norris and Sylvester Stallone, who will restore the lost masculinity of John Wayne's cinematic patriarch in a new regeneration-through-violence pattern. Such a narrative will allow no complexity, only an abstract ahistorical interplay of Manichaean opposites. The enemy now becomes a symbolic reincarnation of those alien nineteenth-century blacks, Native Americans, and women. They exhibit traits of irrationality, hysteria, and madness, as opposed to those strong, virile heroes who will restore American supremacy. This imagery is easily applicable to the black renegade officer in *Missing in Action: The Beginning*, as well as to those stereotypical roles played by Aki Aleong, Soon-Teck-Oh, and Mako in *The Hanoi Hilton, Braddock, Missing in Action II: The Beginning*, and *POW: The Escape* (1986).[20]

Although David Carradine, Chuck Norris, Sylvester Stallone, and the anonymous heroes of *Hamburger Hill* are prime examples of eighties virility as opposed to their seventies predecessors, we must not unnecessarily elevate the latent dialogic possibilities of the latter to the restricted monologic dimensions of the former. A key component of seventies films implies that strong leadership would have resulted in a different outcome. Such is the message of *The Boys in Company C* and *Go Tell the Spartans*.[21] Kurtz's behavior in *Apocalypse Now* can also be traced to the hypocritical, soulless bureaucracy Willard meets in the film's beginning. The strong-leadership element eventually becomes a pattern of the "noble crusade" ideology of the eighties.[22] We must remember that, both politically and cinematically, the 1970s were a time of confusion, not of alternatives equally struggling for control. Patriarchy was in retreat, not defeated. Nostalgia for the world of the "silent majority" infiltrated popular consciousness. The crucial difference between Chuck Norris's earlier Vietnam-influenced movie *The Good Guys Wear Black* (1979) and his 1980s *Missing in Action* films is not the absence of the hero figure. Rather, the hero's movement is so restricted by the depressed, leaderless post-Watergate world that there is no open space for his effective operation. This fantastic realm, with its patriarchal components, returned to the screen (and to the White House) in the 1980s. Hence the male hero's triumphant victory.

Several common motifs in Vietnam films relate to both the eighties and the seventies. Contemporary critical opinion notes a more virulent attack on the media in eighties Vietnam films, where they are blamed as being primarily responsible for losing the war. *Hamburger Hill* treats them with explicit contempt. The grunts have more respect for the North Vietnamese "little man" up on the hill than for the newsmen. "At least they take sides, you just take pictures." Although this comment reflects justifiable footsoldier grievance against the media, it is selective in its direction, ignoring such correspondents as Peter Arnett of Associated Press, who covered the entire war in the front line, earning grunt respect. [23] Also, the media did uncover cases of military blunders, lies, and inefficiency that drew justified attention to the war. However, both seventies and eighties films draw on the same monologic view of the media as does the non-Vietnam film *The Dead Pool* (1988), where Harry Callahan treats the press in the same manner as did *Hamburger Hill*'s grunts. Contradictions are noticeable by their very absence, highlighting the unidimensionality of the text.

The Hanoi Hilton presents the media as silent accomplices of the North Vietnamese. They are always on the other side, filmed prominently with the enemy, their long hair contrasting with the POWs' shorn heads. [24] *Full Metal Jacket* (1987) presents war coverage as merely a media circus. The grunts, fully aware of Vietnam's mythical generic interpretations, treat the television crew with contempt. Joker repeats his John Wayne voice at the appearance of the three-man crew. "Is that you, John Wayne? Is this me?" The rest of the platoon satirize the filming. "Hey, start the cameras. This is 'Vietnam—the Movie!'—'I'll be General Custer!'—'We'll let the gooks play the Indians!' " In *Apocalypse Now*, the media direct the troops through classical Hollywood narrative techniques—"Don't look at the camera"—while Dennis Hopper's hippie photojournalist is as much an undiscriminating camp follower as those long-haired accomplices of "Jane Fonda" in *The Hanoi Hilton*.

In both seventies and eighties representations the media are untrustworthy, unreliable, and uninformed. The genesis of this depiction is *The Green Berets*'s liberal journalist, George Beckwith. He only becomes trustworthy when his heart and mind belong to Colonel Kirby's militaristic discourse. At the film's climax he is in uniform and part of the team—the sergeant yells at him, "If you want to go where the war is, it's this way." However, the actual media could not be controlled in this fictional manner. Later films recognize this, presenting the press in a negative, one-dimensional fashion. *The Hanoi Hilton* judges the press as uninformed, opportunistic, and complicit in treason, while *Full Metal Jacket* sees them as cosmically absurd.

Although a major film about the antiwar movement is conspicuous by its absence (or, like *1969* [1989], conspicuously unsuccessful),[25] both seventies and eighties films agree on its irrelevant and dangerous nature. The emotionally bland *Coming Home* (1978) employs a schematic binary opposition between converted paraplegic Luke and militaristic monster-figure Bob in an incoherent and dishonest manner.[26] Although not perceived as such on release, *Coming Home* presents the same superficial avoidance of historical complexity and use of cardboard characters that would, in an inverse manner, characterize the oppositional messages of eighties films. The script is schematically structured so that the actors can only represent stereotypes. They do not undergo any complex personal development relevant to the changing nature of the historical environment. Luke's paraplegic is a bloodless representation of an actual mass movement whose effectivity is confined to a romantic liberal discourse, thus undermining its political significance. It is an easy step from here to stress the antiwar faction as irrelevant and redundant. Such is the link between *The Boys in Company C*'s Dave Bisbee and *Full Metal Jacket*'s Private Joker. Their respective oppositional stances are merely superficial. Both become trapped within the military apparatus, personally (Bisbee) and cosmically (Joker). In either case, basic training and militaristic education will make them "good soldiers," although Kubrick's view is clearly ironic. Despite Joker's "Front Page" cynicism about the conflict, the seeds of his boot-camp training lie dormant within him.

He will never tell the true story of Vietnam but will eventually succumb to a "world of shit." In *Missing in Action: The Beginning* and *POW: The Escape*, both Nestor and the rebel grunt Sparks are displaced representatives of the peace movement. They respectively embody the black and hippie oppositions to the war effort. However, the films recuperate opposition into eventual American unity since both perform "noble sacrifices" and expiate their sins. This duty ethos lies behind the respective condemnations of the antiwar movement in *Hamburger Hill* and *The Hanoi Hilton*. The latter film assigns war protesters indirect responsibility for the traumas and tortures inflicted upon patriotic American soldiers. American demonstrations are conveniently part of the North Vietnamese ideological offensive. *Hamburger Hill*'s peace movement resembles the press in being worse than the enemy by pelting returning GIs with "bags full of dog shit" and making malicious phone calls to bereaved parents. In *Gardens of Stone* (1987) Bill Graham's cartoonish gargoyle retrospectively debases a historically strategic dedicated and radical mass movement responsible for changing American attitudes toward Vietnam. Again, another key narrative element in seventies and eighties films appears in a monological manner that avoids all complexity in both depiction and characterization.

As Andrew Britton has noted, 1970s Vietnam movies contain narrative structures that preserve "a hero-function, but posit in relation to him a situation ('Vietnam') which is not only radically inexplicable, but which has also destabilized the structure of values which support and justify the hero's agency."[27] Contrary to received opinion, the same is true also of eighties movies, despite the overwhelming masculine presences of Norris and Stallone. The World War II generic movie pattern of John Wayne/Audie Murphy heroism can only function in the imaginary terrain of the post-Vietnam situation. *POW: The Escape* is set before the 1973 cease-fire, but it avoids its humiliating complexities to immerse itself in a typical escapade situation. *The Green Berets* has no relationship to the Tet-offensive period of its production. Amalgamating World War II and western genres, it presented its audiences with familiar mythical codes for reassurance.[28] Despite its anachronism, Wayne's ideological project actually anticipated 1980s movie revisionism involving audience removal from the actual historical situation. The subsequent Norris/Stallone films make no attempt at historical resolution. They depict wish-fulfillment resolutions uncontaminated by the realities of the 1964–73 situation.[29] These works are mythical recreations placing the heroic role not in reality but in fantasy. By their very nature they implicitly condemn the hero role as unrealistic. Although they chose to focus on the MIA issue current in the early eighties, such sequels as *Rambo III* (1988) and *Braddock* selected other "topical" issues, such as Afghanistan and the Amerasians. Since these issues were being resolved when the films were released, they become immediately dated as the ideologically produced wish-fulfillment fantasies they were. Removed from their suspect topicality, they simply evoked audience contempt for heroic posturing.

However, films set in the period after the Tet offensive present complications for the heroic role that also render it impotent or absurd. Both seventies and eighties films present contradictory elevations of the hero. The role is still central to the narrative, but it is beset by historical and personal deficiencies that render it either passive or psychotic.

Significantly, relatively few films (*The Green Berets, Go Tell the Spartans, Good Morning, Vietnam*) are set in the early, "innocent" days of American involvement. With the exception of Wayne, these films have protagonists who are not in the least heroic. Burt Lancaster in *Go Tell the Spartans* is more anachronistic than heroic, a debased father figure similar to Lee Majors's Pop in the 1989 season of the CBS *Tour of Duty* television series. Although Norris and Stallone embody 1980s Hollywood monstrous masculinity, their very heroism is, in itself, contradictory. Braddock and Rambo are really the "throwaway generation" victims depicted by such Vietnam writers as Mark Baker and Charles Durden.[30] In the first *Missing in Action* films Braddock's government is never his friend. *First Blood* and *Rambo* present their protagonist as a Frankenstein monster created by the military machine. Once he has served his purpose, he can easily be discarded. The 1969 Ashau Valley in *Hamburger Hill* presents little opportunity for individual heroism, and as a result "the platoon never emerge as more than anonymous cyphers."[31] POW confinement in *The Hanoi Hilton* precludes individual heroics associated with the typical war movie. The main figures are passive, not active. This may be one reason for the film's disastrous reception. The reality of North Vietnam captivity left no room for the imaginary celluloid Norris/Stallone heroics. Placed in an impossible situation, the World War II heroic model of Major Barker in *Go Tell the Spartans* collapses. Heroism is bullshit in *The Boys in Company C*. Despite the final disciplined march at the film's climax, the viewer has already seen enough to doubt both military values and American involvement in Vietnam. Both Willard and Kurtz call war-film heroics into question by their very personalities in *Apocalypse Now*, while *The Deer Hunter* had also destroyed any notion of an effective charismatic leader–hero.[32]

If we have no reliable hero in Vietnam films this naturally affects our usual tendency to credit first-person narration. In *Apocalypse Now*, *Platoon*, and *Full Metal Jacket*, the narrators are never entirely in control. They are victims of outside forces. In accordance with Kurtz's willed primal atavism, Willard becomes Kurtz's designated executioner. He is the pawn of forces beyond his control, whether military bureaucrats or Kurtz's Frazerian-derived sacral king. Willard's youthful successor in *Gardens of Stone* represents conversely the death of the son. Doubting the war's validity in the opening voice-over sequences, Willow becomes a sacrificial victim to both historical inevitability and technological forces (television) beyond his control. In *Platoon*, Chris Taylor is a passive "child born of those two fathers," Barnes and Elias, fighting for "possession of my soul." He is no hero, merely a pawn in a filmic structure using a banal version of Melvillean archetypes and a *Star Wars* Oedipal trajectory signifying an appropriate tombstone of Hollywood's decline. *Full Metal Jacket* reveals the final death of first-person narration. Unlike Michael Herr's "new journalistic" narration in *Dispatches* and *Apocalypse Now*, Joker's voice-overs are unindividualistic, banal, and uninspired. They anticipate that climactic moment when he will destroy what little is left of his individuality and undergo full integration in the Marine Corps' infantile "Mickey Mouse" world.

That moment of Joker's psychic death parallels aspiring writer Alvin Foster's physical death in *The Boys in Company C.* Joker's predecessor utters the last pages of his projected "true story of Vietnam" in a posthumous narration while his platoon sings the marine marching song, anticipating *Full Metal Jacket*'s communal Mickey Mouse chant.

Bureaucratic betrayal by the political/military class is another common link between seventies and eighties films. Whether represented efficiently in *Twilight's Last Gleaming* or ineffectively in *The Losers* (1970) and *The Good Guys Wear Black*, populist discontent with a treacherous or inefficient establishment reflects Vietnam literature's cynical treatment of the same theme. For the most part, it is usually the Frank Capra motif of the one bad egg ruining a still potentially democratic and viable system. *Twilight's Last Gleaming*, which presents the whole military and government establishment as corporatively responsible, offers an important contrast. It failed at the box office, however, ignored by a public who preferred the well-worn lies. The whole American democratic system, this film insists, is irredeemably corrupt, making any attempt at political and individual heroism ineffective. *The Losers, Go Tell the Spartans, Apocalypse Now, The Good Guys Wear Black*, and *Good Morning, Vietnam* are typical in laying blame on individual figures for the chaotic worlds encountered by the hero. Other films present the cause as nameless. Though *Hamburger Hill* and *Platoon* have scenes depicting soldiers decimated by "friendly fire," the action is usually presented as one of individual, not corporate, incompetence.

Even the most rabid right-wing representations contain radical critiques stolen from antiwar discourses. Addressing his men in *Uncommon Valor*, Jason Rhodes utters the anticorporation attack found in the writings of Durden and Baker. "Because you lost, and in this country that's like going bankrupt—you're out of business. They want to forget about you; you cost too much and you didn't turn a profit. That's why they won't go over there and pick up your buddies and bring 'em home because there's no gain in it."

Trautman makes a similar condemnation in *Rambo*. "In 72 we were supposed to pay the Cong four and a half billion dollars as war reparations. We reneged." Murdock denies that any senator will ask "for a couple of billion dollars for a number of forgotten ghosts." In *Gardens of Stone* the military complains about "rifles that do not fire" and "bayonets that do not stab," while the bureaucracy surrounds itself with the technological apparatus that Norman Mailer condemns in *The Armies of the Night.*[33] It is no accident that Rambo's revenge on Murdock's disavowing post-Vietnam establishment consists in destroying its hated technological apparatus. Such motifs have the potential of disrupting the movie-text's right-wing narrative tendencies, but they are never voiced in such a manner as to call the whole project into question. Although ideology never acts in a rigidly dominant manner within any form of entertainment, these films still contain a monological structure that overpowers any possibility of raising contradictions within the audience's mind. The fast-edited, shock-action effect drowns them within its flow. After all, the films are only action movies!

Another instance where contradictions are present, but never fully articulated in such a manner as to call the whole ideological operation into question, involves the gender motif. Most Vietnam literature features a familiar generic pattern depicting war as sublimated sexual aggression involving denial of feminine qualities.[34] It is a motif found also in seventies and eighties films. Tim O'Brien draws obvious conclusions from the combination of bayonet drill and sexist marine marching songs depicting woman as Other. "There is no such thing named love in the world. Women are dinks. Women are villains. They are creatures akin to Communists and yellow-skinned people and hippies."[35] As Klaus Theweleit has shown, this conditioning is an integral part of military training.[36] It is not surprising, therefore, to find its presence in seventies and eighties Vietnam movies. The role of the patriarchal apparatus predominates in virtually every film. In *The Green Berets* woman's only function is as sexual lure. Although woman violates her assigned patriarchal role, she is recuperated by the fatherly intervention of Colonel Kirby. In *Go Tell the Spartans*, a fifteen-year-old NVA spy's successful mission parallels Major Barker's earlier fall from military and political grace because of his overindulgence in "pudenda." This foreshadows the destruction of his Military Assistance Advisory Group mission. *The Boys in Company C* views Vietnamese women generally as whores or male appendages, while *The Deer Hunter* concentrates on its male as opposed to its female characters. Similar patriarchal mechanisms govern other films that use the rescue motif. MIA films involve either women's absence from the main text or their literal expulsion by death (*Rambo, Braddock*). Both Willard and Kurtz in *Apocalypse Now* ignore the female in favor of the patriarchal sacral kingship bond. They equally disavow the female and home, as had Willard's predecessor. Woman is either the enemy or the "other," the latter envisaged in Kurtz's inscrutable Cambodian mistress always silently in the background. Vietnamese women are whores in *Hamburger Hill* and *Full Metal Jacket*, while the antiwar stances of Samantha and Rachel in *Gardens of Stone* easily collapse before Raymond Bellour's classical Hollywood patriarchal marriage motif.[37] *The Hanoi Hilton*'s "Jane Fonda" is an opportunistic, superficial, treacherous bitch fully on the enemy side. In *Good Morning, Vietnam*, Adrian Cronauer's gaze focuses on an ethereal white-clad Vietnamese woman. He does not recognize that her "other" side is her Vietcong terrorist brother. The remaining women are hookers. This patriarchal Madonna-Whore dichotomy also appears in *Off Limits*, which contrasts a white female novice to dark-skinned prostitutes or Vietcong. Brian De Palma's *Casualties of War* (1989) reductively presents the female Vietnamese as the sexual object of the sadistic male gaze, combining both the misogyny of De Palma himself and of certain Vietnam War narratives. Aptly characterized by the *Village Voice* as De Palma's "atrocity," the film presents the Vietnam conflict as a black-and-white male morality play where the woman functions as a mere pawn for Michael J. Fox's crisis of conscience. Having conveniently disposed of Sean Penn's satanic sergeant, the film just as conveniently resurrects its heroine to forgive the innocent victim of past historical sins in the most nauseating climax of any Vietnam movie so far. In Oliver Stone's *Born on the Fourth of July* (1989), woman becomes subordinated within a male melodrama aiming to return its hero to society and the Law of the Father. The film achieves this by the most manipulative use of patriarchal mechanisms yet revealed in contemporary Hollywood cinema. Stone abruptly removes Ron's former high-school girlfriend from the narrative at the time of his hero's conversion, denying her any share in the process. Such a character does not figure in Kovic's original narrative. Although Stone may avoid the war narrative's stereotype of the disabled veteran resuscitated by the love of a good woman (*Pride of the Marines* [1945], *The Best Years of Our Lives* [1946]), the college meeting has negative associations. This now-politicized feminist is so intent on organizing a demonstration that she is completely oblivious to the man, his disability, and his openness to changing his political views. The movie also uses mother as a convenient scapegoat whom Ron can hysterically blame for both his physical and social castration. Visiting Sam Peckinpah's Mexico, giving a conveniently maternal whore an orgasm, Ron is then able to confront his dark side (Willem Dafoe), confess his sins to the family of the man he shot, and gain the phallus (if not the penis) by speaking at the 1984 Democratic convention before an audience mainly composed of silent (Ron's girlfriend) and admiring, autograph-seeking women. Confirming mother's prophecy of following in the steps of the patriarch (Kennedy) who began the war's escalation as object of the admiring female gaze, Ron becomes masculinized and ready to return "home" to the political society responsible for his actual condition. The implications of this final sequence have ironical overtones. Unlike Kennedy, who stands during his televised inauguration, Ron rolls down the dais, and his message is just the opposite. Because of the text's masculinization process a significant question remains in the viewer's mind. Was it for female approval (leading to symbolic phallic mastery) that Kovic really became involved in the veterans' protest against the war?

Full Metal Jacket contains a scrupulous examination of this gender conditioning familiar from most Vietnam literature.[38] The boot-camp scenes illustrate the inevitable combination of patriarchy and war. Many writers have recognized war's function as an act of ritual cleansing whereby man can purify his masculinity and disavow his feminine side. Sergeant Hartman's patriarchal function is to turn his new recruits into killing machines by stripping them mentally and physically. Woman becomes the enemy. As Joker says in reference to a Da Nang hooker, "You know, half these gook whores are serving officers in the Viet Cong." Significantly, the next encounter with a hooker occurs outside a ruined movie theater with the poster of a Native American outside. Kubrick is conscious of Vietnam literature's use of the western as a mythic-interpretative device. The Vietnam generation was conditioned by westerns from prepuberty, so it was an easy transition to view the Vietcong as Native Americans. We must also remember how the Puritan Captivity Narrative associated Native Americans with a libidinous sexuality. The hooker presents a sexual challenge to the group unity when Eightball and Animal Mother compete for first place. This competition anticipates the female sniper's later temporary castration of platoon effectiveness. The film's final scenes have a deliberate purpose. They depict Joker's final initiation into the male brotherhood by completing the killing of the feminine side that boot-camp training sought to achieve.[39] The Vietcong sniper symbolizes Joker's earlier comments about Jungian duality. She is both soldier and female.[40] Once Joker kills her his look resembles Pyle's earlier expression, as well as Kubrick's alien, dehumanized galaxy of the Star Child in *2001* (1968), Alex in *A Clockwork Orange* (1971), and Jack Torrance in *The Shining* (1979). With final thoughts articulating aggressive sexuality and recognizing his survival in a pregenital anal "world of shit," Joker joins his fellow marines in singing the Mickey Mouse Club anthem.

By concluding in this manner, *Full Metal Jacket* shows its understanding of the important metaphorical significance of cartoon and comic-book imagery continually present in Vietnam literature and film. Many reviews refer to *The Green Berets*, *Missing in Action*, and *Rambo* in terms of their comic-book fantasy form. Despite negative connotations, this condemnation actually notes an important aspect of the conflict's factual and fictional treatment. It recognizes a cinema avoiding political and historical complexity in favor of ideological interpretation. Although the comic strip has antecedents in eighteenth-century satirical cartoons and can function in such alternative, antiestablishment formats as Steve Bell's *If* in the *Guardian* (U.K.), the nearest parallel relevant to our purposes is the DC-Marvel monthlies, like *Sergeant Rock* and *Sergeant Fury*. These often portray an excessive level of spectacular violence resulting in suspension of critical faculties, seducing the reader into the pleasures of danger and easily leaning toward ideological manipulation. As David Huxley and David A. Willson have shown, "the comic artist/author has control over the reader's point of view, presents moments frozen in time, and controls the visual means by which the image is expressed. . . . The greater control available does make the comic perfect as a vehicle for propaganda."[41] Despite the comic strip's possibility of representing any side of the political spectrum, it is an essentially abstract, noncomplicated, bloodless structure that can express ideas only in the most basic sense. The format can also depict a world of artificial absurdity. It is not surprising that several notable works in Vietnam literature have used this device to question the military's definition of reality and its one-dimensional thinking.[42] However, it can also be an important pictorial unit expressing dominant ideological concerns under the mantle of entertainment, very much like the cinema. The very form of an average comic strip is one that denies complexity of form, coloring, and nuance, bringing everything down to uncomplicated meaning. It can be used as a powerful ideological tool in the hands of either Left or Right to emphasize monological messages.[43]

Comic strips, like films, are never just pure entertainment. They can perform ideological functions in any national crisis. It was true of World War II as it was of Vietnam. An important component of the war film involves patriarchal manipulation of sublimated sexual aggression. Crucial links occur between adolescent fantasies, certain cartoon formats, and mythic manipulation in the service of contemporary ideologies. Comics can have a special function in promoting childish dreams of aggression, numbing the mind, and manipulating thought in a desired one-dimensional direction.[44] The format specifically appears in the action-motivated narrational fantastic landscapes of Cannon Studios and Stallone. There is little difference between World War II cartoon grotesques of

"Tojo and his bug-eyed monsters" in *The Fighting Seabees* (1944) and certain treatments of Vietnamese in 1980s cinema.

Close parallels exist between the war movie and comic-strip representation, particularly in the depiction of combat. Claudia Springer has demonstrated that even in antiwar films combat sequences structure emotional signification through their use of cinematic excesses that surpass "the requirements of narrative progression and frequently even undermine and contradict the narrative."[45] This may involve the viewer's pleasurable indulgence in the representation of combat and violence leading to historical disavowal and wish-fulfillment fantasy. Without actually referring to Vietnam movies, Mark Crispin Miller has recently noted the predominance of cinematic cartoon representation in an industry even more under corporate control than before.[46] Such a situation serves to reinforce the spectator's tendency to take gratuitous pleasure in violent representations. The combat sequence itself can appeal to contradictory drives of sadism, masochism, exhibitionism, and voyeurism, leaving the viewer open to emotional manipulation. As Miller notes, "The primacy of stimulation has, in short, made the movies increasingly cartoonlike. In the cartoon world nothing stands between the wish to look at violence and the enactment of that violence: no demands of plot or character, no physical limitations (space, gravity), no mortality."[47] We are once again in the comic-strip realm that sacrificially manipulated the earlier Vietnam generation. Thus, the very nature of the war film, the negative influences of comic strips, and Hollywood's cinematic development into its present state of cartoon wish fulfillment may prevent any adequate attempt at representing the complexity of Vietnam on film.

The conclusion is inevitable that, as presently formulated by Hollywood cinema, the Vietnam genre is a reactionary one. Because of its association with the economic, industrial, and spectatorial mechanisms of corporate control, it is highly unlikely that Hollywood can ever do justice to the conflict to the extent that other representations in prose and poetry can. Will this always be the case? This depends on future films. Springer notes that dominant narrative conventions "are not the only possible techniques for representing combat."[48] A different strategy is possible, one that involves recognizing the presence of the imaginary cinematic representational codes operating within the narrative and using them to disrupt ideological manipulation in favor of an active dialogical practice involving greater participation by both director and audience.[49] At this moment it seems unlikely that this will come from inside Hollywood. As was the case during the actual war, the oppositional movement must come from outside the establishment.

Notes

1. See, for example, Harvey R. Greenberg, "Dangerous Recuperations: *Red Dawn, Rambo,* and the New Decaturism," *Journal of Popular Film and Television* 15 (1987): 60–67; Leo Cawley, "Refighting the War: Why the Movies Are in Vietnam," *Village Voice,* 8 September 1987: 18; Andrew Sarris, "The Screen at the End of the Tunnel," *Village Voice,* 8 September 1987: 19, 26, 28–29, 54; and Raymond Durgnat, "True Grit and Friendly Fire," *Monthly Film Bulletin* 54.646 (November 1987): 326–28. For a contrasting survey of pre-1980 Vietnam films, see Peter McInerney, "Apocalypse Then: Hollywood Looks Back at Vietnam," *Film Quarterly* 33.2 (1979–80): 21–32.

2. See Gary Wills, *Reagan's America: Innocents at Home* (New York: Doubleday, 1987).

3. Steven James Fore, "The Perils of Patriotism: The Hollywood War Film as Generic and Cultural Discourse" (Ph.D. diss., University of Texas at Austin, 1986) 116.

4. Steve Fore, "Kuntzel's Law and *Uncommon Valor*; or, Reshaping the National Consciousness in Six Minutes Flat," *Wide Angle* 7.4 (1985): 23–32.

5. For an understanding of this definition, see Robin Wood, "Eighties Hollywood: Dominant Tendencies," *CineAction!* 1 (1985): 2–5; and Andrew Britton, "Blissing Out: The Politics of Reaganite Entertainment," *Movie* 31–32 (1986): 1–42. For some alternative observations, see Christine Anne Holmlund, "New Cold War Sequels and Remakes," *Jump Cut* 35 (1990): 85, 94–95.

6. Mikhail Bakhtin's ideas have great relevance to film narratives. For the opposition of "dialogical" to "monological," see Mikhail Bakhtin, *The Dialogic Imagination,* tr. Caryl Emerson and Michael Holquist (Austin:

University of Texas Press, 1981), and *Speech Genres and Other Late Essays*, tr. Vern W. McGee (Austin: University of Texas Press, 1986).

7. Stephen Neale, *Genre* (London: British Film Institute, 1980) 59.

8. See J. Hoberman, "Hollywood on the Mekong," *Village Voice*, 8 September 1987: 57.

9. See Peter McInerney, "Straight and Secret History in Vietnam War Literature," *Contemporary Literature* 22.2 (1981): 187–204. According to Dale W. Jones, such a work as *Dispatches* "is not exactly history" nor is it "exactly fiction either." See "The Vietnams of Michael Herr and Tim O'Brien," *Canadian Review of American Studies* 13.3 (1982): 309. Several works articulate the thesis that "the war in Vietnam caused and was caused by a depraved American society," a theme McInerney finds sustained in the film version of Robert Stone's *Dog Soldiers*; see "Apocalypse Then": 21. He evaluates *The Boys in Company C* in this vein: "Furie's America is a breeding ground for imperialism, racism, corruption and death" (28). See also Maureen Karaguezian, "Irony in Robert Stone's *Dog Soldiers*," *Critique: Critical Studies in Modern Fiction* 24.2 (1983): 65–73; and Frank W. Shelton, Robert Stone's *Dog Soldiers*: Vietnam Comes Home to America," *Critique* 24.2 (1983): 74–81. For a comparison between earlier war literature and Vietnam, see Jeffrey Walsh, *American War Literature: 1914 to Vietnam* (New York: St. Martin's Press, 1982).

10. See Gordon O. Taylor, "American Personal Narratives of the War in Vietnam," *American Literature* 52 (1980): 297. See also John Hellmann, "Vietnam and the Hollywood Genre Film: Inversions of American Mythology in *The Deer Hunter* and *Apocalypse Now*," Chapter 3 of this book. On the recognition of generic fusing in *Hamburger Hill*, see Nigel Floyd, "Hamburger Hill," *Monthly Film Bulletin* 54.643 (August 1987): 242.

11. See Mike Westlake, "The Vietnam SubText," paper read at the fall 1979 Manchester Society for Education in Film and Television school on Vietnam. For a critical view, see Paul Kerr, "The Vietnam Subtext," *Screen* 21.2 (1980): 67–72. For the 1970s relationship between Vietnam and the horror film, see Tony Williams, "Family Horror," *Movie* 27–28 (1980–81): 122–26.

12. See Harvey R. Greenberg, "Fembo: *Aliens'* Intentions," *Journal of Popular Film and Television* 15 (1988): 165–71; Adam Barker, "*Predator*," *Monthly Film Bulletin* 55.648 (January 1988): 19; and Holmlund, "New Cold War Sequels": 93.

13. Toby G. Herzog, *"Going after Cacciato*: The Soldier-Author-Character Seeking Control," *Critique: Critical Studies in Modern Fiction* 24.2 (1983): 88.

14. Mikhail Bakhtin, "The *Bildungsroman* and Its Significance in the History of Realism," *Speech Genres and Other Late Essays* 10–13.

15. For relevant criticism of O'Brien's ideological project, see Marie Nelson, "Two Consciences: A Reading of Tim O'Brien's Vietnam Trilogy: *If I Die in a Combat Zone, Going after Cacciato*, and *Northern Lights"* in *Third Force Psychology and the Study of Literature*, ed. Bernard J. Paris (London and Toronto: Associated University Press, 1986) 262–79; Arthur M. Saltzman, "The Betrayal of the Imagination: Paul Brodeur's *The Stunt Man* and Tim O'Brien's *Going after Cacciato*," *Critique: Critical Studies in Modern Fiction* 22.1 (1980): 32–38; Mark Busby, "Tim O'Brien's *Going after Cacciato*: Finding the End of the Vision," *CCTE* 47 (1982): 63–69; Michael W. Raymond, "Imagined Responses to Vietnam: Tim O'Brien's *Going after Cacciato*," *Critique: Critical Studies in Modern Fiction* 24.2 (1983): 97–104; Gregory Stephens, "Struggle and Flight: Tim O'Brien's *Going after Cacciato*," *Notes on Contemporary Literature* 14.4 (1984): 5–6; and Daniel L. Zins, "Imagining the Real: The Fiction of Tim O'Brien," *Hollins Critic* 18.3 (1986): 1–12.

16. See Richard Slotkin, *The Fatal Environment: The Myth of the Frontier in the Age of Industrialization, 1800–1890* (New York: Atheneum, 1985) 281–345.

17. See especially ibid. 343.

18. See Susan Jeffords, "The New Vietnam Films: Is the Movie Over?" *Journal of Popular Film and Television* 13 (1986): 192.

19. On the importance of this motif in the American cultural experience, see Richard Slotkin, *Regeneration through Violence: The Mythology of the American Frontier, 1600–1815* (Middletown, Conn.: Wesleyan University Press, 1973). For a recent article on Vietnam as cultural trauma, see Gaylyn Studlar and David Desser, "Never Having to Say You're Sorry: *Rambo*'s Rewriting of the Vietnam War," *Film Quarterly* 42.1 (1988): 9–16.

20. See, respectively, Jeffords, "The New Vietnam Films": 191, and Kim Newman, who notes "a crazed performance from Mako as the villainous Vinh" in *"POW: The Escape,"* *Monthly Film Bulletin* 54.638 (March 1987): 83.

21. See Tom Milne, *"The Boys in Company C,"* *Monthly Film Bulletin* 45.530 (March 1978): 41, and Richard Combs, *"Go Tell the Spartans,"* *Monthly Film Bulletin* 45.534 (July 1978): 135.

22. See Alasdair Spark, "The Soldier and the Heart of the War: The Myth of the Green Beret in the Popular Culture of the Reagan Era," *Journal of American Studies* 18.1 (1984): 29–48, and Greenberg, "Dangerous Recuperations": 62–63, 69.

23. For information on Arnett, see Thomas D. Boettcher, *Vietnam: The Valor and the Sorrow* (Boston: Little, Brown, 1985) 437–42.

24. For a perceptive argument on the media's role as structuring apparatus, see Michael Clark, "Vietnam: Representations of Self and War," *Wide Angle* 7.4 (1985): 4–11.

25. See Cawley, "Refighting the War": 20.

26. For an excellent analysis of this film, see Andrew Britton, "Sideshows—Hollywood in Vietnam," *Movie* 27–28 (1980–81): 7–9.

27. Ibid.: 5.

28. So John Hellmann, *American Myth and the Legacy of Vietnam* (New York: Columbia University Press, 1986) 90–93. For the dangerous official use of the "John Wayne Wet Dream," see Lloyd B. Lewis, *The Tainted War: Culture and Identity in Vietnam War Narratives* (Westport, Conn.: Greenwood Press, 1985) 19–61.

29. Jeffords, "The New Vietnam Films": 187.

30. Mark Baker, *Nam* (New York: Berkeley, 1983) 242, 269; Charles Durden, *No Bugles, No Drums* (New York: Avon, 1984) 123.

31. Floyd, "Hamburger Hill": 242.

32. On Vietnam "new journalism" narration, see John Hellman, "The New Journalism and Vietnam: Meaning as Structure in Michael Herr's *Dispatches,*" *South Atlantic Quarterly* 79 (Winter 1980): 141–51. For its failure in *Apocalypse Now,* see William M. Hagen, *"Heart of Darkness* and the Processes of *Apocalypse Now,"* *Conradiana* 13.1 (1981): 45–54.

33. For Mailer's understanding of the Pentagon's technological landscape, see Yasuro Hidesaki, "American Conscience and Vietnam War Literature," *Kyushu American Literature* 25 (1984): 46–53.

34. "A gun is power. To some people carrying a gun constantly was like having a permanent hard on. It was a pure sexual trip every time you got to pull the trigger" (Baker, *Nam* 187). See also Tania Modleski, "A Father Is Being Beaten: Male Feminism and the War Film," *Discourse* 10.2 (Spring–Summer 1988): 62–77. For the "forgotten" presence of American women

in Vietnam, see Carol Lynn Mithers, "Missing in Action: Women Warriors in Vietnam," *Cultural Critique* 3 (1986): 79–90.

35. Tim O'Brien, *If I Die in a Combat Zone* (New York: Dell, 1973) 51. The incident of the dying girl sniper penetrated by a bullet "into her buttock and out through her groin" is probably the origin of the climactic scene in *Full Metal Jacket*.

36. Klaus Theweleit, *Male Fantasies*, tr. Stephen Conway (Minneapolis: University of Minnesota Press, 1987).

37. See Janet Bergstrom, "Alternation, Segmentation, Hypnosis: An Interview with Raymond Bellour," *Camera Obscura* 3–4 (1979): 88. For a good analysis of female representation in Vietnam movies, see Cindy Fuchs, "This Is My Rifle, This Is My Gun: Sexuality and the Cinema of Vietnam," a paper presented at the eighteenth annual meeting of the Popular Culture Association in New Orleans, 23–26 March 1988.

38. See Jacqueline E. Lawson, " 'She's a pretty woman . . . for a gook': The Misogyny of the Vietnam War," *Journal of American Culture* 12.3 (Fall 1989): 55–65.

39. See, for example, O'Brien, *If I Die* 51, 52; Baker, *Nam* 173, 187; Ron Kovic, *Born on the Fourth of July* (New York: Pocket Books, 1976) 89–93; Philip Caputo, *A Rumor of War* (New York: Ballantine, 1977) 254, 278; and Gustav Hasford, *The Short-Timers* (London: Bantam, 1985) 12–13. On the crucial significance of gender differences as a structuring motif in Vietnam literature, see Susan Jeffords, "Things Worth Dying For: Gender and the Ideology of Collectivity in Vietnam Representations," *Cultural Critique* 8 (1988): 79–104, and *The Remasculinization of America: Gender and the Vietnam War* (Bloomington: Indiana University Press, 1989); see also the "Gender and the War: Men, Women, and Vietnam" issue of *Vietnam Generation* 1.3–4 (1989).

40. See Krista Walter, "Charlie Is a She: Kubrick's *Full Metal Jacket* and the Female Spectacle of Vietnam," *CineAction!* 12 (1988): 19–22.

41. David A. Willson, "The Enemy's Face: Vietnam War Comics of the 1960s and 1970s," a paper presented at the twentieth annual meeting of the Popular Culture Association, Toronto, March 1990. I am grateful to the author for a copy of his paper. See also David Huxley, "Naked Aggression: American Comic Books and the Vietnam War" in *Tell Me Lies about Vietnam: Cultural Battles for the Meaning of the War*, ed. Alf Louvre and Jeffrey Walsh (Milton Keynes, Eng.: Open University Press, 1988) 88–110, and " 'The Real Thing': New Images of Vietnam in American Comic

Books" in *Vietnam Images: War and Representation*, ed. Jeffrey Walsh and James Aulich (London: Macmillan, 1989) 160–70.

42. See here Philip Beidler, *American Literature and the Experience of Vietnam* (Athens: University of Georgia Press, 1982) 33–34.

43. See Sylvaine Cannon, "Editorial Cartoons and the American Involvement in Vietnam," *Revue Française d'Etudes Américaines* 15.43 (1990): 60–61. For useful observations concerning the comic strip's symbiotic relationship to movies and their relationship to cultural movements within society, see George Perry and Alan Aldridge, eds., *The Penguin Book of Comics*, rev. ed. (London: Penguin Books, 1971) 1–8, 106–8, 231–48. See also Ariel Dorfman and Armand Mattelart, *How to Read Donald Duck: Imperialist Ideology in the Disney Comic*, tr. David Kunzle (New York: International General, 1975). According to David A. Willson's *REMF Bibliography* 2 (March 1990): 91, many Vietnam veterans have created their own oppositional Vietnam comics. For the comic-book formula as applied to viewing Vietnam in the sixties, see Beidler, *American Literature* 39–41 and Hellmann, *American Myth* 57–66.

44. See Baker, *Nam* 168–69, for the parallels between adolescent fantasies and cartoon imagery. "If the mortal slapstick can be kept in a cartoon life, maybe the shadow of inhumanity can be denied a little longer, the personal pain can be buried a little deeper" (169). Note O'Brien, *If I Die* 94—"I remembered an old Daffy Duck movie cartoon."

45. Claudia Springer, "Antiwar Film as Spectacle: Contradictions of the Combat Sequence," *Genre* 21 (1988): 480. Note also the following statement: "When a film attempts to turn the spectator against war by presenting a bloodbath, it paradoxically can evoke unconscious drives and desires that take pleasure in vicarious danger" (486).

46. Mark Crispin Miller, "Hollywood: The Ad," *The Atlantic*, April 1990: 41–54.

47. Ibid.: 54.

48. Springer, "Antiwar Film as Spectacle": 483.

49. The use of cinematic motifs as a device in understanding the Vietnam experience has been common since Graham Greene. See Graham Greene, *The Quiet American* (New York: Penguin, 1955) 83, 110; Kovic, *Born on the Fourth* 32, 49–50, 54–55, 60–61, 74, 86; O'Brien, *If I Die* 53, 94, 148; Durden, *No Bugles, No Drums* 3, 25, 166, 201, 222, 237–38, 259; Baker, *Nam* 5, 15, 23, 31, 41, 61, 64, 75, 84, 151, 168–69; and Caputo, *A Rumor of War* 6, 14–15, 30, 44, 67, 88, 102, 128, 255, 288, 295–97, 300–301. For a perceptive article regarding parallels between

fiction and film in Vietnam literature in Stephen Wright's *Meditations in Green* (New York: Scribner's, 1983), see Donald Ringnalda, "Chlorophyl Overdose: Stephen Wright's *Meditations in Green*," *Western Humanities Review* 40 (1986): 125–40. See also Saltzman, "The Betrayal of the Imagination": 32–25, and Beidler, *American Literature* 11, 39–41, especially in his recognition of Mark Baker and Al Santoli's oral histories ordered by "strategies resembling most closely those of cinematic montage, into a narrative devised thematically to recapitulate in a most general and comprehensive sense the unfolding of one's vision of the experience as a whole before, during, and after." For the imitation of such cinematic techniques as slow motion, fades, and dissolves in Vietnam literature, see also Anne Malone, "Once Having Marched: American Narratives of the Vietnam War" (Ph.D. diss., Indiana University, 1983) 99–100.

John Hellmann

Rambo's Vietnam
and Kennedy's New Frontier

CHAPTER 7   Somewhat tentatively upon the release of *First Blood* in 1982, and definitively upon the release three years later of its sequel, *Rambo: First Blood, Part II,* film reviewers declared the Vietnam veteran played by Sylvester Stallone a dangerous personification of right-wing revisionism and militarism. They portrayed the Rambo character as a vehicle for a version of the "stab-in-the-back" theory with which, in the aftermath of World War I, Hitler persuaded a demoralized people that their defeat must have resulted from betrayal by a decadent minority, specifically Jews, democrats, and leftists. The Rambo films are indisputably revenge fantasies, and both the superhuman masculine power conferred upon Rambo and the cathartic violence characterizing his responses to wrongs are a transparent, and disturbing, strategy of compensation for postdefeat feelings of frustration and inadequacy.

Nevertheless, the Nazi stab-in-the-back analogy is ultimately misleading. The reviewers clearly heard Rambo burst out at the end of *First Blood* that "someone wouldn't let us win" and ask at the beginning of the sequel "Do we get to win this time?" Yet the films never identify the media, or liberals, or even the antiwar movement as the "someone." The reviewers made explicit what they assumed was implicit; in the totality of their reviews, reinforced by their virtual unanimity, they "rewrote" the Rambo films through the same process that the Rambo films rewrote the Vietnam War. The reviewers created a "parallel text" substituting for the cinematic texts.[1]

In contrast to the stab-in-the-back theory, Rambo's fury is not aimed at a minority group or an ideology it would be possible to punish or to exclude but rather at the dominant majority, with its "mainstream" pieties and tendencies—that is, at the moviegoing public itself. A former Green Beret, Rambo aligns himself with nature against the city, with a victimized black comrade against a careless white society, and with a liberated woman warrior against exploitative men. He thus signifies the liberal aspirations of the Kennedy era driven to desperate, and ludicrous, outlaw status in the aftermath of the disillusionment with the New Frontier, including the complacent and money-driven Reagan era.

As a 1960 presidential candidate, John F. Kennedy called on Americans to join him in "boldly" entering what he called the New Frontier. Defining this metaphorical landscape as a "great change" that was already under way, he emphasized the opportunity Americans had to identify themselves with the aspirations of the emerging postcolonial peoples, with the explorations possible in space, and with the demands of American blacks for full participation in American freedom. Above all, he offered a vision of the Cold War as a struggle requiring Americans to recapture the adaptability and willingness to sacrifice characterizing their frontier ancestors, virtues that he argued were threatened by the benefits of affluence. Kennedy's rhetoric and public persona re-created the Old Frontier, but just as importantly revised it into the New Frontier by insisting on the need to center the pioneer values of initiative, self-reliance, and flexibility within the institutions of American society.[2]

Once elected, he sought with the help of a cooperative national press to provide Americans with contemporary heroes—the astronauts, the Peace Corps, and the Special Forces, or "Green Berets"—who could be seen acting out the values of the New Frontier. During 1961 and 1962 such popular periodicals as *Newsweek, Saturday Evening Post, Saturday Review,* and *Look* celebrated the work of the Green Berets in the resonant images of American frontier mythology: the adaptation of a few brave individuals to a wilderness to redeem it from savagery. The setting of Southeast Asia possessed further resonance since it was that of the 1958 jeremiad *The Ugly American.*

A huge and much-discussed bestseller, which Kennedy as presidential aspirant urged every American to read, *The Ugly American* had portrayed a few contemporary American individualists, strikingly similar to such vigorous and egalitarian heroes of mythic history as Benjamin Franklin and Davy Crockett, contending in the complacent Eisenhower years with an overwhelmingly larger number of racist, materialist, and bureaucratic Americans. These Ugly Americans were, through their contemporary faithlessness to the traditional American character and mission, aiding the ruthless Soviet organization men portrayed as misleading the pastoral natives of Southeast Asia.

The new Kennedy administration presented the Green Berets in Vietnam as symbols of a resurgence of the traditional American spirit of the frontier and the Declaration of Independence against this "ugly" prejudice, complacency, and careerism. Thus, Vietnam was drawn in the national media of 1961 and 1962 as a thrilling re-creation of the frontier heritage that also promised a redemptive expiation of the ugly stain of racism upon that heritage. Defying the organizational tables and career ladders of the Pentagon, these "new" frontiersmen were implicitly depicted as following the original pioneers in escaping the restraints and corruptions of civilization to struggle with savagery; unlike their ancestors, however, they would save and help the darker-skinned native peoples rather than dispossess them. Thus Vietnam promised ultimate validation of the American frontier journey as a progress toward the enlightened liberal values of egalitarianism and diversity.

It is against this dreamed Vietnam, this projected western, that we must see the cultural impact of Lyndon Johnson's subsequent escalations. His policies of bombing North Vietnam, of sending large units of conscripted troops on search-and-destroy sweeps through South Vietnamese villages, and of overwhelming Vietnamese society with American wealth, personnel, and technology completely reversed Kennedy's portrayal of his Vietnam policies as an unfolding reenactment and improving revision of the western. Indeed, in the rhetoric of the antiwar movement, the war was by the middle 1960s being redrawn as an exact reversal of the western, one in which a pastoral people were being subjected to the onslaught of a European-like empire. By the end of the decade, the western itself had been largely supplanted by such "Vietnam westerns" or "anti-westerns" as *Soldier Blue* (1970) and *Little Big Man* (1971); by the end of the Vietnam era it had virtually disappeared.[3]

The Rambo films pulse with conflict between the text Kennedy projected and the subsequent texts of the Vietnam era. The first Rambo film is a well-made and for the most part credible action movie, while the sequel is both more and less, a cinematically impressive feat of putting a pulp-adventure comic book on film. But, as cultural documents, the two films vividly trace for us the legacy of Vietnam for 1980s America, specifically how that legacy is bound up with a perceived frustration of America's aspirations. For *First Blood* and *Rambo* address not solely the pain of Vietnam; they provide as well a remarkably clear expression of the haunting specter that Kennedy's New Frontier still constitutes in American memory for Reagan's "city on a hill."

The opening scene of the first Rambo film immediately recalls the defining situation of the western and specifically re-creates the opening of *Shane* (1953). A tall male figure, bedroll hanging from his shoulder, strides down from the mountains of the American Northwest into a valley where a cabin that gives every appearance of being a nineteenth-century homestead sits beside a beautiful lake. No sooner is the western framework of *First Blood* set up, however, than viewers discover a substitution that revises the western in the liberal terms of the New Frontier: the "pioneer" family is black. John Rambo politely explains to the wash-hanging mother that he has come to see her son, Delmore Barry, with whom he served in

Vietnam. But as this kindly stranger tries to overcome the mother's taciturn hostility by humorously showing her a snapshot of himself with her huge son, she answers by sending her daughter into the house, a gesture that reprises many similar scenes in westerns in which the homesteader initially sees the frontier hero as a threat (the opening scene of *Shane* again serves as a perfect example). Finally, she reveals the reason for her bitterness. Her son died the year before of cancer. "Brought it back from Nam," she says, "all that orange stuff they spreaded around—cut him down to nothin'. *I* could lift him off the sheet."

We see here a dark-skinned mother angrily telling a white man that his society has brought disease and death to her offspring by its destructive use of technology upon nature. Within the context of the western setting, this scene resonates with the destruction of another darker people, the Native Americans, through the whites' spreading of alcohol, smallpox, and the railroad across the American wilderness. But by combining the figure of the wronged racial Other with the pioneer mother, who in the classic western is the center of white civilized value, *First Blood* places the western hero in a kind of double jeopardy. Stunned, John Rambo expresses his sorrow, and moves on. The former Green Beret, agent of civilization and lover of nature on the New Frontier, sees that he has somehow become the enemy of both.

The film thereafter radically reverses the terms of the classic western. In the next scene, we move into a small town that proudly proclaims itself "Holidayland," suggesting a conception, one opposite to the New Frontier, of America as ideally a vacation-like utopia outside the threats and disturbances of the rest of the world. A smug sheriff, played by Brian Dennehy, benignly greets a young white mother and daughter as they push a baby carriage. He then observes a morose Rambo walking along the highway. The sheriff pointedly warns the long-haired Rambo that "looking the way you do" and wearing an American flag on his jacket could get him in trouble in this part of the country. The sheriff insists on giving Rambo a ride out of town, and Rambo resentfully complies. But after the sheriff answers Rambo's plaintive questioning by saying that "we don't want guys like you" and "get a haircut and a bath," Rambo at last deliberately crosses back into town in full view of the sheriff, precipitating his arrest.

The sheriff has excluded Rambo from the town for being a hippie antiwar protester. Rambo could have informed him that the flag is a sign of patriotism, that he is a Vietnam veteran, indeed that he is a former Green Beret and a winner of the Congressional Medal of Honor. The sheriff probably would have proceeded to invite Rambo over to a local diner for a cup of coffee.

Rambo, however, has just found himself subjected to the prejudice that such men as Delmore Barry have known throughout American history. In the Vietnam War the white soldier joined the black in being victimized in the service of American society. The United States betrayed the men and women in its service, as well as its own announced mission to save South Vietnam, by carelessly using a destructive technology. Rambo's bitter silence must express his sense of a link between the sheriff's prejudice against his appearance as a member of the counterculture with the society's victimization of his black friend, and of himself as veteran. Yet reviewers rarely alluded to the opening scene, and when they did ignored the crucial element of Delmore Barry's blackness, as, for instance, in the *Time* review in which Richard Schickel told his readers only that Rambo has had "his final mooring cut loose by the discovery that his last surviving buddy from the old unit has died of cancer."[4]

The identification of the veteran with traditional victims of American exclusion, with the dark Other, is the underlying motif of *First Blood*. Like the historical victims of American racial prejudice, Rambo suffers confinement, physical abuse, and mockery. When the jailers hold him with his arms out while one of them approaches him with a razor to "clean him up," Rambo flashes back in his mind to an earlier crucifixion, during which the North Vietnamese tortured him with knife cuts while his arms were bound to a cross. In that flashback Rambo joins Michael (Robert De Niro) in

The Deer Hunter (1978) and Captain Willard (Martin Sheen) in *Apocalypse Now* (1979) in finding himself in Vietnam the captive victim of the antagonist he expected to defeat.

In the two earlier films the tormentors in Vietnam are faces of what the hero must recognize in himself. In *The Deer Hunter* Michael survives the threat of "one shot" in the forced Russian roulette game and kills his Vietcong captors, but on his return to the American wilderness realizes that the lesson of his experience in Vietnam is that he must give up his previous frontier code of seeking to control nature by killing a deer with "one shot." With this self-knowledge he goes back to Vietnam to try to save his friend Nick (Christopher Walken) from the cycle of violence. In *Apocalypse Now* Willard similarly discovers during his captivity by Colonel Kurtz (Marlon Brando), the Green Beret who has "gone native," that his own ideal of a "pure" war is hollow; he ritualistically sacrifices his doppelgänger before returning to civilization from the "mission" he had wanted, knowing now that "I'd never want another."

With the identification between the torturing North Vietnamese and the brutalizing American deputies, *First Blood* also seeks to reveal to the hero in his confrontation with the savage Other in Vietnam a meaning about America itself. But where *The Deer Hunter* and *Apocalypse Now* seek to purge the culture of a central compulsion figured in its ideal hero, *First Blood* absolves the ideal hero of any wrong and shows him to be an innocent victim of a faithless society. Thus the "cross" symbolism is a device for asserting that in its actual practice the larger American society (the deputies) seeks scapegoats for its own evils, but that the cultural ideal (the hero) remains innocent, captured and tormented in Vietnam by the Other, but more profoundly wronged by his own society's betrayal of its cultural ideals of tolerance and equality.

The Christ imagery announces the reformulation in Vietnam of the frontier hero into a scapegoat for the savagery of his own society. And it serves to prepare the link between Rambo and a "higher" father. After Rambo escapes and eludes recapture through feats of extraordinary strength and cunning, the Sheriff rhetorically asks "What ever possessed God-in-heaven to make someone like

Rambo?" An offscreen voice answers, "God didn't make Rambo, *I* made him." We are then shown the speaker, a dramatically silhouetted wearer of a green beret, played by Richard Crenna, who announces himself to be Colonel Samuel Trautman and explains that he recruited, trained, and commanded Rambo as a member of the Special Forces in Vietnam. The clichés about the prowess of the Green Berets that make up Trautman's subsequent commentary about Rambo are simply a recitation of the Kennedy-inspired hyperbole with which the media originally created the Green Beret legend, and with it the expectations that Vietnam would be the setting for a reaffirmation and improving revision of America's frontier character. The "Green Beret" Trautman is thus Rambo's cultural or spiritual creator, the progenitor of Rambo's mythic power who by analogy and icon encodes the legacy of John F. Kennedy.

In the post-Vietnam American forest to which Rambo has had to flee, this "son" of the New Frontier hero is driven into positions that iconographically identify him with the Vietcong and Native American against U.S. society. Pursued by a helicopter, he triumphs over the superior technology through cunning use of the landscape. He terrorizes the police with booby traps and knife-wielding ambushes, while the "posse," as Trautman derisively calls it, of National Guardsmen reenacts the clumsy, callous, and finally ineffectual search-and-destroy policies that during the Johnson and Nixon administrations made American soldiers in Vietnam appear "ugly Americans." After they use a grenade launcher to bury Rambo in a cave, the Green Beret completes his symbolic transformation into a Vietcong, escaping through a tunnel maze full of rats.

Viewers are thus provided an opportunity to experience Vietnam from the side Kennedy had ostensibly cast them in, the side of the wilderness against an oppressive city. With this Vietnam veteran, cast as victim of the wrongs of American history, they return to the frontier, the original American wilderness outside the oppressive American town. From there, through their identification with Rambo, they wage a repetition of both the Vietnam War and the Indian Wars, one in which they become the Green Beret/Viet Cong/Indian against Americans who, as contemporary middle-class descendants of the western pioneers, are far more plausibly, and dismayingly, their own waking selves. The audience has been manipulated into identifying with a Green Beret hero who is, in a nightmarishly alienated way, taking up the frustrated work of the New Frontier: literally fighting against the intolerant, complacent, and materialistic Ugly Americans.

Rambo finally surrenders himself at the request of Colonel Trautman, but not before a final "shoot-out." Bare-chested, with a band of cloth about his head and shoulder-length hair, Rambo comes back to the town an avenging Apache. A Norman Rockwell Santa Claus offers Coca-Cola and a smile from a large billboard hovering over the town, and near it a neon sign advertising a bar announces "The Last Outpost" over a target full of arrows. The Norman Rockwell idea of America is indeed the target of the Vietnam veteran returned as the man whom he could not defeat, the Vietcong as return of the repressed Native American. The conservative vision of America is declared to have been revealed by the Vietnam War to be a lie, and Rambo, the returned Green Beret who was created to be the New Frontier hero, symbolically purges Reagan's "city on a hill" from the viewer's consciousness by returning as an avenging Vietcong who was really Geronimo all along.

Wearing his green beret, Colonel Trautman at last confronts Rambo and tells his "son" that the war is over. Rambo cries, "No, you can't just turn it off. You asked me, I didn't ask you." The echo of Kennedy's famous request in his inaugural address to "ask not what your country can do for you, ask what you can do for your country" articulates the accusation so many veterans, as well as other members of the Vietnam-era generation, have posed to the now-silent creator of the New Frontier.

The spectacular success of the sequel *Rambo* was met by liberal reviewers with dismay, outrage, and ridicule. In *New York* David Denby labeled it "a fascist myth of regeneration," ominously claiming that "it relies on the furious emotional appeal of the 'stab in the back.'" Andrew Kopkind in the *Nation* repeated the analogy to the Nazis' use of the defeat in World War I to elicit a search for demons at home and then abroad, concluding that "until the real thing comes along, we are asked to sublimate our death wishes in the Hollywood version." In *USA Today* Kenneth Hey connected the film directly to the Nixon-Agnew policies by summarizing it as a scenario in which "this time, the soldiers, unencumbered by the nattering nabobs of negativism or by anything as stupid as civilian control of the military, will blow the enemy into oblivion." In *Ms.*, Ari Kopivaara decried the "pure Reaganite revisionism: America could have won the Vietnam war if only our leaders hadn't betrayed our fighting men."

Rambo is certainly a fantasy of violent wish fulfillment, but the wish can be more precisely identified. Just as Kennedy once offered the vision of returning to the frontier in Vietnam to both reenact and revise the old American frontier triumphs, the Green Beret brings Rambo a chance to return to Vietnam for a mission that promises to be the one originally held out by Kennedy: the hero is needed to enter a wilderness and rescue innocent victims from savagery. But here, as in the opening scene of the first film, there is a striking substitution. The innocent victims to be rescued are the heroes who answered Kennedy's call, and who have since been truly missing in action from American mythology. When Rambo asks, "Do we get to win this time?" and Trautman answers, "This time it's up to you," the status of the subsequent film as pure wish fulfillment is established. *Rambo* enacts the desire of the culture to find its way back into the film originally projected by the New Frontier. The implicit promise is that this time the society will not undercut the mission with its corruptions and technology.

Yet Rambo and the viewer soon discover that this dream carries with it nightmarish elements from the memory of the Vietnam experience. The "symbol of the American spirit," as Rambo was described in the advertisements for the film, is being sent on this operation by a smug civilian bureaucrat who drastically limits his mission (he can only take photographs of any POWs he may find) and assures him of the solutions offered by technology (a battery of computers). Thus the prelude to Rambo's reenactment of the Vietnam War already reenacts that to the debacle in Vietnam; it turns out that the New Frontier (Trautman in his green beret) is not really in charge, but has been usurped by a government and military bureaucracy that together lack dedication and competence.

The Vietnam to which Rambo returns has nothing to do with the Vietnam of our historical experience, the one that Rambo recalls in *First Blood* when he anguishes over the memory of a buddy who was killed when a Vietnamese child handed him a booby-trapped shoe box. In the sequel Rambo returns not to the unexpected landscape that revealed itself as the setting of Johnson's and Nixon's war, but rather to the Vietnam earlier projected by the Kennedy administration and the national media as a setting familiar from American myth. South Vietnam is a beautiful and stalwart companion who emblematizes Rambo's "natural" virtue, the North Vietnamese are the dissolute savages against whom Rambo defines his civilized restraint, and the Russians play the role of European oppressors against whom Americans must periodically act as liberators from the New World.

The climactic line of *Rambo* comes when the symbol of the American spirit, surrounded by Russians and North Vietnamese who have ordered him to broadcast to the American bureaucrat that there are no POWs, instead says, "Murdock, I'm coming to get you." Rambo eventually satisfies his vengeance upon the faithless technocracy represented by Murdock when he destroys his computers. Technocracy and bureaucracy—and above all the faithless greed they are seen as serving—are figured as the pervading aspects of contemporary America that in Vietnam stabbed the aspiring heroes of the New Frontier in the back.

The Rambo films are an unhelpful but revealing episode in the inevitable, and necessary, mythologizing of the Vietnam War. Vietnam will either be turned into myth or it will be forgotten, because myth is the only form in which history can be retained in collective memory. The complicated historical facts must be distilled into a coherent narrative and vivid imagery to provide a truth-telling interpretation of the war. The issue is whether the "mythic" Vietnam being constructed will effect a rejection, a revision, or a reaffirmation of the larger American myth into which participants in the country's discourse seek to place it. The Rambo films attempt the third, and they do so by duplicitous strategies. But cultural critics should acknowledge the sources of Rambo's appeal in aspirations that cannot simply be projected onto the liberals' Other of fascism or even Reaganism.

Notes

1. Since the initial wave of reviews in the mass media, three interesting essays have countered the prevailing interpretation. Although having different emphases and ultimate theses, these essays and my own share the premise that the Rambo films are sites of complex ideological work. See Thomas Doherty's review of *Rambo*, *Film Quarterly* 39.3 (1986): 50–54; Gaylyn Studlar and David Desser's "Never Having to Say You're Sorry: *Rambo's* Rewriting of the Vietnam War," *Film Quarterly* 42.1 (1988): 9–16; and John Carlos Rowe's "'Bringing It All Back Home': American Recyclings of the Vietnam War" in *The Violence of Representation: Literature and the History of Violence*, ed. Nancy Armstrong and Leonard Tennenhouse (London and New York: Routledge, 1989) 197–218.

2. See *Final Report of the Committee on Commerce, United States Senate: Part I, The Speeches, Remarks, Press Conferences, and Statements of Senator John F. Kennedy, August 1 through November 7, 1960*, 86th Cong. (Washington, D.C.: GPO, 1961).

3. For a full elaboration and documentation of this argument, see John Hellmann, *American Myth and the Legacy of Vietnam* (New York: Columbia University Press, 1986).

4. Richard Schickel, "Primary Colors," *Time*, 8 November 1982: 85. Reviews of *First Blood* in national periodicals were few in number, while reviews and broader commentaries regarding the sequel constituted a medium even in themselves. In evaluating the Rambo phenomenon, I have studied the following reviews, a number of which I subsequently quote in the text: of *First Blood*, David Denby, "The Thing from Sociology 101," *New York*, 15 November 1982: 108–9; and David Ansen, "Rebels with a Cause," *Newsweek*, 25 October 1982: 119; of *Rambo*, Richard Schickel, "Danger: Live Moral Issues," *Time*, 27 May 1985: 91; Jack Kroll, "A One-Man Army," *Newsweek*, 27 May 1985: 74–75; Andrew Kopkind, "Films," *Nation* 240 (1985): 776–78; Ari Kopivaara, "Grossed Out on the Summer's Top-Grossing Film: Why One Nice Guy Isn't," *Ms.*, August 1985: 71–72; Michael Musto, "Bloody Awful," *Saturday Review*, July–August 1985: 81–82; Kenneth Hey, review, *USA Today*, September 1985: 93–96;

David Denby, "Blood Simple," *New York*, 3 June 1985: 72–73; Loudon Wainwright, "Rambo to the Rescue," *Life*, August 1985: 11; Scott Haller, review, *People*, 3 June 1985: 12; and Fred Bruning, "A Nation Succumbs to Rambomania," *MacLeans*, 29 July 1985: 7. Two additional reviews deserve special mention for perceptive discussion of the use of the western and the significance of the Native American motif, though in both cases the authors conclude that these are only aspects by which *Rambo* perpetrates its "stab-in-the-back" theory. See Tom O'Brien, "Birth of Legends: Unchaining Loss and History," *Commonweal*, 21 June 1985: 374–75; and Stanley Kauffmann, "Now, About Rambo . . . ," *New Republic*, 1 July 1985: 16.

Judy Lee Kinney

Gardens of Stone, Platoon, and Hamburger Hill
Ritual and Remembrance

CHAPTER 8 Unlike their predecessors, many recent films about the Vietnam War, notably *Platoon* (1986), *Full Metal Jacket* (1987), and *Hamburger Hill* (1987), have been dramatizations of combat. Yet two of these films combine combat stories with a tone so elegiac and full of grief that they reflect something quite different from the celebratory heroics of traditional action-oriented American combat films like *The Sands of Iwo Jima* (1949). *Platoon*, called by *Newsweek* "a ferocious Vietnam elegy," concludes with an act of remembrance: "Dedicated to the men who fought and died in the Vietnam war."[1] More directly than *Platoon*, *Hamburger Hill* is an act of memorializing. The action opens with panning shots of the Vietnam Memorial, invoking critic Stanley Kauffmann's reminder "that behind the marble are tens of thousands of individual young human beings. Who were killed."[2] The emerging lexicon of the Vietnam combat film is also the lexicon of the eulogy, a connection clearly stated by Lee Iacocca's speech at the beginning of the *Platoon* videotape.

153

This film *Platoon* is a memorial . . . not to war but to all the
men and women who fought in a time and in a place nobody
really understood. Who knew only one thing. They were
called and they went. It was the same from the first musket
fired at Concord to the rice paddies of the Mekong Delta.
They were called and they went. That in the truest sense is
the spirit of America. The more we understand it, the more
we honor those who kept it alive.

Was it "the same"? Iacocca's mixture of sentiment and commer-
cialism (he delivers his remarks from the side of a Chrysler Jeep)
points toward the ongoing cultural project of erasing distinctions
between Vietnam and other American wars and erasing discordant
political questions that continue to be raised by the expensive and
corrosive defeat in Southeast Asia. For American culture, the act
of memorializing Vietnam is an act of reconstructing history; to
remember is to re-member, to reconstitute the dead in a new landscape, a mythical place. This reconstruction has so far occupied two
distinct stages. In the second, popular films play a major role.

The first stage followed the construction of a literal place of
memory, the memorial to the Vietnam War dead in Washington,
D.C. The erection of the granite slabs and their subsequent dedication as a sacred place opened a new discourse on Vietnam. This
discourse was primarily, although not exclusively, directed toward
remembering and memorializing the war that had been so hastily set
aside after 1975. New books about Vietnam became best-sellers,
and most of them were combat memoirs. The public ceremonial of
the Wall, as the memorial is commonly referred to, established the
outlines of a discourse that would encompass the private (remembering) and the public (memorializing). More importantly, the goal of
this new public discussion was to effect a reconciliation or reunion
between society and the soldier, most frequently described as closing or healing a wound. The designer of the memorial, a young
college student named Maya Lin, suggested that her creation was
"not meant to be cheerful or happy, but to bring out in people the
realization of loss and a cathartic healing process."[3]

At this point, with these particular metaphors in play, the second stage of memorializing continues. What began in a relatively confined arena, the ritual surrounding the Wall being directed mainly to vets, was disseminated through mass culture by an unusual clustering of feature films and network-television films and series, including the NBC docudrama *To Heal a Nation* (1988), the story of the building of the Wall. The memorial films became the communal ritual of recognition that the vets felt they had been denied. The films became their homecoming parades, their yellow ribbons. As a way of exploring the specific dimensions of the memorializing effects of popular films, I shall concentrate in this discussion on *Platoon* and two other films: *Hamburger Hill,* which shares with *Platoon* the aura of a combat elegy, and *Gardens of Stone* (1987), which depicts the military burial rituals at Arlington National Cemetery.

A distinction between Vietnam films of the 1970s and those of the second wave is the absence of strong images of dislocation and disjunction in the second group. Whereas such films as *Apocalypse Now* (1979), *The Deer Hunter* (1978), and *Who'll Stop the Rain?* (1978) are marked by images and narrative strategies of rupture and dislocation, films of the 1980s are driven by the need for closure. These films take their place beside the classic Hollywood dramas of unification described by Robert Ray: "This reconciliatory pattern, itself derived largely from earlier American forms, increasingly became the self-perpetuating norm of the American Cinema."[4] The goal of the illusion of union is to effect a seamless bond between the experience of the Vietnam era and dominant American culture. The tactics of the three films under consideration here involve the resort to organic images of natural unity or symbols whose meanings are presumed to be unquestionable. As a result, the history of the war in the sense of its political contradictions and dilemmas is lost.

The use of photographic artifacts as reconciling objects of sacred memory did not begin with the Vietnam War; indeed, it originated with the very first comprehensive photographic coverage of the effects of war, which occurred during the American Civil War.[5] In describing the persistent power of certain photographs of the Civil War, Alan Trachtenberg notes their ritualizing function. The relationship that he assumes between artifact and culture is one of absorption (or, one could say, consumption) in which the culture imbues the artifact with meaning, in this case a "sacred" one that serves to reconcile discord. Whatever may have been shocking or disruptive about the more gruesome views of the conflict, Trachtenberg suggests, is at last reconciled: "As mementos the pictures are trophies of that therapeutic consummation: by memorializing, celebrating, remembering as sacred, the images participate in the process of making whole again, restoring American society to its familiar place in the bosom of nature."[6] In fact, this resort to Nature is a familiar trope in the reconciliation of cultural opposition and appears poetically at the opening of *Gardens of Stone*. The credits come up on a slow left-to-right pan over rows of gravestones shadowed by huge trees. The pan reveals the irony of the title in the conjunction of the living and the dead in the "garden" of gravestones and trees. The stillness of the moment, the sound of the horse-drawn caisson erase both time and culture. The organic imagery evokes timelessness and universality and directs our attention away from the fact that this is a ritual surrounding a military death, much less that the death occurred specifically in Vietnam.

While the Vietnam War produced a number of unforgettable photographs—Colonel (later General) Nguyen Ngoc Loan's execution of a Vietcong suspect during Tet 1968 (photographer, Eddie Adams), the running girl burned by napalm (photographer, Huynh Cong Ut), and the dead in a ditch at My Lai (photographer, Ronald Haeberle)—by the very nature of their content, exposure of American-perpetrated or supported brutality, they were expelled from the realm of the sacred. Almost without exception, the most-remembered still photographs of the war recall rupture and displacement rather than reconciliation. The site of ritual remembrance in regard to Vietnam has been the movies, especially, but not exclusively, *Platoon*, *Hamburger Hill*, and *Gardens of Stone*.

Quite soon after the war ended many perceived that the popular cinema could have a ritualized, cathartic effect in the cultural process by which the Vietnam War recedes into history. In an unsuccessful attempt to persuade President Jimmy Carter that *Apocalypse Now* should have Department of Defense assistance, director Francis Coppola wrote that the film would help "put Vietnam behind us, which we must do so we can go to a positive future."[7] In another context, Coppola characterized his film as "cauterizing old wounds, trying to let people put the war behind them. You can never do that by forgetting it."[8] Though a grand and beautiful film, *Apocalypse Now* failed to capture the popular imagination or to instigate the kind of communal remembrance that *Platoon* did almost ten years later. Oliver Stone acknowledged this response to *Platoon* in his Oscar-acceptance speech: "But I think that through this award you are really acknowledging the Vietnam veteran, and I think that what you're saying is that for the first time you really understand what happened over there."[9] The mythic roots of *Apocalypse Now* were too attenuated; the ritual murder of Kurtz at the end failed to resolve the film's narrative or to provoke an emotional response from the film's audience. One Vietnam vet explains, "I don't like movies about Vietnam 'cause I don't think that they are prepared to tell the truth. *Apocalypse Now* didn't tell the truth. It wasn't real."[10]

Ironically, it was Coppola's second film about the Vietnam War that built the drama of reconciliation ostensibly sought for in *Apocalypse Now.*[11] Within the explicit narrative pattern of memory (the story is a flashback after Jack Willow's [D. B. Sweeney] funeral at Arlington National Cemetery), *Gardens of Stone* builds a web of false resolutions to conflict or it effaces contradiction altogether. The film is characterized by images and situations of fictitious union. Through its many rituals, the army buries its dead, as well as the cause of their deaths and the political disunity this might uncover. As a first step the narrative establishes the main characters as a surrogate family to create the impression of unity. Jackie is the son of a former comrade in arms of sergeants Clell Hazard (James Caan) and Goody Nelson (James Earl Jones). Upon Jackie's arrival at Arlington, Clell receives a letter from the boy's father asking him to look after Jackie. When the old friend dies, Clell takes a clear fatherly role, imbuing with significance the way he refers to Jackie as "son" in the casual manner older men do with younger men.

Divorced and further estranged from his own teenage son, Clell tells Samantha ("Sam") Davis (Anjelica Huston) that the army is "my family."[12] Sam, too, is divorced, unable to have children and becomes, if not a mother, at least an older sister to the young couple, Jackie and Rachel (Mary Stuart Masterson). The romance between Clell and Sam, which culminates in their plan to marry before he ships off to Vietnam, is the most unlikely union of all between the gung ho soldier and the antiwar *Washington Post* reporter.

As nurturer and caretaker for his surrogate army family, Clell's most pressing desire is to obtain a transfer from Arlington to Fort Benning, Georgia, where he can train combat soldiers for Vietnam. He is convinced that his experience can save lives, that he can teach men how not to die in combat. Clell's conviction that reason (training) can overcome chance (randomness in battle casualties) offers a false succor that seems satisfactory to the characters within the narrative but is undercut by the film as a whole. The film demonstrates the randomness inherent in dying in battle by hiding Jackie Willow's death. The scene of his death is not rendered, except possibly in the mysterious helicopter radio-traffic voice-over at the beginning and near the end of the film: "med-evac here; took two rounds in the chest; I guarantee he's got one round in the arm." No cause is given, no description of the circumstances, no reason at all, just that he does not come home. While Jackie's death solidifies Clell's determination to get to Fort Benning, Clell does not acknowledge the role of chance, that some days "the bear eats you," as his friend Goody says. There was no one better suited to survival than Jackie Willow, son of a good soldier trained by better ones. Yet Jackie dies and the completely inept Albert Wildman (Casey Siemaszko) earns the Congressional Medal of Honor.

Gardens of Stone concludes as it began, with the ceremony of Jackie's funeral. Each step of the ritual is drawn out with perfect timing, from the caisson's journey to the grave to the flag given to the inconsolable widow. Jackie's story is an attempt to individualize the many names in the garden of stones, yet the ceremony obscures the most important fact of his individual suffering.

This is part of the process that Trachtenberg sees at work in the

Civil War photographs as they became sanitized or made "sacred." In the first step we have the photographic record of the effects of war, which is, in its most moving accounts, in its most memorable instances, a record of the dead. The most famous, as well as one of the most gruesome, of the Civil War photos is Alexander Gardner's view of a field of Confederate dead at Gettysburg, entitled in contemporaneous publications "Harvest of Death." For, stripped of ruffles and flourishes and all the other gaudy trappings with which societies convince their young to kill each other, the individual's view of war is one of suffering and death.

Like the Civil War photographs, the fictional Vietnam combat films are successful in erasing the difference between individuals as a locus for suffering and death in war and the larger ideological context of the society that sent them to war. The formal austerity of the static, black-and-white nineteenth-century pictures, a result of limitations in technique and apparatus rather than aesthetic choice, reminds us more of the spare list of names that is the Vietnam Memorial than it does the Vietnam combat films. The films provide a comforting embellishment, which seems a necessity in the same way that the embellishment of the Wall has come about as visitors leave flowers, letters, pictures, and other memories: "So many letters and other artifacts have been left behind—more than 4,900 at last count—that the act of leaving something behind has become a ritual at the memorial."[13] At the same time that these Vietnam films appear to offer us the authentic experience of the grunt, they erase his existence as an individual by subsuming his experience into a readily accepted cultural matrix of meaning. This is what is meant by memorializing the Vietnam War.

The first condition for a successful film memorial is realism or the plausible invocation of a past time. *Platoon* and *Hamburger Hill* were the first popular Vietnam films based on the combat experience of the participants.[14] *Hamburger Hill* is a fictionalized depiction of the historical events surrounding the assault on Dong Ap Bia in May 1969. *Platoon* was explicitly marketed as a memoir, the early ads featuring a wartime photograph of director Oliver Stone with some other grunts. The critics' response to the film, with few exceptions

(Pauline Kael was one), touted its "realism." This presumed authenticity is the primary reason for the greater audience acceptance for the later films.

The question of realism in Vietnam films has never been one of representational veracity, as all films (excepting director John Wayne's error in having an easterly sunset in *The Green Berets* [1968]) have made use of the readily identifiable signs of the Vietnam location—red earth (even if it is that of Georgia or the Philippines), lush jungle growth, and the omnipresent sight and sound of helicopters. The significance of the presumed realism of *Platoon* and *Hamburger Hill* lies in the authenticity of the memoir, that is to say the authenticity of the personalized. The significance of the idea of "realism" in these films is not in the act of replication but in the connection of the authentic with that which draws us close to the individual. What then seems paradoxical, but that I want to argue is at the heart of the memorializing process, is that the realism of the personal memoir is not accepted by the audience as idiosyncratic, as one grunt's view of the war, but accepted as universal, the typical grunt's experience. The single man, in being made to stand for all others, becomes symbolic. And these two combat memoirs come to stand in the public mind for the experience of Vietnam itself. The paradox rests in using the image of the "real" to offer the illusion of reconciliation. At the same time that these new Vietnam combat films offer us the contemplation of the authentic experience of the grunt, they erase his existence as an individual by subsuming that experience into a readily interpreted cultural matrix of meaning. The frequently stunning depiction of combat in these films offers the audience a view of the suffering of the single man while the narratives reconcile his fate within some larger meaning.

The aesthetic and formal mechanisms by which *Platoon* and *Hamburger Hill* accomplish this are quite different. In a more subtle way than some early Vietnam films, *Platoon* uses grand mythic structures to confer meaning on the events of the story. *Platoon* relies especially on symbolic references that are unquestioned and, in some cases, directly sanctified. Although not very many critics noticed it, *Platoon* is quite consciously an artifice relying on its own aesthetic structure and external mythic resonance to create emotional response. *Hamburger Hill* is a more claustrophobic film, manipulating internal signs and symbols. Its narrative structure depends on the gradual depletion of resources for the squad as it goes up the hill again and again, each time with fewer resources, fewer reserves of strength, and fewer comrades, until the end— three guys, a blank sky, and a blasted tree.[15]

Platoon relies on the traditional structure of the bildungsroman, the tale of the education of a young man, within the context of a modern morality play. Seen from the new recruit's point of view, the action of the film becomes intensely personalized. The viewer is drawn to Chris Taylor's (Charlie Sheen) point of view through his recurrent voice-over readings of letters to his grandmother, but more dramatically in repeated close-ups of his eyes during a night ambush. Uncannily, these extreme close-ups bear a strong resemblance to Coppola's similar use of close-ups of Martin Sheen to establish the viewpoint of Sheen's character in *Apocalypse Now*. This personalizing of the action draws the audience toward accepting the film's overall point of view, first through fearing that catastrophe will befall the protagonist and then through sharing his emotional response to the action. Thus, when the wounded Chris is literally lifted up out of the morass at the end when a helicopter bears him homeward, the action evokes a strong sense of transcendence.

Chris's redemption is essentially a false one, coming so quickly after his battlefield murder of Sergeant Bob Barnes (Tom Berenger). This ritual killing ends the morality play between two loci of power— one sacred, one profane—two "fathers," as Chris calls them in his final voice-over. Sergeant Elias (Willem Dafoe) and Sergeant Barnes fight over control of the squad, which in the context of war means power over life and death for the enemy and for their own men. Although himself an accomplished killer, Elias is clearly sanctified by identification with traditional Christian iconography. His death takes place in a small jungle clearing with a ruined church nearby. The death scene, agonizing and prolonged through slow motion, culminates as Elias spreads his arms in the gesture of Christ crucified. This connection of soldierly heroism and sacrifice with the religious figure of Christ has been noted by John Keegan in eighteenth-century battle paintings, especially the work of Benjamin West.[16]

Like Elias, the character of Barnes derives some of its power from a source of symbolism outside the film; unlike Elias, Barnes is associated with the secular pantheon of American heroes. "Our Ahab," Chris's voice-over names Barnes as the squad embarks on what will turn out to be a revenge sack of a Vietnamese village. Barnes carries not only Ahab's lust for revenge and his ruthlessness but also the scar "continuing right down one side of his tawny scorched face and neck."[17] The scar marks Barnes's duality, for the other side of the face is unmarked. The scarred side is turned toward the camera when Barnes is doing something that is morally questionable; otherwise, we do not see it. Barnes's face is the film's most compelling image of rupture, an expression perhaps of the "duality of man" Joker (Matthew Modine) describes in *Full Metal Jacket*.

Strangely enough, many of the same critics who saw *Platoon* as a grand exercise in historic realism also described it as a battle between "good and evil" personified in the two sergeants. The conflict between Elias and Barnes is not exclusively a moral one, as they are both good soldiers and expert killers, but rather a question of control over the squad and control over methods. When Barnes holds a pistol to the head of a little girl (a shot that, of course, invokes the Nguyen Ngoc Loan photograph, as well as the suicide of Nick [Christopher Walken] in *The Deer Hunter*), Elias explodes: Barnes has gone too far. His challenge to Barnes is met as Barnes kills him in cold blood; however, Barnes is killed in his turn by Chris as if that act could expunge all evil in the war or the disconcerting split registered on Barnes's face.

If *Platoon* offers a drama of personal redemption for Chris, *Hamburger Hill* offers the Vietnam War as existential drama and comes closer to touching the edge of nihilism that borders the history of the Vietnam era. *Hamburger Hill* clearly juxtaposes the austere Vietnam Memorial, which offers no meaning other than its long stone recitation of names, with the recounting of an assault that offered no other meaning than the act of ascending a hill that was shortly thereafter relinquished to the enemy.[18] The motif of naming and remembrance recurs throughout the film, most poignantly in the case of the new guy Languilli (Anthony Barrile). Sergeant Frantz (Dylan McDermott) cannot remember his name, so he calls him "Alphabet"—that is until Languilli dies in his arms begging Frantz to remember him.[19]

Visually, the film reinforces the existential trials of the squad as it moves from the lush green jungle to the barren brown mud of the hill. Over and over, the condition of the grunts is described in their own words as an excursion into nothingness. The blacks say "Don't mean nothin'" as a ritual incantation, and a new recruit's early question, "What's the Ashau Valley?" is never answered. The strongest image of futility is captured as the men try to take the hill for the fifth or sixth time. It is raining; both the NVA regulars and the mud keep them from attaining the summit. It is an ascent that is a descent; their temporary defeat is a conspiracy of nature itself. Such a scene reinforces Pauline Kael's claim that "the hill comes to represent Vietnam."[20] The mud and rain conspire to suggest that war is a force of nature about which men can do nothing except roll the Sisyphean rock. To this intensely compacted visual symbolism has been appended a poem requesting remembrance of the "gentle heroes you left behind."[21] The injunction to remember seems inadequate as a gesture toward the suffering we have just witnessed. The question "What is the Ashau Valley?" remains unanswered.

Although they rely on different means, *Platoon* and *Hamburger Hill* ritualize the suffering of individuals, which becomes transformed into the archetypal experience of the Vietnam soldier. A reconciliation is thus effected between the individual and a meaning that persists beyond him. While both films place the single soldier in the familiar context of the combat film, *Platoon* extends its meaning through traditional religious and cultural symbols. *Hamburger Hill* establishes combat as an unknowable natural force against which men can do nothing and in which they can find no meaning. Neither film treats war as a political fact, an endeavor organized by men, amenable to men's control if the desire is there. It is clearly not. Certainly the millions of people who made *Platoon* an extraordinarily popular film prefer the reconciliation of history with myth. The films transform memory into myth. *Gardens of Stone* is the most distant of the three films from the particular historicity of Vietnam, as its narrative depicts a timeless set of military rituals. As "Taps" plays over every soldier's grave, these films, too, seem to say that Vietnam was "the same" as every other war. The cumulative effect of the memorializing films is a collective evasion of Vietnam's tough questions.

The gaping wound is closed but not healed.

Notes

1. David Ansen, "A Ferocious Vietnam Elegy," *Newsweek*, 5 January 1987: 57.

2. Stanley Kaufmann, " 'Don't Mean Nothin,' " *New Republic*, 14 and 21 September 1987: 32.

3. Jan Scruggs, *To Heal a Nation* (New York: Harper & Row, 1985) 147.

4. Robert Ray, *A Certain Tendency of the Hollywood Cinema, 1930–1980* (Princeton, N.J.: Princeton University Press, 1985) 57.

5. British photographer Roger Fenton "covered" the Crimean War but concentrated on portraits rather than the battlefield scenes we associate with the Civil War. See Lawrence James, *Crimea, 1854–56* (New York: Van Nostrand, 1981).

6. Alan Trachtenberg, "Albums of War: On Reading Civil War Photographs," *Representations* 9 (1985): 23.

7. Quoted in Lawrence H. Suid, *Guts and Glory* (Reading, Mass.: Addison-Wesley, 1978) 314.

8. Ibid. 316.

9. Bob Thomas, "*Platoon* Captures Best Picture," *Denver Post*, 31 March 1987: C1.

10. Reginald Edwards, quoted in Wallace Terry, *Bloods: An Oral History of the Vietnam War by Black Veterans* (New York: Random House, 1984) 15.

11. Coppola also received the cooperation of the Department of Defense for *Gardens of Stone*, help that he had failed to secure for *Apocalypse Now*. See Joanne Kaufman, "Pentagon Lends a Hand to Hollywood—Sometimes," *Wall Street Journal*, 23 June 1987: 28.

12. Coppola told an interviewer that the notion of the army as family in the novel *Gardens of Stone* had been attractive to him. *Vogue*, March 1987: 90.

13. "Introduction" in Michael Norman, *The Wall: Images and Offerings from the Vietnam Veterans Memorial* (New York: Collins, 1987).

14. Two earlier television films, *A Rumor of War* (1980) and *Don't Cry, It's Only Thunder* (1983), were adapted from war memoirs but never achieved the popularity of the later films.

15. The final scene bears a strong resemblance to the conclusion of the Korean War film *Pork Chop Hill* (1959).

16. See "The Death of General Wolfe," in John Keegan and Joseph Darracott, *The Nature of War* (New York: Holt, Rinehart and Winston, 1981) 86–87.

17. Herman Melville, *Moby-Dick*, ed. Alfred Kazin (Boston: Houghton, 1956) 110.

18. A moving practice of the antiwar movement was to stage vigils during which the names of the combat dead were recited.

19. The novelization of the film begins and ends with Frantz and his family searching for Languilli's name at the Vietnam Memorial. William Pelfrey, *Hamburger Hill* (New York: Avon, 1987).

20. Pauline Kael, "No Shelter," *New Yorker*, 7 September 1987: 98.

21. Major Michael Davis O'Donnell, quoted in Bernard Edelman, ed., *Dear America: Letters Home from Vietnam* (New York: Pocket Books, 1985) xxxix.

Daniel Miller

Primetime Television's Tour of Duty

We didn't recognize the fact that the Vietnam vets were no different from our heroes in the Second World War, no different from our John Waynes or the people who were taking Iwo Jima, raising the flag at Iwo Jima.
— Z E V B R A U N , executive producer, *Tour of Duty*

CHAPTER 9 CBS's *Tour of Duty* was U.S. network television's first dramatic series specifically about the Vietnam War. Like its cinematic predecessor *Platoon*, it has been described as a first in telling the truth about the real war in Vietnam and in aiming toward healing wounds the nation, the public, and veterans suffered as a result of the war. It premiered on American television in September 1987, only months after *Platoon* won the Academy Award for Best Picture and established the model for film and television representations of the war. Like *Platoon* it is set in 1967 and reconstructs the period of the United States' deepest involvement in Vietnam, before the Tet offensive in 1968 shattered popular illusions and ignited a massive public movement against the war.

Tour of Duty provides a valuable focus for textual and contextual television studies. It provokes consideration of a number of issues concerning war (the Vietnam War in particular), film and television representations of war, representations of cross-cultural minority issues in the context of war, the commercialization of the Vietnam War and Vietnam veterans, and the network's production and mar-

166

keting strategies for its own dramatic presentation of the war. It represents a site of struggle over meanings of the Vietnam War, militarist-interventionist policy, minority-social-rights policy, and minority representation in mainstream media.

In promoting *Tour of Duty*, CBS and the producers, Zev Braun and New World Pictures, emphasized the program's historical documentation of the Vietnam experience, their interpretation of that experience as real, personal, human and apolitical, and their socially progressive integration of various minority subcultures into the content and production of the program. Responses from members of many of these subcultural groups have indicated that there are indeed progressive elements in the program and in the conditions of its production. These elements have encouraged praise and support from many members of various subcultures, but most dramatically from Vietnam veterans, whose initial response generally supported the program's portrayals of combat soldiers and its historical accuracy.

Tour of Duty received the Asian Artists' Pacific Association award, presented by Daniel Inouye, U.S. senator and World War II veteran, for its balanced portrayal of Asian Americans. It received accolades from black publications for its employment of black writers and actors, as well as for the content of episodes concentrating on racial issues and the black experience. Veterans' groups have promoted the program, organized national and local symposia around showings, and generally applauded the portrayals of veterans as real, sympathetic, and healing.

Although analysis of the media's treatment of all subcultural groups is of extreme importance, *Tour of Duty*'s treatment of Vietnam veterans and their response to meanings generated in the program, especially those concerning the "real" nature of war, is of particular importance. There are a number of reasons for this.

First, there is currently a culturewide, cross-media proliferation of war imagery in the United States, much of it portraying the Vietnam War and those who fought in it. These images are intertextually related. They tend to reinforce and to privilege certain meanings over others. The memorialization and valorization of the war and veterans, redefining the event and participants in traditional mythic, heroic terms, is a primary, privileged meaning presented in the new war films.

Second, at the same time that war imagery has proliferated, particularly during the Reagan era, the expansion of militarist political rhetoric, military spending, and militarist interventionist policy has escalated. The successful execution of militarist policies is ultimately reliant on public consent—consensus—as well as the active participation by men and women in military industries and in the United States all-volunteer armed forces. Media representations contribute to the shaping of consensus as well as to decisions to participate in the armed forces and related industries. Although recent global political realignments in the former eastern bloc, as well as social and economic crises in the U.S., have raised serious questions concerning the legitimacy of militarist-oriented social and economic policies, in the wake of the war against Iraq the future of these policies appears headed toward even greater dependence on the military-industrial complex. The popular support for the invasion of Panama, the continued funding and training of the El Salvadoran military, the increasing employment of military force in drug wars, both within and outside the United States, and years of political, economic, and technical support for Saddam Hussein's repressive militarist regime in Iraq, followed by the massive and popular war against that country, raise serious questions about the directions of U.S. domestic and foreign military policy. Media portrayals of war and the Vietnam War in particular continue to be extremely relevant to the development of consensus concerning past, present, and future exercise of U.S. military power.

Finally, Vietnam veterans, predominantly from racial-minority and working-class backgrounds, direct witnesses to the war, and inheritors of a powerful government lobby and the third-largest government bureaucracy, the Veterans' Administration, occupy a unique and powerful position as a legitimating force on various sides of war policy and other minority-rights, social-policy issues (witness the attention paid veterans' organizations and the military in the 1988 presidential campaign). Their voices are powerful. Their lobby for or against particular meanings concerning minority-rights policy and military interventionist war policy substantially influence culturewide consensus, as well as active participation in support of, or in opposition to, these policies.

CBS launched its promotional campaign for *Tour of Duty*, targeted directly at veterans, on 31 July 1987 at the Vietnam Veterans of America national convention in Washington, D.C. At the gathering, postcard-sized black-and-white photos of the program's combat platoon were distributed announcing a special screening of the premiere episode. At the showing, a promotional packet was provided for each participating veteran. It encouraged active participation in publicizing the program and the "issues" it raised, a process many veterans supported and carried out in communities across the United States. The packet included the following items and statements.

- A lengthy description of the actors, characters, setting, historical period, and dramatic scenario.
- A fact sheet describing the production team, including personal histories, with an emphasis on prestige film credits and the real Vietnam War experiences of some of the writers and advisers involved in the production of the program.
- A "Read more about it.—CBS/Library of Congress Book Project" Vietnam War reference-material list.
- A "generic press release" form, designed to be sent by vets to their community press in order to promote the program, that included the following statement: "While the program will be entertaining, it will also be a valuable historical and cultural experience."[1]
- A four-page list of more than thirty suggested community activities designed to publicize *Tour of Duty* and emphasize its social significance. The list includes general procedures, which among other things state: "It is not appropriate for any project about the program to become the focus of a political debate about the Vietnam War."[2]
- A cover letter signed by the Vice President for Programs, Earl

LeMasters, touting CBS's pioneering efforts in bringing the "real" war to dramatic television and stressing that "while *Tour of Duty* is apolitical, it is designed to be real, gritty and, we believe, a sensitive portrayal of the Vietnam experience. . . . CBS is proud to bring this program to primetime television. We hope that our audience will, through its relationships with the characters, come to have a new understanding of what it meant to fight in Vietnam."[3]

· A two-page article—a dramatic narrative in itself—entitled "Executive Producer Zev Braun Searches for the Human Side of the Vietnam War," documenting the "serious, responsible" efforts of the producers to sincerely capture the Vietnam soldier's story. Mr. Braun is quoted as saying, "The political angle just wasn't as dramatic. We decided to take a grunt's point of view, because we were dealing with the reality of war and the inherent dramatic quality of men in wartime situations."[4]

The content of *Tour of Duty*'s promotional packet illustrates important elements common to the program and to the majority of current news, literature, film, and television representations of the Vietnam War. They present the war through the combat soldier's personal experience, "the grunt's point of view." They promote their efforts to document the historical reality of the war, to tell the truth. They present this personalized "truth" as historical and yet apolitical. They focus on traditional themes and narratives—principally derived from the western—of interpersonal struggle between men (independent of women) of mixed class and race surviving the threat of a harsh, primal environment and savage native aggressors through the exercise of individual initiative, heroism, brotherhood, and dedication to a just cause.

The dramatizations of the war overwhelmingly present traditional heroic texts in the trappings of reality. They advertise themselves as simultaneously enlightening dramatic representations of universal human values and important historical documents of the war. *Tour of Duty*'s promotional packet claims the program's purpose is to capture both the "inherent dramatic quality of men in wartime situations" and the "reality of the Vietnam war."[5] The presentation of ideology as history is typical of media portrayals of the Vietnam War, which accurately document particular aspects of the war, represent this partial documentation as reality, and foreground revisionist themes that often distort history within that "reality."

Elements of the production, promotion, and content of *Tour of Duty*, *Platoon*, and other new-phase dramatizations of the Vietnam War that accurately represent people, events, and social relations during and after the war can be read by various progressively minded subcultural groups as subversive of the dominant ideology. Mainstream-media cultural productions, particularly network-television programs designed to appeal to and thus reach the broadest possible audience for commercial sponsors, rely on creating a multiplicity of such readings. However, these readings, especially by veterans—who take understandable pleasure in positive portrayals after a generation of negative ones—may deflect critical attention away from dominant ideology, which now threatens to permanently distort our perception of the Vietnam War.

Although television typically encourages a variety of views, including progressive ones, the dominant ideology is not necessarily at risk, for television "contains" progressive meanings within the context of preferred ones that pose no threat to dominant structures. In fact, presenting a range of views supports the dominant power structure, reinforcing the common perception that it results from free choice. Unfortunately, the range of "free" choice is narrow and weighted. Television typically presents a limited number of different meanings as *all* there are, and hierarchically organizes this limited selection, privileging traditional meanings over others. As Mimi White explains, "This can be seen as a strategy of containment, as minority positions or deviations are framed and held in place by more familiar conventional representations."[6]

All mainstream media, and especially television, manage systemic crises through the repeated presentation of particular social problems in particular ways. A range of social problems, including the disabilities of Vietnam veterans, racism, sexism, economic and educational inequality, the environment, drugs, violence, and institutional crime, are examined weekly on episodic and series television. These problems are appropriate subjects for media treatment. They cause immense suffering in the United States, particularly among minority subcultures, and they signal a crisis in the social fabric of the country. The media's treatment of these problems is potentially progressive. However, progressive treatments would necessarily direct analysis of social problems toward structural inequities in social, political, and economic systems. Corporate-controlled network television traditionally supports the legitimacy of the system by directing attention away from the systemic sources of social problems, isolating them from their political and economic contexts. As such, social problems seem to arise from fate rather than society—that is, from uncontrollable forces rather than social institutions like government, laws, or policy that have been consciously shaped. When social problems are discussed from multiple viewpoints, those viewpoints are variations of traditional outlooks; progressive, innovative solutions—particularly those promoting change in the system—are defined as impractical, radical, or extremist. Similarly, traditional solutions—emphasizing treatment rather than prevention and placing an emphasis on the kind of heroism that reaffirms the system's validity—are demonstrated to be the only satisfying and sensible resolutions of social problems.

The failures of the American social and political system that resulted in the Vietnam War, as well as the major social and political upheavals of the Vietnam War era, are increasingly portrayed in the limited terms of the suffering of Vietnam veterans. The preferred solution to this problem is not one seeking change in the system responsible for the suffering of Vietnam veterans—as well as millions of others—but rather one that casts American soldiers and the American system in the deceptive but familiar and flattering light of conventional heroic American mythologies. These myths tend to overwhelm the discourse when distanced from the contexts of reality, history, and politics. Like most mainstream television series, *Tour of Duty* features crucial social problems each week, but contains the broader implications of those problems by reproducing conventional narrative strategies in which they are either purged or resolved at the end of each program by heroic representations of an ultimately good system.

The "Burn, Baby, Burn" episode, which the producers of the program describe as the most dramatic example of its progressive intent, is based on historical incidents in Vietnam, including mutinies against officers, riots, and such racial disturbances as the raising of Confederate flags after the assassination of Dr. Martin Luther King, Jr. [7] The episode begins with white titles over a black screen, which inform the viewer that "the armed services were desegregated by President Harry S Truman on July 26, 1948— Executive Order # 9981."

In the story, a black private named Tucker, who is new to the platoon, encourages open confrontation with racist white soldiers. The character is played as strong, admirable, and articulate, but ultimately destructive and racist himself. His political militancy is divisive; it eventually costs the platoon casualties, threatens the careers of the platoon's best young black soldiers, and sows discord throughout the core group of black, Latino, Asian, and nonracist white soldiers who make up the regular members of the series' platoon. Racial unrest provoked by Tucker's "over-reaction" to the white bigots is cast as the reason for the troops' failures in battle and, by extension, the losing tide of the war. In the climactic scene, a mutiny is ignited by the arrest of Johnson—the series' most moderate and heroic young black soldier—for the murder of a white racist. The crisis is narrowly averted when the star of the series, the white sergeant, Zeke Anderson, mediates the dispute in true patriarchal fashion by knocking some sense into the headstrong Tucker, humiliating one of the white bigots, and voicing his disappointment in the hotheaded black member of the platoon, a series regular, Taylor. Anderson screams at the troublemakers, "not in my family." The resolution of the problem of Johnson's guilt is handled in the most regressive and yet conventional manner imaginable. A stereotyped South Vietnamese scout is discovered to be the murderer. At the end of the program, Tucker, who, it turns out, previously won a medal of valor and two Purple Hearts, transfers out of the troop after

Zeke alternately scolds him, praises him, and finally counsels him to stop hating. Order and social harmony are restored.

Although the issue of racism is treated with some insight, depth, and even historical accuracy, it is ultimately defined as an aberrational problem caused by outsiders, troublemakers, or deviants (Asians, black militants, and white racists) whom the good system—the patriarchal, desegregated army, administered by sincere white leaders—must either transform, and thus "claw back"[8] into traditional positions, or expel. In the last instance, pivotal narrative positions for black characters remain secondary to those of whites. Progressive treatment and characterizations of black soldiers are developed and carried out, but they are contained within a traditional dominant master narrative that privileges the problem-solving capabilities and legitimacy of the established white, patriarchally administered system. Progressive approaches to racism, including solidarity and protest against the system, are characterized as unsuccessful, misguided, and antisocial. In these ways ideology is promulgated.

As Loren Baritz points out in his book *Backfire*, in spite of the landmark Executive Order #9981, racism was an integral aspect of the armed services during the Vietnam War.[9] A disproportionate number of black men were drafted, sent to the heaviest fighting, and wounded or killed in Vietnam. The military-justice system discriminated heavily against minorities. Typically, half of the soldiers in jail during the war were black, and they were treated more harshly than whites for the same offenses.[10]

There is no doubt that producer Zev Braun is sensitive to the issues of race. He has dealt with the topic in his award-winning productions *A Soldier's Story* (1984) and *The Father Clements Story* (1987). He has hired blacks, including writers Steve Duncan and Travis Clark, both Vietnam veterans, and members of other minorities for key *Tour of Duty* production positions. He has said of *Tour of Duty*: "If anything we don't have enough blacks. It was a black man's war at times. We have what I consider to be a minimum of blacks, Hispanics and Asians in the show and I hope to have more."[11] Although praiseworthy for its atypical efforts to deal with the issues of race and racism and to document the history of black participation in the war, television's *Tour of Duty*—like most mainstream television programs—distorts crucial aspects of the history it claims to document.

The typical treatment of history in mainstream film and televi sion is especially relevant to *Platoon, Tour of Duty,* and other new-phase dramatizations of the war. John Ellis observes that the media traditionally portray history in twenty-year cycles.

> TV is persistent in working over history for us, yet at the same time it cuts us off from our history. It has two very separate forms of historical time: the history-fiction-epic with its broad scope and twenty year periodisation; the current affairs programme with its grip at the distance of one year, where it becomes amnesiac.[12]

Mainstream film and television consistently neglect the historical period between one and twenty years ago. News and entertainment programs deal primarily in the coin of the current year, or the past, removed twenty years—the now and the then. This gap in historical coverage creates a gap in knowledge of those personalities, policies, and events of the recent past that directly and indirectly determine the course and shape of the present and the future. Mainstream media and audiences are thus distanced from history. That distance obscures reality and facilitates revision, mythology, and the portrayal of contemporary events as natural, unmotivated, and beyond the control and understanding of the public.

The twenty-year cycle of media interest not only leaves serious gaps in history but facilitates, especially in fictional entertainment programming, a portrayal of history as a series of generational personal struggles, primarily between fathers and sons. Wars are memorialized as historical backdrops against which these generational battles between past and future patriarchs are played out. It is a man's world and making history is the province of men, as making war is their duty. The fathers of the country gravely administer wars and the sons bravely fight them. In this patriarchal view of history, women's roles are limited to nurturing and grieving, or simply disappearing.

Tour of Duty, like *Platoon*, focuses a great deal of attention on father/son relationships. Two major characters, Lieutenant Goldman and Private Purcell, the cowboy from Wyoming, deal with this generational conflict in various episodes throughout the series. Both must live up to the heroic military exploits of their fathers, one a former combat soldier, the other a general. Lieutenant Goldman, patterned after the character Chris in *Platoon*—educated, noble, introspective, and caring—suffers an emotional crisis over his relationship with his father, a conservative, highly decorated, Patton-like general who earned his stars in World War II and Korea. Goldman is torn between living up to the standards of his archetypal patriarch and rebelling against them. Many of his actions are motivated by this struggle.

The episode "Blood Brothers"[13] deals directly with this father-and-son drama between the lieutenant and the general. In addition, it considers the "aberrational" social problem of the week, drugs. Zev Braun describes this episode as pivotal in the series for its treatment of the drug issue, a treatment that required approval from anxious Department of Defense officials.

In the episode, the young lieutenant, Goldman, is directly confronted by his father, the decorated general. Goldman's father is on a fact-finding mission for Washington. Observing his son's platoon in action, he is both shocked that the troops do not act or fight in a traditional, conservative manner and upset that his son questions his authority. In his opinion, this defiance is what is wrong with his son and with the war. Young Goldman pleads that it is a different kind of war and that his and Sergeant Anderson's less-traditional methods of fighting are born of experience with a treacherous enemy and are designed to save lives, as well as kill enemies and achieve objectives.

As the father and son are about to separate bitterly, unable to resolve their differences, two things occur that bring them together. First, the seasoned veteran, Platoon Sergeant Anderson, who represents a big brother as well as a working-class father figure to the young lieutenant, counsels him to give the general another chance. Then, father and son are forced to cooperate in order to save the young Latino private, Ruiz, from heroin dealers (who curiously resemble stereotypes of Colombian drug lords). The ensuing "western" showdown and gunfight result in the destruction of the drug ring, the rescue of Ruiz, and the reunification of father and son.

The general discovers that the drug trade carried on by the Vietnamese and a few corrupt, deviant, lower-echelon U.S. Army personnel is the reason that this war is a different kind of war. The general, lieutenant, and sergeant cooperate to save Private Ruiz from the evils of drugs. The general and his son find a new respect for one another and a negotiated meaning to the war. The episode ends with the general vowing to seek out the truth of the war and make it known to those running it. The generational problem is solved, the drug problem is solved, the true history of the war's administrative corruption and failure is revised, and, ultimately, the war is portrayed in the same terms as other American wars, a mythological environment where heroic white fathers and sons work out generational problems while fighting a greater evil, in this case uncivilized Vietnamese who fight dishonorably and push drugs on American boys.

Drug abuse has become one of the most important and most publicized issues of our time. It was one of the most important concerns in Vietnam. It is intimately related to the military. The efforts to treat such a relevant and controversial subject on *Tour of Duty* are illustrative of the influence the Department of Defense exerts over the program. The DOD provided support, men, and matériel in exchange for final approval of scripts. The department was particularly concerned about the portrayal of the drug issue and insisted on review of scripts dealing with it. The episode seems to have exhausted the topic as an issue in the series. Drug use is rarely treated or even mentioned in other episodes. It is hard to understand how such an integral part of the Vietnam soldier's experience could be so neglected in a series that promoted itself on the basis of historical accuracy. Troop drug abuse and drug profiteering were out of control during the war. Although in 1967 the abuse of drugs had not reached the catastrophic proportions it would by 1970, the patterns of abuse and official misconduct and corruption were firmly established. Senior officers knew about the problem and did little to stop it. The CIA and various other American agencies aided and abetted drug sales and distribution.[14] In his book *The Discarded Army*, Paul Starr concludes that "the government had simply made a calculation that the continued political and military support of those groups profiteering from the drug traffic was worth the risk of hooking American soldiers."[15] Obviously the DOD considered the subject of drugs a politically controversial one and applied one of *Tour of Duty*'s own general procedures to the issue: "It is not appropriate for any project about the program to become the focus of a political debate about the Vietnam war."[16]

Tour of Duty was promoted for its historical accuracy at the same time as it was promoted and even praised for being apolitical. The strategy of depoliticization is common to most of the new Vietnam media representations, but it is particularly emphasized in television's *Tour of Duty*. The promotional packet distributed to veterans constantly reminds them of their responsibilities to contain political impulses in favor of more "human" ones.

> And although *Tour of Duty* will be an apolitical presentation of the combat experience, it will help Americans to understand what it was like for the young Americans who fought there.

> Beyond the political turmoil there was a human side to the Vietnam war.

> They came up with an apolitical approach to the war, one that wouldn't become bogged down in the debate over whether the war was right or wrong.

> It's very difficult to take a political view and then have to defend it.[17]

In *Tour of Duty*, the characters' most extreme political judgment about the war is that it might be wrong (by no means a settled issue).

In spite of this, they must continue to fight in this "wrong" situation to protect one another and to prove their worth to their buddies, their fathers, and their nation. The reasons for it being wrong are never articulated, as if soldiers in "Nam" had and voiced no opinions. At one point in the series it is stated that the secret to the admirable, goodhearted Sergeant Anderson's survival throughout his three tours is that he has managed to stay apolitical. Black militants, antiwar types, and pacifists are characterized as political. Most often they let the troops down.

In the episode entitled "Soldiers,"[18] three members of the platoon, Taylor, Ruiz, and Purcell, try to pick up three Stanford coeds while on leave in Honolulu. One taunts Taylor, telling him she is writing a thesis on American imperialism in Vietnam. She is portrayed as weak, unpatriotic, privileged, arrogant, and ignorant of the human cost of the war, a true representative of the "permissive society." The men are enraged that she questions the killing and vent their rage by beating up the college "boys" who come to her defense. The issue is, as usual, removed from any larger political context with the assertion that such antiwar sentiments betray Americans suffering and dying for the rights of those who condemn their actions. This assertion supports a now-familiar revision of the war that pins the blame for its suffering, death, and destruction on those in the antiwar movement.

The major theme of the untitled premiere episode[19] is the depoliticization of one such antiwar type, a young blues-playing pacifist from Chicago, Private Roger Horne, the only college-educated grunt in the platoon. The promotional packet of the program emphasizes that the lesson about politics that Private Horne learns in this episode represents the major theme of the series. Perhaps *Tour of Duty* is best described in the way Zeke Anderson puts it to Horne, who is struggling to come to grips with his unwillingness to kill: "This is what it's all about—you're fighting for one reason—to keep yourself and your buddy alive."[20]

The rationale for the destruction carried out in the war is reduced to a traditional, unassailable logic—one fights to protect one's friends and countrymen. The question Why the killing? is deflected. The true heroism of courageous GIs is used as a smoke-screen to obscure the question about the purpose of their sacrifice. This logic is the last defense of the indefensible. The war was fought to impose Western ideological, social, political, and economic hegemony on the region, not to protect American or Asian lives. It resulted in the loss of fifty-eight thousand American and millions of Asian lives, as well as wholesale corruption and destruction of a country, society, and culture.

As the premiere episode opens, the platoon has been searching for a North Vietnamese Army unit responsible for the brutal deaths of two respected members of their group, a white soldier and a black soldier. As in the film *Platoon* and most of the other representatives of the genre, the actions of the young Americans are motivated by a sense of outrage over the murder of their friends. They are portrayed as victims of aggression, fighting back, never initiating violence, only responding to it.

After discovering and destroying the responsible NVA unit in spectacular and explosive fashion, the platoon moves in to mop up. As they walk through the carnage, a surviving Vietnamese soldier rises. In a blatantly stereotypical manner he prepares to kill the platoon's soldiers. Only Private Horne can stop him. Because he has previously abandoned his rifle, he is forced to kill the enemy in particularly grisly fashion with his knife. Agonizing over the act, he is comforted by Anderson, who explains to him that what he did was not a matter of killing someone but rather a matter of saving his buddies. Anderson also explains to him that next time it would be easier to "save his buddies" with an M16 than with a knife. In later episodes, Horne's peace rhetoric deescalates as his firepower escalates. He progresses from killing a single enemy with a knife to killing many enemies with various weapons, including an M16, an M60, and a grenade launcher. As the music and lyrics of Bob Dylan's "All Along the Watchtower" rise in volume, the final lines of this premiere episode are Horne's agonized exclamation, "This war is wrong!" and Anderson's response, "Maybe, but that's not the point." Certainly it is not the point of *Tour of Duty*.

Alongside the producers' claims that the new media representations of the Vietnam War are not political is the even more vigorous claim that they are realistic. In fact, the emphasis on reality is perhaps the most hotly contested assertion of the new depictions of the Vietnam War. The idea of capturing the "real experience" is pursued and promoted so intensely that one film, *Hamburger Hill* (1987), is touted by its distributors as "the most realistic portrayal of the Vietnam war ever. Because it is the only one that is true."[21]

The promotional packet of *Tour of Duty* repeatedly insists on the series' realistic treatment of the war, including numerous references to the contribution of actual Vietnam veterans to the program's authenticity.

> It is designed to be real, gritty, and, we believe, a sensitive portrayal of the Vietnam experience.

> "The Department of Defense was very cooperative in providing equipment and some of their men, which allowed us to achieve a very high degree of realism," Braun says. "Our technical adviser, Master Sergeant James A. Stephens, was a Vietnam vet, and a tremendous help to all of us."

> We decided the best perspective to take was a grunt's point of view, because we were dealing with the reality of war.[22]

Tour of Duty, like its model, *Platoon*, has undoubtedly achieved a high degree of verisimilitude, especially in its treatment of detail.[23] In this sense, the series might be considered remarkable, especially for television. Like *Platoon*, it carefully depicts sensory and environmental detail experienced by combat soldiers in Vietnam. This surface authenticity provides a powerful appeal, especially to veterans, witnesses to the war, who can then fill in political and historical gaps in the program from their complete historical and political, as well as "human," experience.

One source of *Platoon*'s success and its unprecedented support from veterans can be attributed to its careful, detailed, diarylike portrait of the everyday experiences of combat GIs. This re-creation of the detail of the grunt's experience, this "reality," shaped from the memory of war veteran and director Oliver Stone, was one of the film's most significant accomplishments. *Tour of Duty* uses similar strategies to transmit this "reality," relying on veterans in various capacities to re-create the look, tone, and feel of the war. Vietnam veterans respond in much the same way to *Tour of Duty* as they did to *Platoon*: "It's like it was,"[24] they have said. In addition to re-creating the environmental detail, other techniques are employed to blur the distinction between reality and fiction. Like many of the Vietnam films, the premiere episode of *Tour of Duty* mixed actual documentary footage with new dramatic footage. In some episodes, characters watch documentary footage on television. Documentary images, as well as historical incidents and stories now imbedded in the culture, are often quoted or dramatized.

Each new episode begins with a documented historical fact relating to the war, printed in white letters over a black screen, lending an air of authority to what follows. This echoes the stylistically similar opening of *Platoon*. In the process, the program not only alludes to a prestigious film, promoted and generally perceived as real, but creates an aura of "history" as well. As in *Platoon*, the unique language of the war is meticulously re-created—expletives deleted for television, of course. The program's promotional packet emphasizes its faithful treatment of the language.

> "Language was another aspect that came under discussion.
> We decided we are not going to sugar coat the language,"
> Braun asserts. "It's going to be tough, gutsy and expressive,
> but it won't be the profanities we're used to hearing. After all,
> the grunts in 'Nam didn't just use profanity, they used another
> language altogether, which they invented. Just as the GI's in
> World War II and other conflicts did."[25]

Period rock and roll, much of it antiwar and progressive in origin, is an integral part of the program, as it is in *Platoon, Hamburger Hill, Dear America: Letters Home from Vietnam* (1987), and all the Vietnam films and television programs. These techniques reinforce the authenticating period details that the general public and Vietnam veterans respond to as real. However, they do not represent reality as the producers claim. They re-present a version of reality—mediated, worked over, and described as the truth. Truthful though it may be, it is a partial truth. It is isolated from its historical and political contexts and it is focused narrowly. The war is presented as if it occurred in a "time and place no one understood"[26]— a gritty, mythological "never-never land" where American boys "grew up" without their mothers and discovered their "inherent dramatic qualities"[27]—a place where there were no clear reasons for the suffering, no concrete decisions that led to it, and no real way of preventing its repetition. In spite of this, there is no doubt that these techniques, particularly surface authenticity—which John Ellis describes as the first version of media realism[28]—are so powerful when applied to the Vietnam War that they evoke a genuine sensitivity toward the suffering resulting from it. In the current wave of media representations, this sensitivity, as well as the discourse in general, is focused overwhelmingly on Vietnam veterans.

In the majority of films and television programs dealing with the Vietnam War since *Platoon*, a sympathetic, valorizing treatment of veterans has become the dominant theme. Such films as *Gardens of Stone* (1987), *Hamburger Hill*, *Good Morning, Vietnam* (1987), *Bat 21* (1988), *Jackknife* (1989), *Distant Thunder* (1988), and *Born on the Fourth of July* (1989), and such television treatments as *Tour of Duty, Dear America: Letters Home from Vietnam, Vietnam War Stories* (1988), and *My Father, My Son* (1988), pay homage to the courage and heroism of Vietnam veterans. The culture now publicly mourns not only those who served, fought, and died in the Vietnam War but its own abandonment and alienation of them. In a complete turnaround from the attitude between the late sixties and the early eighties, the culture now celebrates the virtue of Vietnam veterans and, in the process, its own "noble" efforts to return them to the social fold.

Returning Vietnam veterans were grievously mistreated by the government, the public, and the media.[29] The government discarded them: it failed to provide the care, money, personnel, and programs required to fulfill its primary responsibilities to those who fought in Vietnam—healing their wounds and assisting their successful reintegration, with dignity, into society. The Veterans' Administration, in particular, subjected returning veterans to deplorable conditions and gross negligence. Massive trauma suffered by Vietnam veterans during the war and the failure of the government to properly treat it, even to acknowledge it in some cases, has resulted in a postwar devastation of Vietnam veterans' populations which rivals that of the war itself.

Like the government, the public participated in the mistreatment of Vietnam veterans during and after the war. Unlike the cases of previous U.S. wars, Vietnam veterans received few victory parades or other public displays of appreciation for their service to the country. They were abandoned, ostracized, and ridiculed by citizens on both sides of the war issue. Some of those who supported the war, including government and business leaders, members of fraternal organizations, and veterans of previous wars discriminated against Vietnam veterans and blamed them rather than institutions, corrupt officials, or bankrupt policies for what was perceived as America's first military defeat. Some of those who opposed the war engaged in misdirected attacks on Vietnam veterans. Their abuse may have been appropriate for the administrators of the war and for those soldiers who participated in war crimes, but not for the majority of twenty-year-old GIs from minority backgrounds who had been thrust into the fighting and had risked their lives for their country. Unfortunately, the worst of these abuses have become etched into the memory of many Vietnam veterans to become mythlike, crucial references in the conservative representations of the war.

Hamburger Hill illustrates the ideology in its most divisive, malicious, and revisionist form. In a telling example, a brave, respected sergeant explains to naïve young troops why he is still in Vietnam after several tours of duty. On medical leave in the United States, longhairs threw dogshit on him, he found that a "hairhead" had moved in with his wife and kids, and when a good friend's son came home from Vietnam in a body bag marked "members missing" "college students" repeatedly called his friend to tell him "how glad they was that his boy was killed in Vietnam, . . . the Republic of, . . . by the heroic People's Army." "And that," he concludes, "is why I am in Vietnam."[30] Such representations lay the responsibility for the betrayal of the country and veterans on the antiwar movement, diverting attention from those who sent them to the war, lied to the American people to keep them there, and abandoned them physically, morally, and spiritually in the field and at home.

Until a major rehabilitation of the image of Vietnam veterans began in the 1980s—in conjunction with the rehabilitation of U.S. military power—mainstream film and television portraits of Vietnam vets were overwhelmingly negative and stereotypical. The predominant stereotype was the sadistic psychopath. The television series *Kojak* typified the situation, depicting a crazed, murdering Vietnam vet almost weekly. Rather than bearing the "mantle of patriotism" traditionally bestowed on returning soldiers, veterans bore the blame. At times, it seemed as if veterans were scapegoats for all of society's ills, including, most significantly, the "failure" of the war. The negative, stereotypical portrayal of Vietnam veterans during this period shifted national guilt and shame over the corruption of the war to predominantly young, relatively unempowered, racial, ethnic, and economic minorities who were direct witnesses to, and visible reminders of, the corruption. Blaming and "damaging the witnesses"[31]—undermining their testimony and credibility—were largely the result of the media labeling of veterans as deviant from the late sixties to the early eighties.

Amending the mistreatment of veterans by the government, the public, and the media during the late-war and postwar periods is essential to healing. In some ways, however, the new trend toward indiscriminate valorization represents a danger to the culture and a disservice to those who fought and died in Vietnam. The danger arises when the warrior and not the person is celebrated, when the homage to those who fought and died is transformed to the homage to those who unquestioningly fought and killed, when the self-congratulatory culture elevates recognition of one transgression, the victimization of veterans, to the level of complete enlightenment, and when the collective struggles of veterans to properly historicize the war and achieve social justice are subverted.

The process of memorializing and valorizing the war and veterans in traditional ways has progressive implications in that it rectifies past portrayals of deviance that damaged the legitimacy and visibility of veterans seeking social rights. But, it has ultimately reactionary implications in that it denies history and politics, and redefines the war and warriors in traditional, glorifying ways that discourage political struggle against militaristic policy and for social rights. In the new-phase representations of the war, veterans, who have been returned in the media to more traditional roles, are now being positioned as promoters, producers, narrators, and consumers of the dominant ideologies that mythologize and revise the history of the war. In this way, regressive revisions of history, and the rehabilitation and reconstruction of the war according to traditional mythologies, are portrayed as originating from Vietnam veterans. They are presented as authors of the dominant discourse, and their potentially progressive voices are co-opted.

In 1987, Vietnam veteran and antiwar spokesman Oliver Stone's powerful Academy Award–winning film, *Platoon*, became to many the "veterans' film," telling their story and speaking their message. Many agreed it was an antiwar message. Chrysler/Jeep CEO and media star Lee Iacocca took it upon himself to interpret that message in his introduction to the film's videotape version, released at approximately the same time as the Chrysler/Jeep-sponsored *Tour of Duty* premiered on television. Portrayed in a rural setting, leaning on a Jeep, Mr. Iacocca states:

> This Jeep is a museum piece, a relic of war—Normandy, Anzio, Guadalcanal, Korea, Vietnam. I hope we will never have to build another Jeep for war. This film, *Platoon*, is a memorial, not to war, but to all the men and women who fought in a time and in a place no one really understood, who knew only they were called and they went. It was the same from the first musket fired at Concord to the rice paddies of the Mekong Delta. They were called and they went. That in the truest sense is the spirit of America. The more we understand it, the more we honor those who kept it alive. I'm Lee Iacocca. [32]

Not only does this tribute commercialize the war and those who fought it, but it suggests that no one understood the war, the war was like all other American wars, all American wars were essentially noble, and all of those who went, went willingly. Surely, this is not the message Oliver Stone intended, particularly on behalf of Chrysler/Jeep.

The final section of the promotional packet for the Chrysler/Jeep-sponsored premiere episode of *Tour of Duty*, distributed at the Vietnam Veterans of America national convention in July 1987, entitled "Executive Producer Zev Braun Searches for the Human Side of the Vietnam War," concludes with Mr. Braun's statement: "We have a deep obligation to reconstruct the war they experienced, and recreate [*sic*] the conditions they actually lived through."[33] Since *Platoon*'s commercial success in 1987, the media have vigorously pursued their "obligation" to reconstruct the war in Vietnam. The proliferation of films and television programs about the war has only recently leveled off. Unfortunately, the majority of these media reconstructions of the Vietnam War—including Zev Braun's *Tour of Duty*—have seemed more "deeply obliged" to reconstruct and re-create dominant ideology than the actual conditions of the war. That ideology has served to rehabilitate and legitimate the war—the social, political, and economic institutions responsible for it and the antidemocratic means employed to conduct it. It has fed on the memorialization and valorization of the war and Vietnam veterans and extended from there to reincorporate the mythological ethos of U.S. political, moral, spiritual, and technological superiority.

The reconstruction process now seems all but complete. In the patriotic afterglow of the "clean" war against Iraq—which resulted in hundreds of U.S. casualties and hundreds of thousands of Iraqi casualties, and which was caused in part by years of Western contributions to Saddam's tyrannous military machine—politicians are once again describing the United States as "the shining city on a hill" and proclaiming a "New World Order" cast in America's image while at the same time declaring a healing end to the "Vietnam Syndrome." Unfortunately, even as Operation Desert Storm ends and the cold war cools down, the social, political, economic, and racial injustices at the root of war heat up. Traditional ideologies concerning war and warriors embodied in mainstream media continue to underwrite popular consent to military solutions. These "solutions" are characterized by support of dictatorial regimes, official secrecy, censorship of the media, censure of dissent, disproportionate minority casualties, acceptable "collateral damage" (i.e., civilian casualties), "sanitized" high-tech violence, massive ecological and cultural destruction, staggering economic costs, and subversion of democratic processes.

Although the program *Tour of Duty* has been canceled, mainstream television's "duty" to mythologize war continues unabated.

Notes

1. CBS Entertainment, *Tour of Duty*, Promotional Packet, "Generic Press Release," July 1987.

2. CBS Entertainment, *Tour of Duty*, Promotional Packet, "Suggested Community Activities," July 1987.

3. CBS Entertainment, *Tour of Duty*, Promotional Packet, "Cover Letter," July 1987.

4. CBS Entertainment, *Tour of Duty*, Promotional Packet, "Executive Producer Zev Braun Searches for the Human Side of the Vietnam War," July 1987.

5. CBS Entertainment, *Tour of Duty*, Promotional Packet, "Cover Letter," July 1987.

6. Mimi White, "Ideological Analysis and Television" in *Channels of Discourse*, ed. Robert C. Allen (Chapel Hill: University of North Carolina Press, 1987) 146.

7. "Burn, Baby, Burn," *Tour of Duty*, CBS Television, 5 November 1987.

8. John Fiske and John Hartley, *Reading Television* (London: Hutchinson, 1978) 87.

9. Loren Baritz, *Backfire: A History of How American Culture Led Us into Vietnam and Made Us Fight the Way We Did* (New York: William Morrow, 1985) 311–12.

10. Ibid. 312.

11. "CBS Announces Vietnam War Series for the Fall," *Jet*, 24 August 1987: 22.

12. John Ellis, *Visible Fictions* (London: Routledge and Kegan Paul, 1982) 17–18.

13. "Blood Brothers," *Tour of Duty*, CBS Television, 12 March 1988.

14. Baritz, *Backfire* 309–12.

15. Paul Starr, *The Discarded Army* (New York: Charter House, 1973) 114.

16. CBS Entertainment, *Tour of Duty*, Promotional Packet, "Generic Press Release," July 1987.

17. CBS Entertainment, *Tour of Duty*, Promotional Packet, July 1987.

18. "Soldiers," *Tour of Duty*, CBS Television, 18 February 1988.

19. Untitled Premiere Episode, *Tour of Duty*, CBS Television, 24 September 1987.

20. CBS Entertainment, *Tour of Duty*, Promotional Packet, "Press Information," July 1987.

21. Video Release, *Hamburger Hill*, Paramount Pictures Corporation, 1987.

22. CBS Entertainment, *Tour of Duty*, Promotional Packet, July 1987.

23. Ellis, *Visible Fictions* 6–13.

24. Bill Bishop, "Vets Review *Tour of Duty*," *Register-Guard* [Eugene, Oreg.], 23 September 1987: C1–2.

25. CBS Entertainment, *Tour of Duty*, Promotional Packet, "Executive Producer Zev Braun Searches for the Human Side of the Vietnam War," July 1987.

26. Lee Iacocca, quoted in *Platoon* video production (Hemdale Film Corporation, 1987).

27. CBS Entertainment, *Tour of Duty*, Promotional Packet, "Executive Producer Zev Braun Searches for the Human Side of the Vietnam War," July 1987.

28. Ellis, *Visible Fictions* 6–13.

29. Starr, *The Discarded Army* 114.

30. Video Release, *Hamburger Hill*.

31. Paul R. Camacho, "The War Film, the Cinema Industry, and the Vietnam Veteran Movement," presented at the War Film: Context and Images conference, Boston, 26 March 1988.

32. Lee Iacocca, *Platoon* video.

33. CBS Entertainment, *Tour of Duty*, Promotional Packet, "Executive Producer Zev Braun Searches for the Human Side of the Vietnam War," July 1987.

Women Next Door to War
China Beach

CHAPTER 10 Vietnam was the first television war, one brought to the dinner table each evening in graphic detail. Images from its verité coverage influenced the iconography associated with the ensuing genre revision of combat war films focusing upon the Vietnam experience. Yet *China Beach*, shown on the very medium that brought the war so close to the millions of Americans who had little other access to its "reality," seems to displace the entirety of the Vietnam nightmare into the realm of romanticized fantasy, one in which historical, political, and social implications are all but erased. Instead one is offered the stuff of which nostalgia is made, in which roles are defined by gender alone and ultimately the heroics of previous war genres are evoked in place of any constructive criticism. In presenting a "female perspective," *China Beach* contributes to a larger attempt to recoup or reconstruct the meaning of heroism and hence offers its audience a referent in the "real" discourse of the U.S.–Vietnam War. A primary goal of *China Beach* is to construct the Vietnam vet as hero in a traditional sense, to attempt to imbue this war with a purpose that history in fact denies it, so as to continue to ease the national guilt and irresolution concerning U.S. involvement in Southeast Asia.

China Beach centers on women's involvement in Vietnam and is set primarily during 1967–69 at the U.S. military recreational facility of the same name and the neighboring Ninety-Fifth Evacuation Hospital (510 Evac Compound) located on the shore of the South China Sea in Da Nang. Unlike *Tour of Duty*, which is modeled after the film *Platoon* (1986) and such earlier television war series as *Rat Patrol* and *Combat*, *China Beach* adopts the structure, style, and tone of melodrama, focusing upon domestic and love-story aspects rather than those issues usually foregrounded in the action-adventure genre. In a highly emotionalized approach to the problem of everyday life next to a war zone, the stories are those of the "woman's film" and soap opera, in which the experiences of women are drawn more in terms of their sexual interactions and social concerns than the actuality of their military/volunteer duties and the importance of those duties for the war effort. The portrayal of these women highlights their "lack"—both in terms of gender and its concomitant roles in war—dramatizing their inability to gain access to either the physical activity or the specific discourse of combat.

As with its predecessor, *M*A*S*H* (1970), *China Beach* constructs characters who represent differing military and moral positions, often sketched in stereotypical, gender-based strokes. The cast includes a range of American female military and volunteer personnel—a dedicated and martyrlike head nurse, Red Cross volunteers (otherwise known as "Doughnut Dollies"), a base prostitute and black marketer, a special-services career officer, USO entertainers, an aspiring film journalist (also a senator's daughter), and an enlisted servicewoman. This last character is perhaps most emblematic of the American woman's position in the Vietnam discourse, in that she has no specific single duty but rather is given a series of odd-jobs for which she is ill-suited or ill-prepared but to which she manages to adapt despite adverse conditions. This and the tongue-in-cheek names of the characters—Cherry White, a naïve nineteen-year-old, who is the first of two "Doughnut Dollies" prominently featured—is only in part an indication of the series' some-what carefree attitude toward its representation of women and their experiences. The representation of Vietnamese women suffers even more; despite the fact that "round-eyed" women were the smallest minority in Vietnam, Vietnamese women are significantly under-represented in the program. Even in the episodes in which they are featured, they seldom speak for themselves; their actions are inter-preted by Americans, much as American women's experiences are defined by men. The program implies that women's accounts can only be told in relation to the men who served in Vietnam, but Kathryn Marshall's book *In the Combat Zone* and Le Ly Hayslip's *When Heaven and Earth Changed Places* speak otherwise.

Despite the touted goal of the series, which, according to Mark Morrison of *Rolling Stone*, is "to see what Vietnam meant to the women who were there (an estimated 50,000 nurses, entertainers, Red Cross volunteers and others served in Vietnam)," the actual representation and discourse of the series are not always controlled by women.[1] Even though the title song is "Reflections" by Diana Ross and the Supremes, it is the actions of men and their visions that are reflected upon the women of China Beach. As well, the inclusion of current contextual references marks a deviation from the solely nostalgic and reminiscent mode of representation. Just whose reflections are these? The question one might ask is why, in exploring the memory of wartime experiences, is *China Beach* about the experiences of predominantly white, American women, who represent a relatively small percentage of women's experiences in the U.S.–Vietnam War? Why use female characters to come to terms with what many see as the worst military experience in U.S. history, especially given the overwhelming male presence in the planning and the execution of the war? Is it only a strategy to include an absent female viewership in a genre dominated by male dis-course?

Susan Jeffords suggests that some Vietnam films use a femi-nized perspective in part to ready audiences for a revisionist attitude toward Vietnam veterans and current military conflicts.[2] She defines a feminized audience as one that is made passive and embraces behavior conducive to functioning in mainstream, nonviolent society; it is one in which the visualization of violence is acceptable but violent action itself is not. Jeffords discusses *Coming Home*, referring to Bill Nichols's argument that "cinematic narrative[s] . . . resolve contradictions and provide models for action in the present," and asks "who was this film's audience?"[3] The same question might be asked of *China Beach*, which in turn raises additional questions. In view of the fact a male Vietnam combat veteran created the series, how should the text be read in the context of the entire Vietnam War genre, both filmic and televisual, which upholds combat experience as the standard for authenticity? What are the expectations of a series conceptualized and produced by a male veteran for a potentially female-dominated audience? What is the significance of telling a story controlled by male "experience" through the eyes of female observers?

China Beach does not simply invert the established conventions in order to regenerate the genre, since the roles of American men and women were not the same during the U.S.–Vietnam War. The series is not the female complement to *Tour of Duty* in the same manner as *Big Valley*'s matriarch stands in for *Bonanza*'s patriarch. But *China Beach* does attempt to regenerate the idea of individual heroism. *China Beach* went into production at the height of the U.S. debate about aid to the "Contras" of Nicaragua. The Reagan administration's argument, framed in notions of heroism and moral obligation, was constructed to persuade the American public to support the government's decision without questioning the political ethics of the decision or the ultimate consequences of providing such support. The figure of the hero, the meaning of heroism, and the matter of justifying heroic actions through their results were at the forefront of a protracted series of televised investigative hearings. Key to the media's construction of Oliver North as a hero was not only the public statements issued by the great mythmaker and male storyteller of the 1980s, Ronald Reagan, but also the testimony of Fawn Hall, North's secretary, who stressed the importance of North's family in his daily life. While her testimony did not directly affect the amount of coverage North received, it shifted the matter from being about only political issues into being about personal concerns as well. His positive role as a family man balanced his tarnished role as a military officer, thus humanizing and individualizing his plight. This strategy sheds some light on the choice by William Broyles, Jr., producer of *China Beach,* to position women as sympathetic and supportive observers of combat. In part to remythologize his own war experiences, about which he had already written both a novel and numerous articles, Broyles ultimately works to remove the individual human soldier from the responsibility for action taken by a large, impersonal military machine—"I was just following orders"—and allowing the concept of heroics to reenter the genre.

In an interview with *Rolling Stone*'s Mark Morrison, Broyles indicates why this shift is not so simple, revealing what is perhaps most disturbing about the recent wave of revisionist approaches to the U.S.–Vietnam War. Discussing both the television series and his novel, *Brothers in Arms,* Broyles says:

> I was able to look at [Vietnam] as a setting and not a story itself. I also thought, most important to me seemed to be the story of the women who were there. No matter how involved you get with the tangled purposes of the war and its moral confusion and its unhappy end, what they did was purely heroic. Not in a sentimental, sappy way. But in a concrete, day-to-day, real-people-in-extraordinary-situations kind of way.[4]

The notion that Vietnam is just a setting, a backdrop against which to tell any number of stories, is as disturbing as Broyles's monolithic notion of the "purely heroic." While Broyles claims that his project is not sentimentalized, the very nature of melodrama, the dominant mode of fictional television, is to reduce various conflicts to an emotional continuum.

To say that the makers of *China Beach* posit a concept of "pure heroics" and insert it into an essentializing melodramatic format does not sufficiently account for how the series works. For one thing, as Lynne Joyrich argues in "All That Television Allows," television melodrama is not a distinct genre but rather a pervasive and dominant mode of many television forms.[5] Certainly, it is the nature of television to create simplistic oppositions and facile solutions in place of complex and vague conflicts. Joyrich concludes that much of current television's varying format is a hybrid between established television genres and the general aesthetic and thematic concerns of melodrama; more specific melodramatic conventions are lost amid the distinguishing features of other genres, but the overall emotional tone remains. Thus *China Beach* can be considered part of a genre of Vietnam texts and yet not wholly adhere to the war-genre format. Perhaps even more significant than changes in generic convention, however, is the new relationship between the spectator and the Vietnam War discourse. In bringing the war into the realm of fictional, serial television, *China Beach* becomes part of television's inherent melodramatic format, in which the audience, already constructed as passive by the medium, moves closer to a feminized position, and an otherwise problematic representation is made consumable and, ultimately, unquestionable.

A "special" episode of *China Beach*, which aired toward the end of the 1988–89 season, specifically addressed how actual women veterans functioned during wartime in South Vietnam. This episode, "Vets," focused upon the narratives of "some of thousands of men and women who served in Vietnam telling their stories in their own words"; the episode begins with this statement in voice-over by the series' lead actress, Dana Delany. This single program attempts to validate the series' own fictional representation as somehow being "truthful," a historically accurate representation. "Vets" intercuts fictional images from the series with excerpts from interviews with a variety of female and male noncombat veterans. Images drawn from earlier episodes often depict events referred to in the immediately preceding or following interview segment. In some instances, the interview serves as a voice-over to a fictional sequence from the series, blurring the boundaries between "documentary," or fact, and fiction. Toward the end of the program, the lack of visual reference to a specific speaker makes it difficult to match the voice-over with an interviewee and allows the dialogue to be linked to a fictional character depicted on the screen. The distinction between what is recounted as truth and what is imagined as truth seems to disappear altogether, especially as reinforced by the uncanny facial resemblance between Delany's character, Colleen McMurphy, the head nurse, and one of the veteran nurses being interviewed.

Howard Rosenberg, entertainment critic of the *Los Angeles Times*, seems to reflect the desired response in a review concerned with both this episode and the series as a whole.

> Their living transcript also affirms the basic truth that "China Beach" has presented during its 10-month run, for it's amazing the way these actual war memories and scenes from the series track and fit together like pieces of a puzzle. A surgeon recalls removing an unexploded grenade from a soldier's chest. Then we dissolve to a scene from a past "China Beach" episode that is almost identical to the surgeon's story, a scene that might otherwise have been dismissed as bizarre fantasy.[6]

The correspondence between fact and fiction is not, however, simple coincidence; the series' producers revealed in a public interview during a March 1989 Broadcast Museum special screening of "Vets" that they had spoken with many of the interviewees, as had the actors, before beginning the pilot episode of *China Beach*. Rosenberg's use of the phrase "bizarre fantasy" does provide a clue, nevertheless, to the program's highly stylized visuals, which distinguish it from the more documentary-like aesthetics of *Tour of Duty* or from actual news footage with which one might associate a more "real" perspective.

"Vets," with its classical narrative structure, presents a clearly organized story with which the viewer can engage. Starting with the recollection of one nurse's departure from the States and subsequent arrival at China Beach, and ending with another nurse recalling her anticlimactic departure from Vietnam after a year's tour of duty, the episode reinforces its strong sense of closure and resolution through its visual presentation. The visuals mirror the narrative structure of the piece as the program begins and ends with the beachfront view of China Beach set against the backdrop of a red sunset.[7] Authentic pictures of nurses, soldiers, and Red Cross volunteers at locations resembling China Beach and its compound link the fictional characters visually with the veterans who are seen and heard reminiscing. The interviews are highly emotional, with some of the women being overcome by tears. With the exception of the male doctor and one nurse, all the veterans' experiences emphasize the roles of the women through their emotional relationship to "the men" more than through their specific duties. These women functioned as surrogates for loved ones left far behind back "in the world," reminders of a soldier's mother, sister, wife, or girlfriend, family, and home. So, for example, a Red Cross volunteer, as a woman, might better explain a "Dear John" letter to an angry and hurt soldier. In another case, a woman's positive reaction to a wounded man, it is suggested, could make or break his recovery; says veteran Jeanne ("Sam") Bokina Christie, "We were their first tests; we were American, we were home, we were family." As might be expected, fictional images are provided that match these and other testimonies; Cherry attempts to console a "Dear John" recipient, while the USO character, Laurette, finds her picture in a dying stranger's pocket, an occurrence that an actual USO entertainer recalls as her most memorable moment in Vietnam.

The frame of reference for the viewer, then, is how these women related to soldiers and how "the men" responded to them. The focus is more on the nurturing aspects of their experience than on the difficulty and enormity of their jobs. Rather than sharing in what these women may have thought of their responsibilities and of the war effort overall, one shares instead in the somewhat glamorized depictions of romantic and family concerns. In positioning the spectator to identify with predominantly female veterans, whose function is defined simply as being next to the soldiers, next door to the war, *China Beach* offers the viewer the opportunity to identify herself or himself as a surrogate family member. The viewer is then able, if not to understand, perhaps to have compassion for the veteran combat soldier in a personalized, intimate manner. Both the "Vets" episode and the series as a whole use a lingering, static close-up that hovers for emotional impact, working at an intensified level to emphasize intimate moments. Thus, what was previously foreign and inaccessible to the majority of the American public becomes more familial and more readily consumable. In presenting the experiences of veterans on television, not only in the documentary fashion of "Vets," but also in the more mediated form of fictional narratives, *China Beach* works to bring the war back into the living room, into the realm of the personal, in a way contemporary films cannot, and at the same time takes a significant step toward refiguring the war's impact on the psyche of the American public.

The program presents some of the women in archetypal roles most often associated with femininity in Western ideology—the mother (both Lila Gerraeu, the base commander and career special-services officer, and McMurphy) and the whore (K.C. in particular, together with a number of faceless Vietnamese female characters). In their role as surrogate family, the women often serve a maternal function, emphasizing not only their duty as caregiver but their "instinct" as caretaker. In separate episodes, Lila mothers an orphaned leopard cub, while McMurphy oscillates between being a fantasy mother and acting as a mother to Dodger, a severely wounded infantryman who is a regular in the series. In "Afterburner," Lila agrees to take care of a package for a young soldier bound stateside until it can be shipped to him. The package turns out to be a wildcat, and Lila displaces her maternal affection for the absent soldier onto the young, orphaned feline, becoming more attached to it than she would have liked. During a monologue, overheard by the head surgeon, she addresses her maternal instinct; she apologizes to the cat for her necessary abandonment of it, speaking of her loneliness and how the cat reminds her of that fact. The surgeon remarks on the betterment of the cat's life through Lila's intervention and acknowledges the difficulty of seeing them "grow up." Lila has sublimated her maternal instinct for the sake of her career, making the army a replacement family for which she cares. Her promotion to base commander during the second season prompts Lila to fuss about the appearance of the base, as it seems to reflect directly on her abilities as a caregiver. She demands that the base be in "tip-top shape" and that those on leave there behave themselves properly.

"Limbo" is the second of three episodes that deals with Dodger's

near-fatal injury and resulting paralysis. As the title implies, in this
episode Dodger, a mysterious figure who lurks on the perimeter of
the camp, hovers between life and death while McMurphy obsessively watches over him. Included in the visual imagery are a
number of flashbacks that show Dodger being injured as a child. In
these scenes, the actress who plays McMurphy is also cast as the
boy's mother. One of the flashbacks ends with Dodger's mother
leaning over him; as Dodger comes to in the army hospital, McMurphy duplicates this action, blurring the distinction between herself
and the mother. The viewer is left to wonder if it is McMurphy who
has cast herself in the mother role, causing Dodger to dream of her as
his mother, or if, through the process of displacement, Dodger has
come to identify McMurphy as his substitute mother. It is McMurphy, however, who is traumatized when Dodger is temporarily evacu-
ated to another hospital.

For Lila and McMurphy, the process of letting go is difficult.
Mary Ann Doane, in *The Desire to Desire*, writes of motherhood as
being "conceived as the always uneasy conjunction of absolute
closeness and a forced distance."[8] The separation trauma experienced by these female characters is clearly a maternal one. It is also
not unlike the process that hundreds of thousands of mothers underwent during the war, nor is it very dissimilar from the experience
both veterans and the American public are undergoing in recovering
from the scars of the U.S.–Vietnam War.

In addition to the process of healing, the series initially explored just where the Western woman's place, both her emotional
and physical space, was in Vietnam. At the end of the debut
episode, McMurphy is left in the first of a series of emotional and
physical quandaries. Having finally decided to stay on for another
year's tour, she finds that an enemy strike has destroyed the hut she
had been living in. In the following episode, "Home," she is caught
between homes: she will not return to her home in the States and
cannot return to her "home" in Vietnam. As she reluctantly bunks
in cramped quarters with Laurette, space becomes a crucial issue
not only for McMurphy but the other women as well. A search for a
space where the women can commune becomes a running plot line

for the remainder of the first aired season after a haphazard night is spent in an underground bunker where the women find themselves alone for the first time since they all arrived. Because they are rigidly defined by the space they work in, providing for the various needs of the men—whether physical (nurse, prostitute), emotional ("Doughnut dolly," USO showgirl), or military (base commander)—the women seek refuge from men in order to be "themselves." On the eve of her departure, in the "Chao Ong" episode, Laurette finally succeeds in constructing a special place for the women called "This is It!" On the walls are painted the names of the women who remain behind. "For women only!" "no makeup!" "no men!" remark the women as they toast her ingenuity. This, however, is the first and last time the room is shown.

The series is slippery about the issue of women's solidarity. The uniting of disparate personalities, who are thrown together by circumstances, is a combat-film convention addressed both in the "Vets" episode and in the series in general. As with World War II films that look at women in the combat zone, such as *Cry Havoc* and *So Proudly We Hail* (both 1943), attempts are made to give communion among the women a positive representation; yet the result is merely a displacement of the male bonding necessary in the male combat genre onto women, with a little hysteria thrown in for good measure. The issues discussed and the tone of specific conversations either imitate male discourse or are projections of male fantasies about women, as in the episode "Hot Spell," in which the women talk about their first sexual experience. This is not to say that women do not speak about their sexuality, but rather to suggest that the dialogue in this instance smacked more of the locker room than of the intimate confiding experienced in feminine discourse. Furthermore, much of their coming together is undercut by plot lines in which the women are consistently separated and subsequently brought back together over various, and sometimes rivaling, romantic involvements. There is no equivalent to this dynamic in the male combat film, although it is seen to a lesser degree in the other television series set in Vietnam, *Tour of Duty*. In later episodes, the women find comfort in a man's arms, in a bottle, or out on the beach, away from the compound. (Needless to say, lesbianism is never even hinted at.) The bottom line for the women is that their solidarity is tenuous; they cannot achieve a permanent bond of trust as long as they are heterosexually competitive—not a terribly positive message about women who made severe sacrifices to be in Vietnam.

In the first season, for instance, both the USO singer, Laurette, and the base prostitute, K.C., vie for the attentions of the beach lifeguard, Boonie. Both women are redheads, and in the "Chao Ong" episode, as Laurette readies to leave China Beach and go on tour, both women appear wearing the same short-cut, Chinese-style, blue silk dress, a gift from Boonie to each at separate times. Their appearance underscores their reduction to substitutable objects of Boonie's sexual desires. To him they are interchangeable, yet they are strikingly different in personality and physicality. Important to this triangle is that Boonie receives a medal for valor, creating the "hero" as the women's object of desire. In a later episode, Wayloo Marie Holmes, a film journalist introduced in the second season, K.C., and Lila all desire the attentions of the same man—a visiting officer who is a decorated war hero. Lila's eventual winning out over the other two women has an additional dimension, as she is undergoing the first stages of menopause and being desired by an eligible man somehow alleviates her anxiety.

What is emphasized in the series, then, whether the women are vying for the attention of the same man, or displacing their maternal instincts into their careers, is that these women are caring for men, who, by the very act of being involved in an absurd war, are heroes. What women do in their jobs and in their private lives is important *because* of the men with whom they interact. *China Beach* constantly refigures the idea of the hero and notions of the heroic; despite what Broyles claims to be heroic, the activity of men and their ability to comprehend and adapt to their situation makes it all the more apparent just how out of place the women truly are. "'Nam" is presented as a combat experience that, according to the male characters, they, unlike the women, did not choose to be a part of; yet they are the only ones who can understand it. Women cannot speak to this part of their own history because there are no books, movies, songs, or stories about combat in Vietnam that can accurately or fully place them within the grasp of the male experience, and there are fewer means in which their own experiences can be truly represented.

Most emblematic of how outside of events, how next door to war, these women are is Cherry, who has come to Vietnam as a Red Cross volunteer to find her missing brother Rick, who apparently has gone AWOL. In the episode "Brothers," Cherry turns to Dodger for help in locating Rick. Dodger informs her that she is unsuccessful because she *looks* wrong—Cherry cannot "walk the walk" or "talk the talk." This use of the word "look" not only implies that her appearance makes her stand out but also suggests, as feminist theorists argue, that because she is a woman she is not allowed within traditional male-dominated representation to be other than the object of the gaze; she herself cannot do the looking nor enter the discourse of combat soldiering in Vietnam. Instead, she must rely upon Dodger to interpret what is going on around her. He becomes the strong yet silent active figure in the search for Rick, and only when Cherry and McMurphy dress seductively and deliberately attract the male gaze does Cherry succeed in finding her brother. Even then, Dodger is needed to decode the events. Like great war heroes before him, Dodger can survive because he has the experience of combat behind him.

The result of these narrative choices is to return the soldier to the realm of hero, hence bringing the war as well to a redefined arena of Western myth. The U.S.–Vietnam War continues to become more completely contained within the confines of a dominant discourse, and its deeply troubling and disruptive reality is rendered essentially impotent. The potential for a minority experience to speak outside of or in contradiction to a majority voice is denied. One wonders whether Le Ly Hayslip will also remain voiceless once Hollywood's most prolific Vietnam storyteller, Oliver Stone, brings her memoir to the screen. Instead of allowing women to tell their own story in their own words, *China Beach* draws upon a camouflaged generic experience to affirm what has already been said and what is already known.[9]

Notes

1. Mark Morrison, *"China Beach* Salutes the Women of Vietnam," *Rolling Stone,* 19 May 1988: 76.

2. Susan Jeffords, "Friendly Civilians: Images of Women and the Feminization of the Audience in Vietnam Films," *Wide Angle* 7.4 (1985): 13.

3. Ibid.: 19.

4. Morrison, *"China Beach"*: 79.

5. Lynne Joyrich, "All That Television Allows: TV Melodrama, Postmodernism, and Consumer Culture," *Camera Obscura* 16 (1988): 131.

6. Howard Rosenberg, "Viet Vets Add Drama to *China Beach, Nightline,"* *Los Angeles Times,* 15 March 1989: 6, 1.

7. This image has been adopted as the program's logo, rendering the Vietnam experience ironically beautiful. The remainder of the credit sequence draws the viewer in with images of Delany sunbathing and playing volleyball. The approach of a med-evac helicopter from around a hill brings in the horrific reality of the war, from which there is no true escape. The women, like the beach, are things of beauty amid the ugliness of wounded and dying young men and are, themselves, also an ironic presence.

8. Mary Ann Doane, *The Desire to Desire* (Bloomington: Indiana University Press, 1987) 76.

9. This chapter was first presented at the 1989 Society for Cinema Studies conference in Iowa City, Iowa. Subsequently, *China Beach* brought a number of talented and versatile women to its staff who functioned as writers, directors, and producers, notably Mimi Leder and Lydia Woodward. Carol Flint, who began as a production assistant, wrote, directed, and produced, and served as executive story editor. These women, along with writer-producer Georgia Jeffries, had an enormously positive influence on the series' representation of women, in contrast to the first, abbreviated season (1988–89), with which this chapter deals.

In January 1991 *China Beach* was put "on hiatus," although production continued. New episodes included material that dealt with posttraumatic stress syndrome as experienced by female veterans. However, the series never touched upon the issue of rape or other acts of violence against American women by American troops, documented in Kathryn Marshall's *In the Combat Zone.* In the spring of 1991, *China Beach* was cancelled.

Susan White

Male Bonding, Hollywood Orientalism, and the Repression of the Feminine in Kubrick's *Full Metal Jacket*

Nature was miraculously skilful in concocting excuses, he
thought, with a heavy, theatrical contempt. It could deck a
hideous creature in enticing apparel.

When he saw how she, as a woman beckons, had
cozened him out of his home and hoodwinked him into holding a rifle, he went into a rage.

He turned in tupenny fury upon the high, tranquil sky.
He would have like to have splashed it with a derisive paint.

And he was bitter that among all men, he should be the
only one sufficiently wise to understand these things.
— STEPHEN CRANE, *The Red Badge of Courage*

CHAPTER 11 *Full Metal Jacket* (1987) was
marketed as a traditional war film, basking in the reflected glow of
Kubrick's ambiguous reputation as an eccentric genius. Like most
war movies, this film is, at least superficially, unconcerned with the
representation of women. However, in the Warner Brothers press
kit, the reviewer David Denby articulates a return of the issue of
femininity repressed from the film's manifest content.[1]

> The first law of moviegoing happiness in the eighties is this:
> *Anticipate nothing.* Because if you dream about an important
> upcoming movie, if you expect it to save your life or even the
> movie season, the picture will turn out to be *Dune* or *The
> Mosquito Coast* or *The Mission.* Burned, you'll feel like the
> high school nerd who gets his hands on the class cheerleader
> only to discover she's wearing falsies. Which serves you right
> for caring so much about boobs, you boob.[2]

Reprinted, in revised form, by permission, from *Arizona Quarterly* 44, no. 3
(1988). Copyright 1988, Arizona Quarterly.

There is here a curious coincidence between Denby's critical approach and the male fantasies both made available by and powerfully critiqued by this film text—as I hope to begin to make clear in what follows. And yet this passage from Denby's review also, despite itself, echoes a deep suspicion toward the film medium that is one of the most profound meditations carried out by this film: you cannot any longer use film as a simple facilitator of fantasy, especially fantasies about women. If you do, you will get burned. A detail from *Full Metal Jacket*: in one of the many "metacinematic" moments in the film, a Vietnamese whore is taken for sex into a gutted movie theater that is advertising a Vietnamese feature as well as a rerun of *The Lone Ranger* (1956).

Like *2001* (1968) and *Barry Lyndon* (1975), Kubrick's *Full Metal Jacket* divides into two distinct parts, punctuated (in the latter film) by a fade to black and a drastic change of location: from the Parris Island boot camp that is the setting of the first half of the film, to Da Nang and then Hue City during the 1968 Tet offensive. Both parts feature a timeworn combat-film formula—the adaptation of the individual to the demands of a ritualistic male group.[3] In both cases that adaptation fails spectacularly, though for radically different reasons. In the first instance this failure stems from what is termed, *pace 2001*'s Hal computer, a "major malfunction" in the brain of Private Leonard Lawrence (Vincent D'Onofrio), otherwise known as Private Pyle (as in "Gomer Pyle, U.S. Marine Corps"), who becomes a suicidal maniac at the end of his humiliating boot-camp experience. The second failure of adaptation concerns the film's protagonist, ironically named Private Joker (Matthew Modine) by the foulmouthed Sergeant Hartman (Lee Ermey) because of his imitation of John Wayne. This reference to John Wayne is hardly a casual one in a movie set during the days when *The Green Berets* (1968) was a gung ho promotion for the U.S. Army.[4] Clearly, Joker is easily influenced by the movies, despite his semblance of being a freethinker. At the end of the film Joker is marching into the reddened Vietnamese night, speaking in voice-over of his "homecoming fuck fantasies" and joining in as the troops sing the "Mickey Mouse" theme song after a full day in the urban trenches.[5] Joker is lost in the masses of men marching against a backdrop of burning ruins, whose towering shapes call to mind the McGuffin of Kubrick's *2001* (a film released in 1968)—the monolith from outer space was there the emblem or figure of a peculiarly human enigma that might be expressed by means of one haunting question: What is human violence? Are we, as Joker's helmet claims, "Born to Kill"?

In this final scene, as he sings along with the gang, Joker has accommodated himself to the group, all right. But Kubrick seems to be implying that the "major malfunction" is no longer—or perhaps never was—an individual one. The men, renamed, repackaged, and, as the sergeant puts it in boot camp, "born again hard," now move as one, as devoid of what we ordinarily call human response as are the bullets encased in the "full metal jackets" that give the film its title. Even Hal singing "Daisy" at the moment of his greatest verbal regression was more human. One could go even further and say that Kubrick in that film as in this one is breaking down any simple binary opposition between the technological and the human, showing rather how man has produced himself as inextricably technologized and violent.[6] And this production of man is, at least in *Full Metal Jacket*, as concerned with gender as it is with species. Having passed through the unholy waters of masculinization—the construction of a masculine identity—where anything infantile, female, or homoerotic is expelled with horror, Joker now finds himself deep in a "world of shit" (one of the catchphrases of the film) joining in a celebration of mass infantilism and reveling in Technicolor fantasies about "Mary Jane Rottencrotch's" breasts. Such are the contradictions of masculinity.[7]

The violent rejection of the female, of the racially "other," and of anything reminiscent of infantile susceptibility to maternal mastery is spelled out in the scapegoating scenes that structure this film. From his first encounters with Sergeant Hartman, the woefully inept Private Lawrence fails to measure up to the standards of male behavior as gauged by the bodily disposition required of a marine. Overweight and incompetent, he is verbally abused as a "disgusting fat body" and linked by the sergeant through his name to that Middle Eastern "faggot," Lawrence of Arabia.

HARTMAN: "What's your name, fat body?"

PRIVATE: "Sir, Leonard Lawrence, sir!"

HARTMAN: "Lawrence? Lawrence what? of Arabia?"

PRIVATE: "Sir, no sir!"

HARTMAN: "That name sounds like royalty. Are you royalty?"

PRIVATE: "Sir, no sir!"

HARTMAN: "Do you suck dicks?"

PRIVATE: "Sir, no sir!"

HARTMAN: "Bullshit. I'll bet you could suck a golf ball through a garden hose. I don't like the name Lawrence. Only faggots and sailors are called Lawrence. From now on you're Gomer Pyle."

Although the other men (specifically Cowboy—Arliss Howard) are also abused as "queers and steers," Pyle's limpid demand for love from Joker, his masochistic enjoyment of the first harsh words from the sergeant, reflect his unique inability, in this group, to shake the menace of the unmasculine.

The name Gomer Pyle is, of course, another timely detail in this film narrative: the television show of the same name was at the height of its popularity in 1968.[8] It featured the antics of the incompetent but lovable Private Gomer Pyle, played by the actor Jim Nabors (whose alleged homosexuality was a topic of pervasive rumor during that period), forever consigned to boot camp under the irascible eye of his drill instructor, Sergeant Carter. One of the subtly disturbing elements of *Full Metal Jacket* is its rewriting of canonical cultural texts such as this television program: here we are forced to acknowledge both the pathological nature of the private's ineptitude and the repressed homoerotic desire that serves to shape these men in the image of the lackeys of the "beloved Corps." (One might note, in this context, the scatological connotation of the name "Pyle.")[9] In the television show, Pyle's bumbling continually arouses the infuriated though distinctly maternal, even loving ministrations of Sergeant Carter, who, to be sure, keeps the proper male perspective through his relationship to his hyperfeminine girlfriend, Bunny. In both the film and the television program, to be part of the Body (the Corps) one must shape oneself in its image. One's body must not be disgustingly or alluringly "other." The Corps is both mother and father, functioning according to group dynamics that fall distinctly within the Imaginary order as Lacan describes it, with the consequent aggression directed toward the body itself insofar as it is the threateningly powerful maternal body; this aggression is directed only secondarily against the enemy. The men are also, we have seen, *renamed* by the sergeant, who here and elsewhere obviously exercises the prerogative of bringing the men under the sway of the group superego that stands in for the Lacanian Symbolic function. At every juncture, however, the line between male bonding and the baldly homoerotic is a fine one. As the drill sergeant puts it in his Christmas speech, "God has a hard-on for Marines."

The film's Private Pyle is finally put under the charge of Private Joker, who is to instruct him in all the practices of soldiering, which Joker does both reluctantly and tenderly. At first this task is carried out with some success. In a series of standard boot-camp scenes (some of which, like the shoe-tying episode, are also to be found in Coppola's *Gardens of Stone* (1987)—the failure of the latter film can be gauged in part by its leaden use of this and other stock scenes), Pyle is shown making slow but steady progress. Then, in one of the many stylistically astounding barracks inspection scenes, Pyle commits an error that he will never live down—he is caught with a jelly doughnut concealed in his footlocker. Hartman declares that from now on the entire group will suffer for Pyle's mistakes and has the men do push-ups while Pyle eats the doughnut. Later, Pyle is made to suck his thumb (for the second time in the film) while the other men do "squat-thrusts and side-straddle hops"[10] as penance for their association with this now marginalized baby. The interdependency of group and individual—which, according to the World War II film formula outlined by Robert Ray, must always be shown to be a *resolvable* opposition—is brought into stark relief, then finally dissolved at the end of the film as Joker melts into the now irrevocably infantilized group. In this film Kubrick has it both ways: he fulfills combat-film formulas as he rewrites them.

Both major segments of *Full Metal Jacket* are marked by what we might term, following Girard, the "violent unanimity" of the group against the individual.[11] In the marine boot camp the event occurs as follows: on an eerily blue moonlit night, Pyle is held down and gagged while each man takes a blow at his body with a bar of soap wrapped in a towel. Joker at first holds back, does not want to hit this boy he has nurtured, but, in the first moment of his moral collapse, he finally joins in and delivers six particularly vicious blows. Pyle is himself transformed into a monster by this victimization. It is only when he is clearly insane that Pyle begins to "fit in" to the Corps (this is one of the film's more obvious messages): soon after this scene he develops into a crack rifleman. Having been inculcated with the ethos of the assassin by Hartman, who "jokingly" offers as models to the men the former marine riflemen Lee Harvey Oswald and Charles Whitman, Pyle later turns his rifle on himself and the sergeant in the barracks head. "I *am* in a world of shit," Pyle declares to Joker, who tries to talk him down with a warning. Although he has at this point graduated from boot camp, Pyle cannot leave behind the confusing miasma of his own infantilism, the blood and violence and desire for male love (the toilet on which he kills himself, like his name, might be seen as a sign of his fixation on the anal) that form the infrastructure of the Marine Corps but must be externalized onto women and the enemy. So Joker spends the rest of the film seeking to externalize this action—to take it out of the men's head, so to speak.[12] For example, the "properly" adapting apprentice marine uses the head in this way: In the very same restroom where Pyle dies on a toilet with his brains blown out, Joker and his buddy Cowboy had exchanged the first in a series of ritual insults of the women in their families—Joker to Cowboy: "I wanna slip my tubesteak in your sister. What'll you take in trade?" Cowboy: "What d'ya got?" The "head" is a place where male control of "tubesteaks" and the consequent devaluation of the women available for barter is paramount. In this woman-rejecting and expelling process, there are no more taboos: even though the sergeant at one point attempts to force Joker to acknowledge the sacredness of the Virgin Mary, this ritualistic invocation of the name of the Mother of God only anticipates the discovery that there is no "elsewhere," no place where the good mother still prevails unassailable in her purity. One could scarcely imagine, in the diegetic world of *Full Metal Jacket*, the existence of a character like the grandmother (unproblematically) addressed by the protagonist of *Platoon* (1986) in his letters home.

Although Joker is a witness to Pyle's act of suicidal homoeroticism—Pyle has, in effect, offered his body to the drill sergeant—he goes off apparently unscathed to Da Nang as a reporter for *Stars and Stripes*, the newspaper of the armed forces. Ordered up-country for smarting off during an editorial meeting after the Tet offensive, Joker and his overly eager buddy Rafterman (Kevyn Major Howard) join up with Cowboy's combat unit in the days following the Tet offensive. The film's second scene of what I am calling "violent unanimity" against the "other" is foreshadowed by an earlier event, where a prostitute (Leanne Hong) poses and talks dirty for Joker and his buddy. Her swaying progress across the screen is the first action of the second half of the film and is accompanied by the theme song of country-western feminism, "These Boots Are Made for Walkin'", a sassy woman's song about taking control of her life (by stomping on a man). Suddenly, in one of Joker's only direct encounters with a living male Vietnamese, a young man (Nguyen Hue Phong) grabs Rafterman's camera, going through some karate moves obviously derived (anachronistically) from Bruce Lee films in a kind of mimeticism of Asian masculinity—moves that are amiably imitated by Joker. [13] This admiration for the Vietnamese warrior is borne out in another scene in the film, when Joker encounters a dead North Vietnamese (Duc Hu Ta) who is the "mascot" of the unit he joins. The dead man's American buddy praises the North Vietnamese Army, the gooks who are a worthy enemy, like "slant-eyed drill instructors"—not like the ungrateful South Vietnamese who bring them whores and hide bombs in babies' diapers. If this were a world of men, of drill instructors, slant-eyed or otherwise, the warrior ideal could prevail. [14] It is the South Vietnamese, not the NVA, who are associated with a degraded femininity.

Later in the film, another prostitute is brought before the men of the unit by a South Vietnamese Army pimp. The woman agrees to have sex with all the men for $5 each after some complicated negotiations, including an argument about the size of black men's penises, in which it is concluded, reassuringly, that black men's penises are *not* larger than white men's. Here the sexual threat posed by the racial "otherness" of Eightball (Dorian Harewood), the "nigger behind the trigger," as he puts it, is recuperated; so, too, is he recuperated in his "otherness" by belonging to the Corps, although the potential threat he offers is never far from the surface of the narrative. The scene of a group of men and a single woman ends "humorously," with "Animal Mother," the quintessence of man-as-fighting-machine, taking first honors with the whore, displacing the black soldier.

Animal Mother (Adam Baldwin) is an arresting character. With a helmet that reads "I AM BECOME DEATH," he seems to be the reincarnation of Pyle in the form of a fighting man, as though that repository of infantile or animal instincts could not be entirely repressed, but may in fact be necessary for the group's survival, even as walking dead.[15] A crack shot, as was Pyle, Animal Mother looks like a "hard" version of the dead recruit. And his name is an index of that never quite completely expelled "maternal" force that seems to haunt the film: Animal Mother is the fighting man (a particularly ruthless one) who must wear the banner of the fertile female principle if he is not to be subsumed by it. Pyle, who wanted to be mothered, is now a mother himself. We could, once again, invoke the notion of a return of repressed ideas, or, in a slightly more deconstructive mode, note how the dominant term in the binary pairs set up by the film (in this case "adult-infant" and "mother-son") depends upon the logic of the repressed term.

The climax of the film takes place when the men of the unit suffer horrifying casualties from the assault of an unseen sniper, located, like the former marine crack shots Oswald and Whitman, in a building somewhere above the victims. These not-quite-dead victims squirm in the dust, their screams tormenting their fellow marines. Here at last is the true test of war: enraged by the violent loss of Cowboy, Joker tries to become a real warrior. He makes his way into the sniper's building—only to find that "he" is a young, austerely dressed Vietcong woman.[16] Joker is paralyzed when he sees her: when he recovers, his rifle jams, then he fumbles the pistol he had drawn for his defense. Leaping into the breach, Rafterman blazes away with his M16, felling but not killing her. There ensues a strange dialogue between the men, who stand over the woman's body as though this were a gang rape, as they had stood over Pyle when they hit him, as they had stood over their dead comrades, and as they had figuratively surrounded the $5 whore. They are clearly confused by this woman who embodies both the repulsive and castrating "otherness" of womanhood and the ephemeral virginal/warrior ideal (she is praying—or at least the men think she is—and they are curiously restrained in their treatment of her). Animal wants to leave her to rot, but in an act of "mercy" Joker puts her out of her misery. "Hard core, man," comment his fellow marines.

In point of fact, the symmetry with the earlier scenes indicates to us that Joker has inexorably succumbed to what Girard might term the machine-logic of victimization, if indeed Joker's status as outsider in conflict with the group, as he who raised the question of "man's duality," was ever genuine. He lifts his hand against the woman as he had against Pyle, as had the human ape against his fellow ape in *2001*. Caught in a double bind, Joker can perform an act of mercy only as a gesture of scapegoating, one for which he must now take personal responsibility. Social unanimity involves violence against the "other": in a capitalist-imperialist society that "other" is a third-world Communist; under patriarchy it is a woman. While the woman is obviously not the only "victim" Kubrick portrays (indeed the women in these films are often complicitous with the powers of oppression), his films almost always show that Western social structures are based on ejection of and contempt for female sexuality. This contempt is curiously coupled with a pervasive desire for regression to the womb, as the last scene of the film (where the men sing "Mickey Mouse"—Hollywood as matrix) seems to indicate. In *Full Metal Jacket* we see the production of man—the storm troopers of America at the apogee, perhaps the final moment, of its imperial power—as a killing machine, whose violence finds

its model in that inflicted on women. This is not a film that specifically represents the struggle of the Vietnamese people: it is a film
about the construction of the racist woman-haters who walk, as
Animal Mother puts it, "like Jolly Green Giants with guns" across
the face of the earth. Woman is troped, in this and other films by
Kubrick, as the "Virgin Mary," whose name is invoked in all seri-
ousness by the drill sergeant, and simultaneously as the cloacal shit
from which the fighting men are trying to emerge so that they can
become "real" men. Clearly, the woman-sewer or woman-fosterer-
of-regression must be destroyed, but we have seen that, to their
confusion, the men find that in doing so they have also destroyed
both the virgin-mother and the warrior ideal that silently pervade the
film's ideological structure.

In *Male Fantasies,* his book on the formation of the protofascist
"soldier male" in Germany after World War I, Klaus Theweleit
describes the Freikorps soldier's fear of the terrifying Communist
riflewoman. These riflewomen were perceived as being endowed
with a fearful instrument of castration: "The men experience communism as a *direct* assault on their *genitals*," according to Theweleit.[17] Thor Goote, a fascist author whose works Theweleit closely
examines, describes a battle in the Baltic, where rumors were rife of
armed Red Army women on the warpath after men.

> [T]he worst thing is not to die from a head wound, as this boy
> has just done; it is far worse to be captured by this bestial en-
> emy, to suffer the most drawn-out, bitter and tortured death
> imaginable at the hands of sadistically grinning rifle women.

> [T]he dead continued to scream, though they were already
> cold. They will scream into eternity, those twelve savaged
> men of the Iron Legion, each drenched in black blood be-
> tween hips and thighs, each with that terrible wound with
> which the bestial foe has desecrated defenseless, wounded
> men.[18]

So, too, in *Full Metal Jacket,* does the sniper woman lure the men
one by one to their bloody doom, set in opposition to the clean "head

wound." Of course, Kubrick is both alluding to and undermining this image of the sadistic riflewoman by surrounding us with conflicting images about her. Theweleit continues: "The sexuality of the proletarian woman/gun slinging whore/communist is out to castrate and shred men to pieces. It seems to be her imaginary penis [whose visible representation is the rifle] that grants her the hideous power to do so."[19] The female phallus is, in *Full Metal Jacket*, fully feminine: Hartman orders his men to name their rifles after women (Pyle's is "Charlene") and to sleep with them each night.

The castrating riflewoman is menacing not only because of her phallic attribute but in some cases because of "something else, too," as Theweleit puts it—that something being racial or ethnic "otherness."

> SALOMÉ, RUTH, ESTHER: she stands there, a half-flight above
> him. Tight, tucked in shirt; left hand planted on her hip;
> right hand brandishing a pistol. The woman who enticed them
> to come up, with her shouting and crying.[20]

The beautiful, castrating Jewess is like her silent Vietnamese counterpart; both stand above the men, armed and dangerous.

Kubrick's representation of the enemy woman is, as I have indicated, a complex one. The Vietcong sniper, allied with the North Vietnamese, presents a sharp contrast to the whores of capitalism, as though Kubrick wanted us to make no mistake about the conditions of women under the two social systems in operation in Vietnam. The liberal Kubrick (one could also argue for a "radical" and for a "libertarian" Kubrick) makes sure that we get the opposite message to that given by the Freikorps officers who confront the Communist whores. And yet Kubrick's sniper is a Communist riflewoman who mutilates the men squirming on the ground beneath her. Joker has reached both a moral impasse and the point where it is no longer possible to conquer the woman, even through gang rape or execution. And having this woman of iron beg for death is no relief, either. The idealized virginal woman and the destructive Communist whore cannot finally be separated.

Full Metal Jacket is not Kubrick's first antiwar film. In 1953

Kubrick directed *Fear and Desire*, an abstract meditation on certain existential issues of war.[21] *Dr. Strangelove* (1964) is, of course, a black comedy about nuclear annihilation. The (seemingly) more traditionally humanistic 1957 antiwar film, *Paths of Glory*, is structured, like *Full Metal Jacket*, on the scapegoating of individuals within a military context. And in the former film, as in each of Kubrick's films dealing with war, women play a significant, if liminal, role.

In *Paths of Glory*, Colonel Dax (Kirk Douglas) defends his men against charges of cowardice in the face of the enemy, brought by the lunatic "bad" father figure General Mireau.[22] Mireau's paranoia and lack of conviction in his leadership lead him to irrational behavior, for which he himself is finally cynically weeded out of the French Army at the end of the film. As in *Full Metal Jacket*, the men are propelled in forward motion toward a deadly objective—in this case they must conquer "the Anthill," a name indicating the dehumanizing effect of the forced assault. They fail in their attempt and then are psychologically tortured by their commandant, who arbitrarily executes three of their comrades. At the end of the film we find the remaining soldiers seated in a tavern watching an enemy woman (in this case a German) perform on stage. Their lewd catcalls quickly turn to tears as the woman sings a touching ballad instead of the torch song they had expected. This victimized "enemy" woman is in fact doubly the object of a spectacle, since Dax is outside watching his men watch her, paternally or paternalistically concerned with the nature of their response to her. But unlike *Full Metal Jacket*'s men, *these* men are able to make the moment of scapegoating itself into one of community, sharing this sad song with the woman as they would a lullaby, accepting her mastery of a language they may not understand. The men in *Paths of Glory* remain "human" because they can accept their own infantilism without violently punishing the woman who makes them aware of their helplessness. (One of the lyrics in the German song is "Please, Mother, bring a light.")

Earlier in *Paths of Glory*, Mireau had struck a man, a victim of shell shock who was acting like a "baby." Mireau cannot bear to see his own fear reflected in the outside world. Obviously we are not to take him for the hero he believes himself to be. Still, in this film Kubrick seems to posit, though ironically, that "real men"—neither babies nor afraid of babies—might exist, and he offers Dax as a stand-in for that possibility. Mireau had earlier declared the Anthill "pregnable." Dax replies—"It sounds odd, like something to do with giving birth." Real men can look without fear into the abyss of female sexuality and reproduction—and still respect the purity of women. Such is the doublethink of old-time gallantry. However, even in this early film, what it means to be a man, to be human, to be a spectator are never simple givens, but are, as I have indicated, continually problematized. While Dax's men seem to accept their own infantilism without violently punishing the woman who brings it to their attention, they can only express their "humanity" in response to a markedly maudlin spectacle. We in turn must question our spectatorial relationship to Kubrick's close-ups of the tears on Dax's men's faces: the meaning of the sympathetic response as evoked by cinema is cast into doubt in the earlier as in the later film, though the political situations represented by the films are radically unlike.

In the title of this chapter I allude to a phenomenon that I have termed "Hollywood Orientalism." By this qualification of the notion of Orientalism, I mean to indicate that I do not wish to invoke the entire history of Western dealings with that heterogeneous "other" that it has called "the Orient," but simply to contextualize the representation of women in *Full Metal Jacket* by pointing to a tendency in *film noir* and in films about Vietnam (to name only two genres) to conflate various Eastern cultures with corrupt sexuality, a degraded or treacherous femininity, and male homoeroticism.[23] I will now take advantage of a textual cue in *Full Metal Jacket* to turn briefly to a late-colonial Orientalist text where a masochistic and homoerotic "turning in on oneself" is presented in the guise of a glorious form of male bonding among Arab men.[24] Lawrence of Arabia, who, as we have seen, is specifically named in Kubrick's film, is one well-known colonialist man who acted out the fantasy of "going native" (in this case, in the Middle East) in explicitly masochistic and homosexual terms.[25] T. E. Lawrence's works bring to the surface the deepest fears (and desires) of white colonialist and postcolonialist men everywhere.[26] As Rana Kabani has written, "Lawrence's 'heroic' epic begins with a passage that seems at odds with the lofty title [*Seven Pillars of Wisdom: A Triumph*]. It describes the homosexual relations that Lawrence claimed took place all around him in the desert."[27]

> Friends quivering together in the yielding sand with intimate hot limbs in supreme embrace, found there hidden in the darkness a sensual co-efficient of the mental passion which was welding our souls and spirits in one flaming effort. Several, thirsting to punish appetites they could not wholly prevent, took a savage pride in degrading the body, and offered themselves fiercely in any habit which promised physical pain.[28]

Kabbani suggests that this "unlikely description of quivering bedouins" may represent "Lawrence's subconscious portrayal of his own desires." In projecting such a lurid fantasy about Oriental male relationships, Lawrence seems to be attempting to do his Eastern brothers one better, exaggerating the homosociality/homoeroticism of Arab men to suit his fancy. One is reminded of Colonel Kurtz, in *Apocalypse Now*, whose reinterpretation of Asian customs is inscribed in violent rather than in explicitly erotic terms.

The view of the Middle and Far East discernible in *Full Metal Jacket* echoes the Hollywood Orientalist ideology at work in a number of films from the 1940s through the 1980s, where certain issues of gender, race, and war are covertly or overtly addressed. I will concentrate here on the films where the Far East, rather than the Middle East, is the geographical area indirectly or directly under scrutiny.[29] In many of the films in this rather inchoate category, there is a bizarre coincidence of *gesture* that caught my attention. The gesture is one of annihilation, and seems to be strongly overdetermined, an intertextual allusion that expresses the Western man's externalization and vicarious destruction of his own fears and desires.

Film noir has offered a rich field for the observation of sexual role playing to theorists of gender. And, as is well known, *film noir* has its own historical tie to World War II. Howard Hawks's *Big Sleep* was, for example, made at the end of World War II; indeed, it was previewed by men overseas on the front. Annette Kuhn has observed an intriguing pattern of movement in this hermeneutically dense film.[30] During its last few minutes, we return to a site that was obsessively investigated earlier in the film by the protagonist, Philip Marlowe. The place is Geiger's house, a den of corruption, where blackmail, pornography, drug dealing, and other unsavory activities were carried out by the now-deceased homosexual tenant, Arthur Gwynn Geiger. A young woman, Carmen Sternwood, had been blackmailed by Geiger with pictures taken by a camera concealed in an Asian statuette, one of the many generically Asian art objects decorating Geiger's sinister home. Indeed, Carmen is found at one point in the film in Geiger's house wearing Chinese clothes. (In Chandler's novel she is naked, obviously not a choice for Hawks— Chinese clothing is thus a permissible though still, we are apparently to gather, sleazy substitute for nudity.) Philip Marlowe loves Carmen's older sister, Vivian—but even at the end of the film Vivian is still too closely associated with Carmen's disturbing sexual and infantile behavior to be considered a reliable potential sexual partner.[31] In this last scene of the film Marlowe must solve, once and for all, the enigma that Kuhn terms *the* enigma of female sexuality, here, as is often the case, conflated with the mysteries of the Orient and the perversions of effeminate men.

Is Vivian a good woman? What is her secret allegiance to Eddie Mars? In the last scene of the film, Marlowe (with Vivian's help) sets up Geiger's house as a place where he will ambush and kill Mars. In this crucial scene, the Asian statuette, of indeterminate, possibly feminine appearance to the eyes of the Westerner, is first linked to Vivian by means of a dissolve over *her* head, then shot by Marlowe in an uncharacteristically hysterical burst of anger at Eddie Mars. Mars is then sprayed with machine-gun fire by his own men, an act that has foul incestuous or homoerotic overtones (penetration, orgasm, death). Vivian has earned her spurs through her passive cooperation with Marlowe. This bit of quintessentially Hawksian teamwork, where the woman seems to be an equal partner but is in fact subordinated to the man, makes the symbolic point of resolving through violence the enigma of what we might call the Orientalized woman. Interestingly, as the scene was first scripted, Carmen (the naughty sister) herself was to have been shot. Instead, she will simply be put away somewhere. In 1945, when *The Big Sleep* was first shown, the United States was on the verge of winning World War II. The Japanese menace will surely be beaten back—the "disturbance in the sphere of sexuality,"[32] curiously conflated with the Asiatic, also appears more resolvable in 1945 than it does in 1968, as seen, in *Full Metal Jacket*, through the lenses of 1987. At the end of World War II, the Japanese were defeated and, on the home front, women left the factories to return en masse to the domestic sphere. The specters of the spread of Asian Communism and of the increasing autonomy of women in the American work force were not so readily vanquished or contained after the war in Vietnam.

The destruction of the "Orientalized" woman has, as I have implied, a *gestural* as well as thematic relationship to later cinematic purges of dubious characters. The gesture is simply a shot to the head, a common enough suicidal or homicidal modus operandi, but strangely insisted upon in this body of films I am examining. In a discussion of *The Deer Hunter* (1978), Robin Wood lays particular emphasis on the film's quasi-mystical treatment of what the protagonists call the "one shot," that pure, masculine single shot that kills the deer stateside, but in Vietnam is transformed into the suicidal, Asianized, and homoerotic Russian roulette subculture used by the Christopher Walken character (Nick) as a way of "going native."[33] The "one shot" is thus transformed during the course of the film from an "emblem of control"[34] to "a monstrously perverted enactment of the union he [Nick] has always desired [with Mike]."[35] It is, I think, important to emphasize that this (probably mythical) game is presented as an *Asian* one, forced upon the men when they are held prisoner by the Vietcong.[36] Nick takes possession of the game as a masochistic expression of his desire for the sexually reticent Mike: the turning inward of sexual aggression is thus once again troped as a process of "Asianization." According to Wood, Mike's attempt to save Nick from the addiction to this perverse game (which he likens to Chance's rescue of Dude from alcoholism in *Rio Bravo* [1959]) can only spell to Nick a return to repression, a return to the externalized, aggressive, and "masculine" meaning of the "one shot."[37] Obviously, Wood sees *The Deer Hunter* very much as a "male love story,"[38] though he seems to see the subversive treatment of male sexuality in this film as less a deliberate act on the part of Cimino than as a product of larger cultural determinants.

A film that, by contrast, works in what is clearly a self-conscious and deliberately citational mode is Roman Polanski's *Chinatown* (1974), which to some extent deconstructs the *film noir* conflation of the enigma of feminine sexuality with the cultural "otherness" of the Chinese. *Chinatown*'s female protagonist, a victim of paternal incest, cannot be salvaged—she is doomed to remain a victim of her hopelessly contorted past. Like Carmen in the original screenplay for *The Big Sleep*, Mrs. Mulwray (Faye Dunaway) is finally shot in the head (her eye is shot out, as is the camera eye at the end of *The Big Sleep*), only in this case the "one shot" is not fired in the shady home of a homosexual man, but, more directly, in Chinatown itself. The ending of Polanski's film shows that Gittis (Jack Nicholson) is precisely *unable* to purge himself of the evils associated with the "Asianized" woman by means of this act of violence. Rather, the scene reveals that Gittis is caught in a repetition compulsion that (by nature) is both out of his control and a deliberate choice he has made: he had lost a woman in Chinatown in the past, and now it is he who has asked Evelyn Mulwray to meet him in Chinatown, where she is killed by the police. A group of Chinese passersby watches the tragic spectacle, obviously not directly implicated in the events unfolding before them (though our discussion of spectatorship in *Paths of Glory* might indicate a need to examine further the meaning of "looking on" in this scene, as well). In this way Polanski wryly comments on *film noir*'s use of Chinatown as a figure of *Western* corruption.[39]

Although Cimino's recent film *Year of the Dragon* (1986) treats many of the same issues that come up in *Chinatown*, its presentation of the sexual and ethnic material it unearths is, as one might suspect, muddled.[40] *Year of the Dragon* is a strangely anachronistic film about a cop's extended flashback of Chinatown-as-Vietnam, as a place that can only be purged of its corruption by all-out warfare. (The references to Vietnam are explicit, as when Stanley White [Mickey Rourke] declares that "this is a fucking war and I'm not going to lose it—not this one.")[41] Not surprisingly, the detective's mission includes saving a woman from the evil influence of the Chinese, of Chinatown. Oddly, the woman, Tracy Tzu (Ariane), a television reporter, is herself Chinese, as White vehemently reminds her throughout the film. At the end of the film the white man does manage to save the Asian woman from the threat of her native culture, after having vigorously dragged her back to Chinatown from the assimilated place in white society she had earlier achieved. While Chinatown-as-Vietnam remains allegorical in Polanski's film, *Year of the Dragon* depicts Chinatown as the literal locus for working through the post-traumatic stress experienced by the Vietnam vet, who rescues/exorcises the woman held captive by her own ethnicity. Like Vivian Rutledge, Tracy will be domesticated—but, true to the reigning ideology of the 1980s, domesticity has been portrayed as even more threatening than Chinatown. The film's plot is predicated on an initial conflict between the detective and his wife, Connie (Caroline Kava), an aggressive woman (she constantly tells her husband not to "break her balls") who wants badly to have a child. This desire sends her husband into paroxysms of doubt and evasive behavior. Before she manages to become pregnant, Connie is killed by Chinese gangsters. The final rescue of Tracy is thus both a displaced rescue of the wife and a more sinister replacement of the phallic mother (a woman with balls who wants to get pregnant) by the more salvageable (because finally less demanding) assimilated Asian yuppie. The "one shot" is also in evidence in this film: in a final, climactic scene White permits a Chinese gangster to commit suicide with his gun. Asian sexuality—both masculine and feminine—as well as Chinese upward mobility are thus punished and brought back under white control at the end of the film.

In his analysis of *Dr. Strangelove*, Peter Baxter describes the

"ineradicable tendency towards self-abasement, even self-destruction, that is almost universally repressed in the construction of masculinity."[42] The joyous self-annihilation of male-dominated Western
culture is made hilariously explicit in that film (viz., its subtitle,
"How I Learned to Stop Worrying and Love the Bomb"). Baxter's
reading of *Dr. Strangelove* concentrates on "the one woman" in the
film, Miss Scott (the bikinied secretary), who, like the "single
women" in *Paths of Glory* and *Full Metal Jacket*, functions to reflect
and transmit various masculine concerns. Baxter notes that "the
comic conceit" of *Dr. Strangelove* derives from the fact that "between
men and the reality of politics and war intervenes the realm of sexual
phantasy,"[43] a phantasy focused on "the nostalgic desire for a past
that cannot be reached except in death. Doomsday echoes with the
voice of the one woman we once upon a time all knew."[44] As I have
already indicated, Baxter, like Kaja Silverman and a number of
other critics, emphasizes the primacy of masochism in this (male)
phantasy,[45] in which a desire for pain, humiliation, and death is
attributed to other beings, generally those of lower social (i.e.,
ethnic or sexual) status. *Full Metal Jacket* incorporates both the
"turning inward" of male masochistic homoeroticism and its aggressive turning outward in the form of projection and denial that we have
observed in the films discussed above. In *The Deer Hunter*, male love
of other men is a disruptive force, capable of tearing apart the social
fabric of the homophobic, working-class American community. It is
also shown to be strongly linked to a self-destructive fantasy that is
attributed to the Vietnamese. In *Full Metal Jacket*, male homosocial
bonding forcibly expels its homoerotic content—and yet Pyle's self-
annihilation under the eyes of his buddy/mother remains the erotic
focus of the film. *Full Metal Jacket* progresses from that image of
violence and eroticism turned *inward*, to its outward infliction on a
woman, as part of a chain of violent group actions against marginal
figures. From fantasies (and phantasies) about male homosexual love
entrenched in violent projections of masochistic desire, from hetero-
sexual interactions irremediably founded on denigration and fear, to
homo- and heterosexualities less marked by patriarchal victimization patterns: these are social and political gains that will not have

been achieved by the time the next Kubrick film is released (even if it is as long in the making as was *Full Metal Jacket*). In the meantime, we can expect to continue to see works in which the Western male's desire to abase himself to the great white father is put off on Arabs, Asians, and women, the "natural" masochists of the world.

Notes

1. It is, I think, significant that the press kit has no pictures of any of the three women who appear in the film.

2. David Denby, "Waiting for Stanley," *Premiere*, July–August 1987. Included as an insert in the Warner Brothers promotional packet for *Full Metal Jacket*.

3. For a succinct and informative discussion of the functioning of this formula, see Robert B. Ray, *A Certain Tendency of the Hollywood Cinema, 1930–1980* (Princeton, N.J.: Princeton University Press, 1985) 112–25.

4. This connection with *The Green Berets* is made much more explicit in Gustav Hasford's novel *The Short-Timers* (New York: Harper and Row, 1979), from which the film was adapted. In "Full Metal Genre: Kubrick's Vietnam Combat Movie," *Film Quarterly* 42.2 (1988–89): 24–30, Thomas Doherty notes that the grunts in Hasford's novel laugh at the naïveté of Wayne's film. Kubrick's Joker comes off as more credulous, regarding the media, than is his novelistic equivalent. And like the journalist in *The Green Berets*, Joker is also a reporter who begins by being "cynical" about the war but becomes a believer by the end of the film.

5. Mickey Mouse makes his appearance at least two other times in the film—once when the sergeant asks the soon-to-be homicidal Pyle, "What is this Mickey Mouse shit?" and once as a figure in the background of the *Stars and Stripes* "office," next to the lieutenant.

6. The "technologized" man is neither machine nor human, but something called a "killer" (another of Joker's nicknames). Joker describes the sergeant as proud when the men grow beyond his control: "The Marine Corps does not want robots. The Marine Corps wants killers. The Marine Corps wants to build indestructible men. Men without fear."

7. The ending of Kubrick's film is only very loosely adapted (by Kubrick, Michael Herr, and Gustav Hasford) from Hasford's novel. Elements of dialogue in this sequence and the group march itself are garnered from other sections of the novel. The final product, in *Full Metal Jacket*, is an ending that very much resembles that of Stephen Crane's *Red Badge of*

Courage, as Ed Dryden indicated to me and as I have hinted by using an epigraph taken from that novel. (The "derisive paint" to be splashed against the sky by Crane's protagonist anticipates the haunting lyrics of the Rolling Stones's "Paint It Black," which is played over the film's final credits.) Kubrick's is an ironic version of the already ironic Crane text— both film and novel achieve a peculiar impersonality of tone despite their close recounting of a young man's experience of a war whose political implications are (directly) dealt with almost not at all. See James A. Stevenson, "Beyond Stephen Crane: *Full Metal Jacket,*" *Literature/Film Quarterly* 16 (1988): 238–43, for a more extensive discussion of Kubrick's reworking of Crane. The most striking differences between Hasford's novel and Kubrick's film are structural ones: by expanding the boot-camp episode Kubrick gives as much weight to the construction of the soldier mentality as to the "Vietnam experience," and by emphasizing certain pivotal scenes of violence he achieves a more economical effect than does Hasford, who, it seems to me, adds a note of ideological confusion when he has Joker "mercy kill" Cowboy, as well as the Vietcong sniper.

8. In *Comic Visions: Television Comedy and American Culture* (Boston: Unwin Hyman, 1989), David Marc notes that although the show paralleled precisely the worst years of American combat deaths in Vietnam, the word was never mentioned in the series (129).

9. The motif of anality reappears when the men laugh at Private Snowball for calling the structure from which Oswald shot Kennedy a "book suppository building."

10. Hasford, *The Short-Timers* 16.

11. See, especially, René Girard, *Violence and the Sacred,* tr. Patrick Gregory (Baltimore, Md.: Johns Hopkins University Press, 1977), for Girard's most far-reaching discussion of the social origins of scapegoating.

12. Moments before he is shot, Sergeant Hartman asks Pyle, "Just what are you doing in my head?" The significance of the image of the "head" in *Full Metal Jacket* has been more fully explored by Elaine Marshall in a paper entitled "Looking into *Full Metal Jacket* and the Problem of Cinematic Representation" presented at the Florida State University thirteenth annual Conference on Literature and Film, January 1988. In "*Full Metal Jacket* and the Beast Within," *Literature/Film Quarterly* 16 (1988), Claude J. Smith, Jr., notes that in *Strangelove* the "probably homosexual General Jack D. Ripper similarly committed suicide inside his latrine, apparently via a head wound" (228).

13. That Kubrick is willing to use such an anachronism in his film is

characteristic of the suspicion pervading *Full Metal Jacket* about the ability of media (including television and newspapers) to "mimetically transfer truth" (Gerri Reaves, "From Hasford's *The Short-Timers* to Kubrick's *Full Metal Jacket*," *Literature/Film Quarterly* 16 [1988]: 236). In the television interview scene and elsewhere, "we get Kubrick's comments on the creation of a gigantic media event and on the obvious discrepancies between the reality of the war and the soldiers' perceptions of the war" (234). The Bruce Lee citation serves to remind us that we are looking at a depiction of the Vietnam War filtered through twelve years of postwar media representations.

14. "The more socially 'efficient' scapegoating is, the more capable it is of generating a positive transfiguration of the scapegoat, as well as the negative transfiguration of fear and hostility. The positive transfiguration is still present in the feudal and even the national traditions of military warfare. The enemy is respected as well as intensely disliked" (René Girard, "Generative Scapegoating" in *Violent Origins: Ritual Killing and Cultural Formation*, ed. Robert G. Hamerton-Kelly [Stanford, Calif.: Stanford University Press, 1987] 94).

15. I owe this insight about the "identity" of Pyle's and Animal Mother's character, as well as aspects of my analysis of the role of spectatorship in *Paths of Glory* (below), to a discussion with Mark Crispin Miller. I thank him here for his many useful comments both after screening the film and when this chapter was in manuscript form.

16. In Hasford's novel the sniper is described as Eurasian; see Hasford, *The Short-Timers* 116. In Chapter 6 of this book, "Narrative Patterns and Mythic Trajectories in Mid-1980s Vietnam Movies," Tony Williams comments that the woman's Eurasian ethnicity makes it possible to read her as Joker's feminine double. Although Williams's is a powerful reading of this scene in the novel, I see little evidence in *Full Metal Jacket* that the woman is meant to be partly European.

17. Klaus Theweleit, *Male Fantasies*, vol. 1: *Women, Floods, Bodies, History*, tr. Stephen Conway, in collaboration with Erica Carter and Chris Turner (Minneapolis: University of Minnesota Press, 1987) 74. As this essay was first going to press, I discovered that Tania Modleski had also written on *Full Metal Jacket*, using Klaus Theweleit's *Male Fantasies* as one of her tutor texts. See Tania Modleski, "A Father Is Being Beaten: Male Feminism and the War Film," *Discourse* 10.2 (Spring–Summer 1988): 62–77. Modleski's placement of *Full Metal Jacket* within the context of other recent war films' depictions of the relation between sexual and military

conquest is extremely useful. She comments on Kubrick's refusal (in contrast to Stone in *Platoon*) to validate the "father": "the authoritarian nature of military training is [shown to be] positively disenabling" (72), as is indicated by Cowboy's strategically disastrous misreading of the map. "Thus," she continues, "Kubrick extensively undermines male authority; the father is not resurrected after he is killed off" (74). Still, the "paternal" power undermined by Kubrick is to a certain extent "recuperated in the signature of the filmmaker himself, the man who has the power to undertake the critique of authority in the first place" (74). Ironically, the overall effect of *Full Metal Jacket* may have been to glamorize the Marine Corps, through the intervention of this authorial signature.

18. Theweleit, *Male Fantasies* 74 is citing Goote (Johannes M. Berg), *Kamerad Berthold der "unvergleichliche Franke": Bild eines deutschen Soldaten* (Hamburg, n.d. [copyright: Braunschweig, 1937]) 286, 297.

19. Theweleit, *Male Fantasies* 76.

20. Ibid. 78.

21. Like *Full Metal Jacket*, this early film also focuses on the interaction between a group of men and a female hostage. See Thomas Allen Nelson, *Kubrick: Inside a Film Artist's Maze* (Bloomington: Indiana University Press, 1982) for details.

22. Oliver Stone's *Platoon* might be seen as a (simplistic) rewriting of the good-father, bad-father dichotomy in *Paths of Glory*.

23. For an encyclopedic overview of the Orient as "an integral part of European *material* civilization and culture," see Edward W. Said, *Orientalism* (New York: Vintage Books, 1979). Said's discussion of the Occident's sexual obsession with the Orient has strongly influenced my own treatment of the subject. See also Rana Kabbani, *Europe's Myths of Orient* (Bloomington: Indiana University Press, 1986).

24. In my discussions of male bonding I am referring implicitly to the work of Eve Kosofsky Sedgwick, especially to *Between Men: English Literature and Male Homosocial Desire* (New York: Columbia University Press, 1985), where she explores the importance of male homosocial bonds in British culture and literature and the related repression of male homosexuality in Western culture.

25. The reference to Lawrence of Arabia by Sergeant Hartman seems to be a deliberate choice in Kubrick's film, although I do not know which of the collaborators on the script (Kubrick, Herr, Hasford) came up with the idea. In Hasford's novel Leonard's last name is "Pratt."

26. It would take me too far afield to examine the complex situation of

the female colonialist. Obviously, the position of the white middle- or upper-class woman differs entirely from that of the (dominated) colonial subject, male or female, although a conflation of these positions seems to take place in some of the texts I am describing. In a more complete discussion of the relationship between colonialism, Orientalism, and gender politics, it would also be important to consider the function of lesbianism and of colonial female sexual adventurism in the Orient (cf. *Emanuelle* [1974], which takes place in Thailand).

27. Kabbani, *Europe's Myths of Orient* 110–11. In *Between Men*, Sedgwick discusses T. E. Lawrence as "charting the alien but to him compelling geography of male homosociality in the Arab culture" and remarks that "he had moved from intensely charged but apparently unfulfilling bonds with Englishmen, to bonds with Arab men that had, for political reasons, far more space for fantasy and mystification and hence for the illusionistic charisma of will" (195). Those "political reasons" for the Englishman's sense of a greater freedom to act out his sexual fantasies in the Orient include the dominance of the British Empire over the Arab world. For Sedgwick, Lawrence's experiences among the Arabs represent a "kind of postgraduate or remedial Public School," where the homosexual component of homosociality is explored without risk to class or gender privilege. See also Kaja Silverman's detailed discussion of the nature of Lawrence's homosexual masochistic fantasies and their complex relation to British imperialism in "White Skin, Brown Masks: The Double Mimesis; or, With Lawrence in Arabia," *Differences* 1.3 (1989): 3–54.

28. T. E. Lawrence, *Seven Pillars of Wisdom: A Triumph* (London, 1935; repr. 1965) 29.

29. I will not attempt rigorously to delineate the often composite profile of the ethnically "other" that is found in the films under discussion. A recent Hollywood film offers a good example of the difficulties involved in sorting out Hollywood's representations of ethnic and racial groups. *Who Framed Roger Rabbit?* (1988) is largely a remake of *Chinatown*, except that the oppressed social group in the film consists of "Toons," indestructible, marginally human cartoon figures housed in a ghetto called Toontown. As the film industry's most exploited entertainers, the Toons are modeled on black musicians and actors. At the same time, Toontown is the structural equivalent of *Chinatown*'s Chinese enclave, living according to its own alien laws (cf. the Chinese bordello in Wenders's *Hammett*). Finally, the film harks back (with twenty-twenty hindsight) to the question of World War II era anti-Semitism, invoking images of the Holocaust by depicting its

villain as plotting the genocide of the Toons. Although it is obviously useful and important to distinguish between the depiction of, say, Chinese sexuality in *Broken Blossoms* and Arabic sexuality in *The Sheik*, my purpose in this chapter is to point out the very slippage, concerning the various "orients," that occurs in Hollywood and Hollywood-style cinema. For a discussion of race and gender in *Broken Blossoms*, see Julia Lesage, "Artful Racism, Artful Rape: Griffith's *Broken Blossoms*" in *Home Is Where the Heart Is: Studies in Melodrama and the Woman's Film*, ed. Christine Gledhill (London: British Film Institute, 1987).

30. Annette Kuhn, *The Power of the Image* (London: Routledge and Kegan Paul, 1985) 74–95.

31. Like Pyle in *Full Metal Jacket*, Carmen sucks her thumb.

32. Kuhn, *The Power of the Image* 89.

33. I am drawing these arguments, rather loosely, from the chapter on Cimino in Robin Wood's *Hollywood from Vietnam to Reagan* (N.Y.: Columbia University Press, 1986). On the question of "going native" and of Orientalization as making feminine, see Eve Sedgwick's chapter "Up the Postern Stair: *Edwin Drood* and the Homophobia of Empire" in *Between Men*. Discussing *Edwin Drood*, Sedgwick remarks that, contrary to the American black-and-white dichotomy of racism, "Colonials . . . can 'go' native: there is a taint of climate, morale, or ethos that, while most readily described in racial terms, is actually seen as contagious" (183). Sedgwick notes that, in *Edwin Drood*, John Jasper wakes up "in a London opium den on a bed with a Chinaman, a Lascar, and a haggard woman." The woman has even " 'opium-smoked herself into a strange likeness of a Chinaman.' " Jasper will later become "orientalized by his contact with the Princess Puffer—and, by the same toke [*sic*], insidiously feminized" (184). I would submit that the black-white dichotomy of race in American film and literature is not as clear-cut as Sedgwick contends—see, for example, John Stahl's and Douglas Sirk's *Imitation of Life* and Faulkner's *Absalom, Absalom!* for similar enunciations of the problem of racial "contamination."

34. Wood, *Hollywood from Vietnam to Reagan* 294.

35. Ibid. 296.

36. Judy Lee Kinney has observed that Michael "presides over the ritualizing of one of the most famous visual icons of the War, General Nguyen Ngoc Loan's execution of a Viet Cong suspect during the 1968 Tet offensive by a shot to the head" ("The Mythical Method: Fictionalizing the Vietnam War," *Wide Angle* 7.4 [1985]: 40).

37. Wood, *Hollywood from Vietnam to Reagan* 296. He also mentions (278) the more widely remarked intertexts for *The Deer Hunter*: Ford's *The Searchers* and James Fenimore Cooper's *The Deerslayer*. Both of these narratives are of interest in that they involve what Richard Slotkin (see below) has termed the "feminization" of the white captive held by Indians. Many critics, including Tony Williams (in "Narrative Patterns and Mythic Trajectories") and Thomas Doherty (in "Full Metal Genre"), have noted the explicit "cowboy and Indian" themes in *Full Metal Jacket* and in other recent Vietnam War films. Richard Slotkin's *Regeneration through Violence: The Mythology of the American Frontier, 1600–1860* (Middletown, Conn.: Wesleyan University Press, 1973) explicitly addresses the role of the "hunter and captive myths" in the selling of the war in Vietnam to the American public. In 1965 President Johnson himself "invoked the characteristic imagery of the captivity myth, in which the family—symbolic embodiment of social order, centering on the figure of the mother and the child and associated with the cultivation of the soil—is assaulted by dark and savage forces from beyond the borders" (562–63). South Vietnam was the mother to be saved from outside invasion. In films like *The Deer Hunter* and *Full Metal Jacket* it is evident that the fear of engulfment by this mother is at least as strong as the fear of the "dark opponent." I will also note my disagreement with Susan Jeffords's assertion that women "disappear" from Vietnam in the recent films under discussion. I realize, on rereading her thought-provoking article "Friendly Civilians: Images of Women and the Feminization of the Audience in Vietnam Films" (*Wide Angle* 7.4 [1985]: 13–22), that my notion of the "repression of the feminine" is a direct citation from Jeffords (17), but in her description of how in these films the Vietnam soldier "denies the feminine" Jeffords does not seem to recognize that this repression is unsuccessful: a threatening (not simply a *passive*) femininity resurges to the forefront of the text. Since my essay first appeared Susan Jeffords has vastly expanded her reading of femininity in relation to Vietnam in *The Remasculinization of America: Gender and the Vietnam War* (Bloomington: Indiana University Press, 1989). In her section of *Full Metal Jacket*, she unfavorably contrasts Kubrick's film with Hasford's novel, claiming that the changes introduced move the screenplay "into a more definitive depiction of the feminine as enemy and rewrites the novel as a story of a gendered opposition between masculine and feminine" (174). I disagree with this reading insofar as I see this move as one analytical of American attitudes about race and gender, rather than one that "allows for the repression of the violence that underlies the gender

system" (176). Whether Jeffords's interpretation or mine is more convincing must be determined by our readers. See also Michael Pursell, "*Full Metal Jacket*: The Unraveling of Patriarchy," *Literature/Film Quarterly* 16 (1988): 218–25, for a discussion of the "gynophobia" shown by the characters in the film.

38. Wood, *Hollywood from Vietnam to Reagan* 294.

39. For further discussion of the depiction of Asians in Polanski's film, see William Galperin, "Bad for the Glass: Representation and Filmic Deconstruction in *Chinatown* and *Chan Is Missing*," *MLN* 102 (1987): 1151–70.

40. In fact, *Year of the Dragon* was picketed by Chinese Americans in many cities when it was released. Complaints focused, for the most part, on the representation of the Chinese-American community as corrupt and controlled by gangs. Most prints now begin with a disclaimer regarding the representation of Chinese Americans in the film.

41. In discussing the use of Chinatown as a metaphor for Vietnam in *Year of the Dragon*, I should note that Oliver Stone (writer and director of *Platoon*) cowrote the film with Cimino, basing it on Robert Daley's novel of the same name.

42. Peter Baxter, "The One Woman," *Wide Angle* 6.1 (1984): 35–41.

43. As is the practice among some psychoanalytic critics, Baxter is using the term "phantasy" to indicate that this is a preconscious or unconscious mental process, rather than a conscious "fantasy."

44. Baxter, "The One Woman": 41.

45. For a discussion of the theoretical grounds for claiming a primary, projected masochism, see especially Kaja Silverman, "Masochism and Subjectivity," *Framework* 12 (1975): 2–9; "*Histoire d'O*: The Story of a Disciplined and Punished Body," *enclitic* 7.2 (1983): 63–81; "Masochism and Male Subjectivity," *Camera Obscura* 17 (1988): 31–67; and "White Skin, Brown Masks."

Owen W. Gilman, Jr.

Vietnam, Chaos, and the Dark Art of Improvisation

CHAPTER 12 The Vietnam War has proved to
have remarkable staying power as an unsettling experience. By the
time of the South Vietnamese government's collapse in 1975, a great
many Americans had been compelled to relinquish their illusions
about managing the war to an ordered, reasonable resolution. Con-
sequently, a panoply of assumptions about power and control was
virtually swept aside, and a kind of existentialism at last became
more real than theoretical. Old truths no longer offered assurance,
and the Vietnam War has shrouded every turn of events in U.S.
foreign policy to the present day. The specter of Vietnam was
evident throughout the Persian Gulf crisis of 1990–91, even at the
conclusion of the 100-hour ground war, even at the moment when
the United States and its allies claimed victory over Iraq. Even in
victory, President Bush was compelled to deliver a funeral oration
for the doubts sown by the earlier war.

The legacy of the Vietnam War will extend, however, far beyond
the end of Operation Desert Storm, challenging American life for
decades with cautionary stories about the fragility of certainties

from the past. With those disturbing revelations also will come valuable insights about how the habit of making meaning survives setbacks. The most provocative texts from the Vietnam War convey a way of being that is, at the heart, dependent upon nothing more (and nothing less) than the vitality of spontaneous creativity—of something made of nothing. The truths of these texts are informed throughout by the dazzling, and sometimes daunting, spirit of improvisation.

Danger lurks at every turn in the interior space of this hyperkinetic realm. Nothing is guaranteed. And nothing planned makes any sense. In fact, plans are always discovered to be in error, flawed by definition. Life is given over to instincts. Everything is made up in motion through time and space; no pattern of meaning holds from one moment to the next. Unless, of course, one is prepared to accept the primacy of chaos itself as a system with a strange kind of meaning. Such was the experiential reality of soldiers in combat in Vietnam, as countless narratives attest, though in asserting this particular reality and arguing for its primacy we must be mindful of the hazards of trying to reduce the Vietnam War to any single, comprehensive theme or meaning.

The Vietnam War has generally been resistant to such reductive efforts, and therein lies a key part of the challenge represented by the war for the American people, who had previously built their history out of a handful of operative myths and symbols justified by the experience of several successive generations. Whenever a creative text about the Vietnam War appears (and, at least since 1975, the novels and films related to the subject have been particularly bountiful), someone is sure to stand up and scream one of two things: first, "I was in 'Nam, man, and this dude is telling the truth. It happened just like that"; or, second, "I was there, baby, and I never seen nothing like that. Crazy as the 'Nam was, I don't know where they got the idea it was like the junk I saw up on the screen. No way." The most likely target of these responses is film, since movies reach a much larger audience than other texts (much more quickly, too), and they often enjoy a few weeks of high-impact visibility. In such moments we wind up listening to a veteran of the war, a person claiming to speak from the temple of experience and reality, with all the conviction that an eyewitness can muster, a person who is enraged by some other person's effort to reduce the experience of Vietnam to a body of material that can be effectively handled in a three-hundred-page novel or a two-hour film but that does not agree in its particular details with his or her Vietnam. Anyone who has ever created anything knows the imperative of reduction that the shaping process mandates. Decisions have to be made, sometimes in terms of factual reality, but at other times primarily in terms of aesthetic coherence or thematic integrity. Those decisions will not please everyone, and the various texts of Vietnam have pretty well run the gamut of possible reactions. Some texts have simultaneously met with harsh hostility and warm embrace—all from the camp of the veterans alone.

Most of the texts from the Vietnam experience have nevertheless tried to convey the essence of what was lost in the war. From text to text, of course, the essence of loss varies. Innocence was clearly a victim of the war—a story told in Philip Caputo's novel *A Rumor of War*, in Oliver Stone's *Platoon* (1986), in *Born on the Fourth of July* (Ron Kovic's memoir [1976] and the film version by Stone [1989]), and in a host of other stories. Some texts have focused on the loss of all good things and the subsequent approach to absolute horror (for example, Francis Ford Coppola's *Apocalypse Now* in 1979 and perhaps Gustav Hasford's *The Short-Timers* in 1979, which became Stanley Kubrick's *Full Metal Jacket* in 1987). And some others have attempted to tell the story of how fragmented life came to be in the wake of Vietnam. Perhaps that last "truth" is most comprehensive, most representative of the reality of the war and its aftermath. The idea of fragmentation, developed pointedly in Jack Fuller's novel *Fragments* (1984), takes us to the threshold of chaos as described earlier in this chapter; the idea of things breaking up in chaotic ways, even in the compulsive renaming process that soldiers went through as they joined their units in Vietnam, hovers ubiquitously over the various texts of the conflict. But some narratives succeed better than others in placing this notion within metaphor. Perhaps the best metaphor for the war thus far—for showing the encroaching presence of chaos with all its thrills and chills—is the dark art of improvisation.

To consider how improvisation has been used provocatively and profoundly to represent the Vietnam War, we can turn to Ward Just's novel *Stringer* (1974) and to Barry Levinson's film *Good Morning, Vietnam* (1987), with Robin Williams in the central role. These two works are not perhaps as well known (or as celebrated) as some others that have appeared in the last twenty years, but I would argue that they strike hard at the chaos/fragmentation issue, thus deserving careful scrutiny, and they certainly turn on the dizzying point of improvisation as a mode of being. Levinson's film is the better known work—partly because of the large reach of film in American culture, partly because of the appeal of Robin Williams—but it makes sense to take up the issue of chaos and improvisation first with *Stringer*, not only because Just's novel appeared more than a decade earlier than Levinson's film but also because the novel explicitly pinpoints the improvisational theme, whereas the film registers the point implicitly. *Stringer* thus makes an argument about improvisation, while *Good Morning, Vietnam* embodies improvisation in its form.

Stringer, Just's protagonist, is adrift, a figure disconnected from community codes. At the end of his Vietnam experiences—as a CIA-type operative used on covert missions into the wilderness—Stringer is held in captivity, somewhere. His tendency to live in a world of his own, with his own rules and codes, has resulted in a breakdown. Stringer's "in-country" experience has collapsed inward. While he sits in captivity, he recalls certain events of his past, and his recollection of a Mike Nichols and Elaine May improvisational comedy routine from the early 1960s in Chicago serves as a parallel (paradigm) for Stringer's war experience. By relying on instincts and by operating in a state of open vulnerability without the security of a prepared routine, Nichols and May ironically anticipated the reality of existence for American combat soldiers in Vietnam. In his Chicago days, Stringer found improvisational jazz to be equally fascinating. Thus, improvisation became all, past and present, for Stringer, symbolic American at war in Vietnam, late in the twentieth century.

When *Good Morning, Vietnam* went into production, Robin Williams re-created imaginatively the war experiences of Adrian Cronauer (an actual DJ in Vietnam) by means of the intense fury inherent in improvisation. When Williams enacted Cronauer's role with the Armed Forces Radio Network, he trusted his instincts, going into the record of film without benefit of a prepared script. In the film's production notes, coproducer Larry Brezner observed that "the dream was to make *Good Morning, Vietnam* as a metaphor for the war."[1] The film brought Barry Levinson and Robin Williams together for the first time, but "both felt that Williams' talent for improvisation would mesh perfectly with Levinson's well-established reputation as a writer/director of engaging ensemble comedies."[2] Once the film was in production, Williams's instincts were given free rein and, according to producer Mark Johnson, this improvisational mode brought the desired objective: "Nobody else works with the inventiveness, the quickness and the zaniness of Robin Williams. When he sat down in the control booth to do the scenes involving Cronauer's broadcasts, we just let the cameras roll. He managed to create something new for every single take."[3] A Williams take, then, becomes a metaphor for the feel of sending helicopters loaded with an infantry company into a hot landing zone; or of sending a platoon-sized patrol into a Vietnamese village, never knowing what would transpire; or of sitting on a compound perimeter through an endless night of anxious watchfulness, with no guarantee of what or how something might happen. In this way, without actually showing the devastation of bloodshed on battlefields, a powerful contemporary art form was able to mimic the essential condition of Vietnam, mimesis of a more perfect nature than the frequently praised "realism" of Oliver Stone's *Platoon*.

Levinson's film has nevertheless been criticized as superficial—emphasizing comedy and oldies rock—and as evading the political and military realities of the war.[4] Echoing the reservations of several reviewers, William Palmer observed that the film "is a shallow, plotless combination of a Robin Williams comedy concert and an extended music video masquerading as a biopic. *Good Morning, Vietnam* fails as a Vietnam War film because it is dependent completely on monologue rather than the kind of dialogue which can explore such a complex issue as was the Vietnam War."[5] I disagree with Palmer's assessment of *Good Morning, Vietnam*. The war forced the participants into a kind of near-solitary confinement, an existence of interior space, space that brought the individual face to face with chaos. This realm was bristling with intensity, and imaginative forces of extraordinary power were unleashed in defiant acts of language. The intensity of this era, with the war at its core, is registered in words, and the performance of Robin Williams, a man going solo under pressure, taking possession of a moment in time, may represent the Vietnam ethos as truly as any created text can.

Improvisation is a dark art because it maximizes the use of uncertainty. There is motion in space. Time advances. And whatever happens, happens without plan. For a world in which the claim to order and reasonableness has never been completely assured, improvisation stands for the horror of chaos. Yet this kind of horror has an attraction for us; we need the intensity it affords. It has a weirdly intoxicating appeal. As a metaphor for the war itself, improvisation demands our considered interest, even though we know that filmed improvisation can be reshot if it fails to produce the desired results, significantly unlike the case with moments of improvisation in life.

Lurking behind improvisation is chaos, a line of derivation known well before Americans floundered into Vietnam. Improvisation as a fundamental attribute of creativity is a Romantic precept, part of the sweeping nineteenth-century refutation of neoclassical order as it had been promoted by many eighteenth-century thinkers and writers. But a powerful figure of the seventeenth century, John Milton, must be recognized for his role in designating chaos as the original state of being. Just a few lines into the text of *Paradise Lost*, as part of a request for inspiration from the "Heavenly Muse," Milton acknowledged—heretically at the time—"In the Beginning how the Heav'ns and Earth / Rose out of Chaos,"[6] and thereby gained for himself an additional prophetic role, that of proto-Romantic. The first book of *Paradise Lost* deals with the state of hell, which is all part of the epic structure's pattern of beginning "in medias res" but which is even more significantly an indication of how indelible the nature of chaos must be in the grand scheme of things. Of the many descriptions offered by Milton to characterize the nature of this hell-from-chaos-everlasting, perhaps the oxymoronic phrase "darkness visible" (I, 63) best stands for the way we are haunted by uncertainty. Even as we attempt to live in the light and with perfect order and purpose, certain experiences make darkness visible. And the creative imagination itself represents that process, at least as long as we remain in the enduring grasp of Romanticism.

Twenty years after *Paradise Lost* appeared, Newton published his *Principia*, and the comforting illusion of general laws and order gained the upper hand. Now, after two centuries of nearly unrelieved Romanticism, with individual darknesses abundantly manifest, Newton has been many times supplanted. The American system of government, product of a Newtonian world, still struggles to maintain the illusion of coherent order; but in the world of science proper, the most significant recent field of inquiry is chaos. The reach and impact of this development were recently the subject of a study by James Gleick; his introduction makes a clear case for the protean possibilities afforded by this new field.

> Now that science is looking, chaos seems to be everywhere. A rising column of cigarette smoke breaks into wild swirls. A flag snaps back and forth in the wind. A dripping faucet goes from a steady pattern to a random one. Chaos appears in the behavior of the weather, the behavior of an airplane in flight, the behavior of cars clustering on an expressway, the behavior of oil flowing in underground pipes. No matter what the medium, the behavior obeys the same newly discovered laws. That realization has begun to change the way business executives make decisions about insurance, the way astronomers look at the solar system, the way political theorists talk about the stresses leading to armed conflict.
>
> Chaos breaks across the lines that separate scientific disciplines. Because it is a science of the global nature of systems, it has brought together thinkers from fields that had been widely separated.[7]

Although Gleick himself does not build a bridge from matters of science to matters of creativity in fields apart from science, such a bridge naturally exists, there for anyone who wishes to cross it. What Milton divined, what the diverse Romantics in their passionate assertions of the individual self pursuing interior demons have posited, and what the Vietnam War in the experience of many eventually came to mean—all is cued on chaos, the state where everything is made up as one goes along, with proliferating choices, fragmentary and fleeting meanings, and inevitable solitariness.

The protagonist of Ward Just's first novel about the Vietnam War embodies such a state of chaos. His name, Stringer, derives from a phenomenon in contemporary journalism, not surprising since Just spent eighteen months in Vietnam as a correspondent. A "stringer" is someone who serves a news organization on an ad hoc, temporary basis; nothing permanent is assumed in the relationship, which can be dissolved at any point. In fact, Stringer's whole existence is based on the ad hoc principle. He has been a drifter, moving from New Hampshire and marriage on to Chicago and eventual dissolution of his marriage ("they were not determined people").[8] He has tried his hand—for a year—at journalism ("sounded glamorous and vaguely racy, a voyeur's dream or nightmare"),[9] but that line of work became tedious, and he was fired. He studied history at the University of Chicago for a year; that interest, too, proved not satisfying, although he made acquaintances there that figured significantly in his later adventures. As Ward Just develops the character, Stringer becomes the epitome of indirection, the site of virtual chaos.

Stringer eventually signs on for assignment with a covert operation backed by the Central Intelligence Agency, not because he has any certainty that the Vietnam War is necessary, right, or justifiable in any way but rather because he feels an impulse to move into something new and different. That impulse started in Chicago, while he was still married. His wife suggested a move east. Stringer's response, " 'West is new, East is old,' "[10] comes straight out of American mythology in its westward orientation. Stringer goes so far west, of course, that he winds up in the Far East, a manifestation of the prophecy embedded in Walt Whitman's poem "Passage to India," which envisioned a world unified and joined together, with New World settlement playing a key role in completing the circle, west to east.

Thus Stringer, creature of chaos in his individual life, seems to be a possible emblem of the whole system of history and political affairs in the world. At the beginning of the novel, Stringer is deep in the jungle, far in alien territory. Although he is paired with a regular-army major named Price, in essence Stringer is "a loner, on his own, the way he liked it."[11] At every point, Stringer is a total contrast to Price. Price believes in the need for an American presence in Vietnam; his West Point background makes him supremely dedicated to the idea of command, which presumes the desirability of detailed plans, standard operating procedures, and precise efforts to execute orders. Stringer, on the other hand, is used to "running on instinct alone."[12] His instincts prove marginally superior to Price's adherence to "hard, straight lines of command and control,"[13] a dimension of being that Price finds absent generally in civilians. On the mission to place sensors beside infiltration trails so as to ensure maximum results from interdiction air strikes, Stringer survives Price. Price is surprised by a North Vietnamese soldier, and when Stringer returns from putting a sensor on a nearby trail he finds Price and the enemy locked in death.

With the mission complete, Stringer has only to make his way to a designated pickup site for extraction. He knows his business, and his instincts have served him well up to that point. Yet a drink of unpurified, contaminated water—water, so crucial for life— proves to be sufficient to bring Stringer fully to the heart of uncertainty. He falls ill and falls prey to hallucinations, including one that involves a conversation with an enemy soldier. During that conversation Stringer's minimal degree of control dissipates: "He couldn't tell where the conversation was going. He was following it, wherever it was going."[14] By this point, the improvisational nature of Stringer's life has become evident, and even though he has met the enemy one on one, in individual combat, with nothing but his instincts for a guide, he simultaneously fits into a larger improvisational scheme.

The idea was to create a pocket of disorder, or misrule. It was tightly enclosed, a piece of its own, a world apart, like a chessboard or a playing field. Nothing else was germane, Command saw the war in that way, "the only war available to us." Ways and means. The means were carefully stylized, but subject to revision and modification, improvisation. A musical theme, becoming ever more cacophonous. What began as a simple child's melody was now a crazy symphony, with every instrument in the orchestra horning in.[15]

Improvisation was all, large and small.

In Stringer's estimation, "One maneuvered inside the details. There was no possibility of making sense of the whole. The thing simply *was*."[16] And so it is with readers of Just's novel at this juncture, for the phrasing is brilliantly suggestive, with all the action cloaked in uncertainty. In their darkest moments, Hawthorne's narratives are no more shadowed by ambiguity than is the story line in *Stringer*; Melville's fascination with ambiguity, too, comes to mind, particularly as manifested in *Pierre; or, the Ambiguities* and in *The Confidence Man*, a daunting work that many find to be the quintessence of chaos. From Stringer's unraveling in wilderness isolation to the end of the narrative some fifty pages later, the novel duplicates in its form the chaotic, make-it-up-as-you-go-along essence of the war in Vietnam.

The penultimate chapter concludes with a surrealistic sequence involving Stringer's apparent effort to shoot down the helicopter that has been dispatched to gather him back into the fold. But Stringer has been hallucinating, and the language is indefinite. The noise and wild confusion may all be within Stringer; at the end he "was not truly conscious, his eyes were closed, and it could have been a dream."[17] The uncertainty of this moment sets up the absolute confusion of the novel's final chapter, which has for its setting a location "forty miles west of the capital,"[18] though the other details make it rather equally possible for the capital to be either Hanoi or Washington.

It is known, however, that Stringer is a captive. And he is

subject to confusion: "He lived inside a thicket. Words and emotions came to him in fragments, of no use whatever."[19] For a society driven by dire necessity to maintain order (or its illusion), the Stringers of the universe are problematic. Despite some purposeful obscurity about the location of Stringer's imprisonment, he does clearly seem to be held subordinate to an American effort to resurrect control and order in the aftermath of combat confusion/chaos in Vietnam, for he "reports" to an American. He is held with several other fellow countrymen, all of whom once served Command in Vietnam and who were somehow "lost" on an assigned mission. Camp life in captivity revolves around efforts to add structure and order. The men, including Steinberg, Stringer's old Chicago pal— the one who brought Stringer into clandestine work—are obliged to come to terms, if possible, with rudimentary facts; their discussion groups are supposed to focus on known and knowable facts from the recent past, their past.

But minds wander, and Stringer and Steinberg are often out of synch with the program of the group. They reminisce fondly of their student days in Chicago, often trying playfully to recall details about players in improvisational jazz groups—who played what instrument, in which club, under the watchful eye of which bartender. It seems trivial, but the form of their mental games to reconstruct another, deeper past is free, itself improvisational. Stringer is told that jazz talk is out of bounds, off limits, not permissible.

Equally unwanted by the controlling authorities is the discussion Stringer and Steinberg have regarding a routine by Mike Nichols and Elaine May that they once joined in Chicago—joined in the sense of providing a few basic details to be used in an improvisational mode to make (or find) comedy out of nothing, the nothing that is chaos. In reflecting on this scene from the past, a portentous beginning, Stringer senses that "'this was something entirely new, and it was happening in our time, in our town, at our university. A comedian taking chances with the public, taking his themes from the audience. It was new and novel. . . . Daring, what they did.'"[20] With this passage, Just bows quickly to Hemingway (*In Our Time*) and Wilder (*Our Town*), thereby invoking the power of symbolic texts meant to represent Americana of an earlier era.

Before being silenced by Fowler (who determines what is fair, what is foul), Stringer further observes about Nichols and May: "'They played to the crowd, brought it to its feet, tears of laughter. Some of their laughs were in bad taste. *They angered the powers that be.* These were brave transactions.'"[21] What Nichols and May did at the Compass Club, Stringer tried to do in Vietnam; and what Stringer did in small scale, America did on a large scale. The essence of Vietnam was a free-fall into chaos, and the best texts of the war show the wild excitement that attended entry into the heart of the creative impulse.

Robin Williams's Adrian Cronauer brought this dimension of the Vietnam experience before the American public on the large screen. With an irony that is not always noticed by those who have studied *Good Morning, Vietnam,* the method of making the film brilliantly parallels American involvement in Vietnam. The idea of control has always been a crucial issue in the dramatic arts, of which modern film is a technology-bound variation. Who controls the reality that is eventually brought before an audience? Whose authority—and what degree of authority—is made manifest in the produced text? In the last two decades especially, the idea of a produced text has been made more complicated still by the recognition that each and every member of a receiving audience effectively "produces" his or her own text, with the whole process being subject to an almost infinite array of possible nuances and shifts in signification. The major attraction for deconstructionist (or reader/viewer response) criticism came upon American culture just as the Vietnam War was winding toward its conclusion, a conclusion that turned the idea of American authority inside out, dispersing power from the cultural center out toward the fringes where isolated individuals dwell.

But even when life was simpler, there was anxiety over the control of a text. We know, for example, that control and authority in drama was a serious concern for Shakespeare, for Hamlet's instructions to the players who will reenact his father's murder (III,

ii) clearly show that players often took liberties with the ordered texts of the dramatist. To avoid any such possibilities, Hamlet warns: "And let those that play your clowns speak no more than is set down for them, for there be of them that will themselves laugh, to set on some quantity of barren spectators to laugh too, though in the mean time some necessary question of the play be then to be considered."[22] For critics of *Good Morning, Vietnam,* Hamlet's antagonism toward players who operate with too much freedom seems applicable to what Robin Williams did in Barry Levinson's film.[23]

Yet those who see only Robin Williams doing an act that made him a well-known comic presence in the 1980s miss the point. In seeking to represent truly a state of being in time, Barry Levinson recognized that he had to give up a degree of control that had been part of his prior work (*Diner,* 1982; *The Natural,* 1984; *Tin Men,* 1987). Levinson's release of control has to be measured in the context of earlier film history, particularly that related to the American film industry. The major studio producers of the 1930s and 1940s tried to maintain—with general success, if not always with happy colleagues—absolute control over all the ingredients of the finished work. But inevitably there were struggles, some of them violently contentious, as budgets brought pressure to bear on producers, as producers sought to keep directors in line, as directors sought to keep actors in line, and even as actors sought to keep themselves in line with what they wanted to achieve. The whole process of film might be taken as an object lesson in the elusiveness of control and authority—as much perhaps as the war in Vietnam could be seen to provide illumination on this point.

Later, in light of the "auteur" theory of the 1950s, film directors were seen as having the key to control, but, in practical fact, all of the possibilities for breakdown of control were still present. Money was still an indefinite but crucial factor, the director might never obtain the actor wanted for a part, the actor might never realize what the director sought, the film itself might fail to capture what the director saw, and so on. Subsequently, sometimes with the purpose of making the film process draw as close as possible to the unpredictability of life itself, a number of directors (for example, Eric Rohmer and John Cassavetes) have consciously experimented with an improvisational mode, using an ensemble of actors to explore possibilities for developing a narrative line, thus allowing for considerable freedom to be part of the filmmaking process. In the 1990 film *Cadillac Man*, another Robin Williams vehicle, director Roger Donaldson attempted to maximize freedom in moments of improvisation; describing the character (a car salesman) that Williams plays in the film, Donaldson declared: "I wanted the audience to feel like Joey was making it up as he went along. You know, 'How's he going to talk his way out of this one?'"[24] For the tightest experiences of life, there is no predicting how they will turn out, and nothing captures that sensation more truly than improvisation. Barry Levinson's effort in *Good Morning, Vietnam* is a variation on such a pattern. In its essence, the Vietnam War placed people, sooner or later, in situations where control from any authority was virtually nonexistent. By having Robin Williams go into the radio broadcast booth without a script, Levinson represented a fundamental truth of the war.

The soldiers in the film who are shown listening and responding to the on-air manic intensity of Robin Williams's version of Adrian Cronauer (whose name the actor appropriates and who becomes, in the process, a nominal shadow behind the blazing intensity of a filmed figure in improvisational overdrive) intuitively recognize the way in which the linguistic pyrotechnics coming to them over the airwaves reflect the realities that will be theirs as they attempt to do the jobs assigned to them. Although it is very early in the buildup of American forces—and many soldiers seen in the film have not yet had combat experience—Cronauer's condition as portrayed by Williams will soon enough be realized in the fighting experience of many of his listeners. Like him, they will meet insanity. Like him, they will feel the terror of chaos. Like him, they will come to depend on the vitality of unfettered humor to serve as an antidote to the war. And like him, they will find in the intoxicating, passionate improvisations of language a means to survive hell—to rise out of chaos/hell on the spirit of the spoken word.

Perhaps the problem for the critics who do not find the movie satisfying comes from the fact that the disc jockey's mad-minute, full-automatic bursts are not a product of his experience in Vietnam; he is not transformed into a figure of prescient lunacy by engagement with hostile forces in-country, he simply *is* that kind of figure from the outset. His essence precedes his experience. For this reason, viewers of the film may sense that all they are getting is an artificial overlay of an actor's stage persona upon the domain of Vietnam at war.

However, the immediacy of Cronauer's antiauthoritarian radio routines is justifiable. Some folks who ventured to Vietnam, even as early as 1965, were quick studies. Looking at official pronouncements and grand strategies, they saw incompetence, delusion, and nonsense—sometimes all simultaneously. Michael Herr's *Dispatches* (1977), a brilliant exercise in new journalism, is chock full of such realizations, often drawn right out of the words of soldiers themselves. Thus it is in the case of Williams's Adrian Cronauer, who roars with irreverence and who sees immediately through the facades of officialdom. His first observations? About the oppressive weather, discomforts of an unavoidable sort that were intimately known to all the suffering soldiers in the field, quite regardless of any "official" position on the climate. As a natural point of departure, nothing could be finer, nothing more real, nothing more true than Cronauer's assault on the fundamental fact of heat. He refuses to dissemble, and for this attribute he is embraced by his listeners. He feels what they are feeling, he senses what they are sensing, he roars at the very conditions that sooner or later set many soldiers in Vietnam to roaring. And yet from one minute to the next, not one listener knows the direction in which Cronauer—or the fates—will move. Thus does improbability inhabit probability.

But the military model depends upon maximum control; all of the various levels and links in the chain of command are meant to have tidy, predictable, ritualized, and responsible relationships with each other. Free-form individuality does not have a place in the military, and so Cronauer's independence places him at odds with his immediate supervisors, Sergeant Major Dickerson and

Lieutenant Steve Hauk. Admittedly, these characters are carica-
tures to a degree, but they clearly serve to dichotomize order and
chaos (they are to Cronauer what Price was to Stringer). Dickerson
is one type of old-school army man, as evident in his bearing, his
language, and his malice toward anyone who manifests an individual standard. The sergeant major loves norms, and he wants them
clean-cut, unimaginative. Hauk is similarly disposed, with a gov-
erning penchant for carefully ordered routines—including his own
efforts in comedy, all tediously worked out on paper and eventually
broadcast when he takes over Cronauer's DJ slot. Hauk's deliberate
methodology rings false on the air; it was not fit for the time, the
place, the chaos that was Vietnam. Many texts from the Vietnam
War have Dickerson/Hauk characters, invariably trailing clouds of
grief in their wake, often the victims of a particular chaos: "frag-
ging" by a disenchanted subordinate. Vietnam proved the fallibility
of authoritarian structure, and anyone watching *Good Morning,
Vietnam* gets a good sense of the reasons for this failure. Reality
was elsewhere.

A more positive, sympathetic position is represented by General
Taylor, the man of responsibility above Hauk and Dickerson in the
chain of command. Taylor has something of a split personality. He is
"old" army, of Sergeant Major Dickerson vintage, but he has an
independent streak, which allows him genuinely to like what Cronauer says (no matter how irreverent) and to realize that the conditions of battle in Vietnam are virtually mirrored in the improvisational nature of Cronauer's work on the air. Even more than
understanding or recognizing that the listening troops enjoy the DJ's
wild indulgences, Taylor discerns that something in Cronauer's
moments of brilliance comes out of necessity—something that might
stand in the face of hollow emptiness, something to stare down the
darkness of the war. Cronauer's work satirizes orthodoxy, makes a
mockery of official standards of decorum and serious bearing; satire
by definition implies the existence of a higher standard, and, as
Americans are creatures of self-improvement, always needing a hint
of possibilities for a better state, Cronauer's satire finds a receptive
audience. With this point, however, there is no guarantee of im-

provement. The art of improvisation depends upon darting motion, the pursuit of possibilities. Nothing is guaranteed, not even that the tonic of energy from improvisation would compensate for the manifold losses in America's most recent war. But the magic of the live word holds out the prospect of possibility.

The great texts of Vietnam have one thing in common: a pulsating, scintillating, rhetorically charged, hard-driving rhythm of language in overdrive, pursuing frenetically the hope of life. Herman Melville observed in *Moby-Dick* that "to produce a mighty book, you must choose a mighty theme. No great and enduring volume can ever be written on the flea, though many there be who have tried it."[25] Vietnam is no flea-sized subject, not by any means, and its significance demands a mighty text. Melville set the standard on that count—an extravaganza or bazaar in language, with cosmic range in tones. There must be a host of voices, diverse aspects of the common source, exactly what Melville built into his mighty book. The natural talent of Robin Williams allowed for the rhetorical range in *Good Morning, Vietnam* to be substantial. The shifts in rhetorical level happen like lightning, and so on this point, at least, Levinson's film not only can be put in the company of Melville's novel (though undeniably *Moby-Dick* is a far greater text) but also linked to such other major texts of the war as Michael Herr's *Dispatches*, Gustav Hasford's *The Short-Timers* (adapted well for film in Kubrick's *Full Metal Jacket*), and Tim O'Brien's *Going after Cacciato* (1978).

The extraordinary rhetoricity of the Cronauer character as created by Robin Williams clarifies another problem noted by some critics of *Good Morning, Vietnam*: the unbelievable or unsatisfying sentimentality of Cronauer's infatuation with a Vietnamese maiden named Trinh. Admittedly, the line of development for this effort in romance has certain flaws. As soon as Cronauer's eyes fall upon the young women of Vietnam—and this occurs during the ride from the airport to his post of duty in Saigon—he is smitten by lust. So it was, assuredly, with many American soldiers. When Cronauer makes Trinh's acquaintance, his shift in interest to something virtually platonic is little short of unbelievable, and almost everyone in the viewing audience chafes at the distraction involved in Cronauer's renascent innocence. Still, such innocence has been a regular ingredient in studies of the American from the beginning to the present, and perhaps the film honors reality by showing innocence in affairs of the heart as a complement to Cronauer's assault on programmatic untruth, for even in that regard his intentions are quixotic.

Moreover, our disenchantment with the romantic, sentimental motif of *Good Morning, Vietnam* is a signal to an even deeper truth of the Vietnam escapade. We lust for the intensity of Cronauer's inspired performances; the rest is minor, lacking in intoxication value, perhaps just too ordinary, too tinged with what is already too well known. We lust for a taste of original chaos. Again, Melville's text might be instructive as a paradigm of the American desire for exorbitant adventures, which is indeed how we must take Ahab's quest for the white whale. One of the joiners to the quest, Ishmael, eventually comes to a momentary perception that pursuits of this order ought to be rejected in favor of more temperate, more moderate ambitions:

> For now, since by many prolonged, repeated experiences, I have perceived that in all cases man must eventually lower, or at least shift, his conceit of attainable felicity; not placing it anywhere in the intellect or the fancy; but in the wife, the heart, the bed, the table, the saddle, the fire-side, the country; now that I have perceived all this, I am ready to squeeze case eternally.[26]

For a fleeting second, Melville has Ishmael give voice to the idea of a comfortably settled life of domesticity. But even as this vision is concluded, Melville's tone starts to shift to whimsy, and the passage becomes ironical at best. Readers of Melville, too, are right ready to move on, for they are in the midst of something profoundly perplexing, full of wonder and danger.

So it was with the minor fantasy of romance between Cronauer and Trinh. Matters far more exciting push love into the background. The wonder and daring danger of Vietnam reach viewers of *Good*

Morning, Vietnam most vibrantly when Robin Williams takes flight in the character of Adrian Cronauer via the dark art of improvisation. And we are ready to soar, virtually out of control, on the wings of that art where anything can happen, launched into a flight pattern that takes us deep toward the heart of the creative impulse . . . chaos . . . Vietnam. Better art than reality. Art doesn't kill you.

Notes

1. *Good Morning, Vietnam* production notes (Touchstone Pictures, 1987) 5.

2. Ibid. 6.

3. Ibid.

4. Those who found more problems than success in the use of Williams's natural talent for improvisation included John Nangle, *Films in Review*, March 1989: 167, and Jay Hoberman, *Village Voice*, 29 December 1987; 63; however, some reviewers, such as Michael Wilmington, *Los Angeles Times*, 25 December 1987: 1, and Mike McGrady, *Newsday*, 23 December 1987: part 2, 9, found this use of improvisation to fit the needs of the movie in its effort to reveal something important about the reality of Vietnam.

5. William J. Palmer, "The Vietnam War Films: 1987–88," paper presented at the 1988 MLA convention, New Orleans, Louisiana, 29 December 1988.

6. John Milton, *Paradise Lost*, ed. Helen Darbishire (London: Oxford University Press, 1958) 5.

7. James Gleick, *Chaos: Making a New Science* (New York: Viking, 1987) 5.

8. Ward Just, *Stringer* (Port Townsend, Wash.: Greywolf Press, 1984) 32.

9. Ibid. 33.

10. Ibid. 35.

11. Ibid. 20.

12. Ibid. 49.

13. Ibid. 87.

14. Ibid. 113.

15. Ibid. 123.

16. Ibid. 102.

17. Ibid. 129.

18. Ibid. 133.

19. Ibid. 132.

20. Ibid. 149.

21. Ibid. 150.

22. William Shakespeare, *Hamlet,* in *The Complete Works,* ed. Alfred Harbage (Baltimore, Md.: Penguin Books, 1969) 952.

23. See Palmer, "The Vietnam War Films." As noted earlier, Palmer's position is not entirely representative of reviews given to *Good Morning, Vietnam,* although the spirit of his observation can be seen in Pauline Kael's general dissatisfaction with the film (*New Yorker,* 18 January 1988: 78–79); a more approving stance was taken by Richard Schickel, who found in his review, "Motormouth in Saigon," that the monologuist routine was indeed appropriate for the subject (*Time,* 28 December 1987: 74), a viewpoint sustained by Wilmington and McGrady in reviews mentioned previously.

24. Desmond Ryan, "The Wild Steering of *Cadillac Man,*" *Philadelphia Inquirer,* 27 May 1990: H2.

25. Herman Melville, *Moby-Dick,* ed. Harrison Hayford and Hershel Parker (New York: W. W. Norton, 1967) 379.

26. Ibid. 349.

Thomas Doherty

Witness to War
Oliver Stone, Ron Kovic, and
Born on the Fourth of July

CHAPTER 13 Alone among bankable Holly-
wood directors, Oliver Stone lends the Vietnam film the moral
authority of the witness. No matter what the cinematic standing of
Michael Cimino's *Deer Hunter* (1978), Francis Coppola's *Apocalypse
Now* (1979), Stanley Kubrick's *Full Metal Jacket* (1987), or Brian De
Palma's *Casualties of War* (1989), none comes close to the stature,
verisimilitude, or moral weight of Stone's *Platoon* (1986) and *Born
on the Fourth of July* (1989). All are the imaginative re-creations
of big-gun auteurs who never knew firsthand the terror or thrill of
live ammunition fired in anger. Like the classical Hollywood filmmakers who most movingly and credibly brought the combat action
and home-front readjustments of the World War II veteran to the
screen—John Ford in *The Battle of Midway* (1942), *They Were
Expendable* (1945), and *The Wings of Eagles* (1957); John Huston in
Report from the Aleutians (1943), *The Battle of San Pietro* (1945),
and *Let There Be Light* (1945); and William Wyler in *Memphis Belle*
(1944) and *The Best Years of Our Lives* (1946)—Stone's work is
imbued with the simple and undeniable integrity of Whitman's
declaration: "I was the man, I suffered, I was there."

This is not to say that Stone's vision of Vietnam is always better or more compelling than that of his nonveteran colleagues—only that personal testimony lends his films an aura of, if not art, then at least authority. On *Wall Street*, talk radio, or rock music, Stone warrants no special hearing; on Vietnam, attention must be paid. In fact, Stone's two Vietnam films—one about frontline combat, the other about home-front rehabilitation—take full advantage of his veteran's benefits. (A third entry, the last in a promised Vietnam trilogy, is reportedly forthcoming.) In both films, public image impinges on popular entertainment—veteran/director Stone in *Platoon*, activist/autobiographer Ron Kovic in *Born on the Fourth of July*. In a war that has itself been preconceived and mediated by images—of the World War II combat film, television news, and finally back again to where so much of it began, Hollywood—the presence of the veteran himself may be the most moving image.

In *Platoon* the Vietnam veteran first put himself into the picture. Even in a trade given to hyperbole, the film was greeted with a special kind of rapture, the advertising blurbs dripping superlatives and four-star ratings. Truth to tell, *Platoon* was something special: the first Vietnam War film written and directed by an actual participant, a true "veteran auteur."[1] The film's publicity campaign made much of Stone's unique status as a witness to war. "In 1967," read the ad copy, "a young man named Oliver Stone spent 15 months in Vietnam as an infantryman in the United States Army. He was wounded twice and received a bronze star for gallantry. Ten years later Stone was a screenwriter in Hollywood, author of *Midnight Express*. It made him the only man in Hollywood with both a purple heart and an Oscar."

That last claim may have surprised Lee Marvin, but the ballyhoo made a point. Though Vietnam veterans had been singularly successful in literature and politics, none had yet entered the first ranks of American pop culture. In movies and music at least, nonsoldierly surrogates on the Right (Stallone) and the Left (Springsteen) had usurped celebrityhood from the genuine item—perhaps because while Sly and Bruce were refining their respective chops in gymnasiums and barrooms, Stone and company were stretching their legs in a very different kind of run through the jungle.

With *Platoon*, Stone changed all that. Too starkly violent and too shamelessly "adult" ever to reach the box-office stratosphere of *Rambo* (1985) and *Top Gun* (1986), the film nonetheless became something of a cultural landmark, its creator an honored inductee into the pages of *People* and the monitors of *Nightline*. Obviously, Stone has paid his dues in the trenches (in 'Nam and in the Industry), and no one begrudges him his entry into the pop pantheon. But in the near-universal praise for the iconoclasm and originality of *Platoon*—see *Time*'s cover story "Vietnam As It Really Was"— Stone's debt to the classical Hollywood combat film has been generally overlooked. Allowing for updates in lingo, locale, and license, *Platoon* has a tight kinship with the very tradition it seeks to dispell.

In *Platoon*, rather than fall prey to the imitative fallacy and make a confused film about a confusing war, Stone works within the conventions of the Hollywood combat film to anchor a recollected experience that is by definition disorienting. In this sense his continuance of a cinematic tradition is more noteworthy than his departure from it. Doing double duty as narrator and Stone's autobiographical self, young Chris (Charlie Sheen) deplanes in-country— his C-130 transport is booked up with body bags for the return trip—and embarks on a rite of passage with sources that predate Homer but whose immediate frame of reference is World War II Hollywood cinema.

Sheen *fils* is eerily evocative of his father in *Apocalypse Now* (talk about intertextuality), but he has none of that character's burnt-out nihilism. Despite the freak-outs, dope smoking, and periodic bloodlust, he is a moral center, not a dead one. Indeed, unlike most historians of Vietnam, Stone sees little moral ambiguity in a wartime landscape as psychic as it is physical. His Manichaean vision is dramatized by two dueling extremes of evil and good: the scar-faced, satanic Sergeant Barnes (Tom Berenger) and the sensitive, ethical Sergeant Elias (Willem Dafoe, at the time playing against a screen psycho persona). Though the outcome of their battle for Chris's soul is sometimes in doubt, the director's preference, and the spectator's sympathies, never are.

Of course *Platoon* would not have generated so much excitement if it were merely a *Sands of Iwo Jima* makeover. The "genre work" of the World War II combat film—personal sacrifice for a larger cause, the cooperative warmth of a team effort, and ultimate victory over an external foe—cannot be sustained in Vietnam.[2] The Vietnam genre promises no larger purpose, rips apart the union of the combat platoon, and turns inward to face the ultimate enemy. Stone's most jarring break with World War II territory, and the film's most controversial sequence, depicts the war-weary platoon's "pacification" of a Vietnamese village, a destroy-in-order-to-save mission. Stone may have had in mind the Jean-Luc Godard remark about the trouble with antiwar films—that, on screen, war is always exhilarating—because, throughout *Platoon*, the brilliantly staged firefights, nerve-racking jungle treks, and thrilling helicopter dust-offs make for great entertainment. But even from the comfortable vantage of a theater seat, the pacification sequence is unsettling. Frazzled and vengeful, the troops enter a village and, led by the murderous Barnes, begin a series of depredations that fall just short of a My Lai massacre. Perhaps only such a former infantryman as Stone could get away with a dramatization of the greatest calumny to follow the Vietnam veteran. Certainly only a self-described former grunt could render the action understandable, if never justifiable. (There is one added, terrible irony: Barnes's military judgment is sound, for the platoon has found a cache of weapons and food. Willingly or not, the villagers *are* helping the VC.)

In the end, though, for all its terror and tension, Stone's fidelity to cinematic expectations is a calming influence. He signals as much by planting, VC-like, a series of "genre convention" booby traps, only some of which go off: the fresh-faced kid with the girl back home, the short-timer waiting out his last days, the soldier with the premonition of death, the inexperienced lieutenant. Likewise, Chris's first-person voice-over ensures his physical survival, if not moral salvation. (Compare the epistolary voice-over to the funeral opening to Francis Coppola's *Gardens of Stone* [1987], where the retrospective cast of a posthumous narration dooms the young soldier from the outset.) Above all, the ultimate success and sanity of the writer-director undermines the defeat and dementia portrayed on screen. Stone/Chris may be the first Vietnam film figure not just to endure but to prosper in the World, a soldier/auteur honored in both uniforms. In his person, the cultural reconciliation yearned for so palpably in the Vietnam vet "backstory" of *Magnum PI* and *Miami Vice* was at last fulfilled for real.

Born on the Fourth of July is even more cluttered with generic ghosts and real-life corporeal presences. The very title—lifted from a lyric in Warner Brothers' patriotic musical of the life of George M. Cohan, *Yankee Doodle Dandy* (1942)—signals the elaborate conflations of public image, screen image, and Vietnam reality. It is at once a war memoir, a critique of Hollywood "combat," and a Vietnam version of the classical and the Hollywood "returning veteran" film. Not least, it is the culmination of the real-life rehabilitation of its inspiration and coauthor, Ron Kovic, paraplegic antiwar activist and autobiographer.

More schematically than *Platoon*, *Born on the Fourth of July* is a personal rite-of-passage story, playing off the conventions of the war memoir. (Not for nothing is Kovic's popular autobiography, first published in 1976, already a standard on undergraduate reading lists.) It traces a familiar, albeit nonchronological course from innocence (induction) through experience (combat) to knowledge (disillusionment). But just as Vietnam broke up America's perfect war record, the Vietnam combat memoir contributes its own permutations to a venerable literary tradition. One might observe, for example, a presentation of self that tends toward isolation and catatonia, a prevailing bitterness in tone, a surrealist sensibility, and a rock 'n' roll heart. However, one quality announces itself immediately. For the Vietnam narrator, the process of disillusionment is as much an insight into media as morality, the sudden recognition of the difference between on-screen and in-country combat. Like the Vietnam films, virtually all Vietnam war memoirs preconceive war in Hollywood terms and continue to mediate the combat experience in those same terms.

This is new. Turn, for example, to the memoir of the definitive case study for any discussion of the strange confluence of Hollywood and war, Audie Murphy. The most decorated combat veteran of World War II, the baby-faced Texan reaped the fruits of heroism and

Life magazine publicity as a postwar motion-picture star. In his biopic, *To Hell and Back* (1955), Murphy reenacts his entire combat story, including his Congressional Medal of Honor-winning battle atop a flaming tank, an experience that for psychological and metaphysical convolutions beggars the imagination. For Murphy himself, though, and for the balance of World War II memoirs, the frame of imaginative reference was never filmic combat. In *To Hell and Back*, published in 1949, one of Murphy's rare childhood memories is of a grizzled World War I vet enchanting little boys with tales of poison gas and machine guns.

> That afternoon in Texas I had followed the veteran of World War I into the field. The sun beat down and the rows of cotton seemed endless. But I soon forgot the heat and the labor.
>
> The weeds became the enemy, and my hoe a mysterious weapon. I was on a faraway battlefield, where bugles blew, banners streamed, and men charged gallantly across flaming hills; where the temperature always stood at eighty and our side was always victorious; where the dying were but impersonal shadows and the wounded never cried; where enemy bullets always miraculously missed me, and my trusty rifle forever hit home.

He concludes the revery with a ready interpretation.

> I was only twelve years old; and the dream was my one escape from a grimly realistic world.

During his first action in the North African campaign, after shedding first blood and witnessing first death, Murphy undergoes a realization that, in one form or another, is the trajectory of all combat memoirs.

> So it happens as easily as that. You sit on a quiet slope with chin in hand. In the distance a gun slams; and the next minute you are dead.
>
> Maybe my notions of war were all cockeyed. How do you pit skill against skill if you cannot see the enemy? Where is the glamour in blistered feet and growling stomach? And where is the expected adventure?

What is different about Murphy's movement from combat dreams to combat reality, from adolescent innocence to adult experience, is not the awakening, but the source of the dream. Murphy takes inspiration from an actual survivor, a firsthand report backed up with fits of coughing from the lingering effects of mustard gas.[3]

Murphy's combat memoir in prose has little of the guts-and-glory that might appeal to the adolescent male spectator of the memoir on screen. A searing portrait of ground-level combat, *To Hell and Back* (a phrase that would adorn thousands of silk jackets in Vietnam), is a bleak night-sea journey through the European theater and the narrator's own troubled psyche. As the Allied campaign moves across Africa, through Sicily and Italy, and into the heart of Germany, Murphy tells his story in a cold, disembodied voice that belies romance or emotion. One can detect the hand of an amanuensis—long passages of suspiciously witty dialogue, "buddy" scenes that by 1949 had become stock in generic trade—but the tone of the book captures the burnt-out lot of the survivor who knows he is less a hero than a statistical anomaly. For a World War II narrative it is shockingly blunt and heartless, the narrator a robotic killing machine. The last-minute epiphany—"My country. America!"—rings so false that the narrative cannot support it and collapses into an abrupt sign-off. At the close of *To Hell and Back* Murphy has not made the round trip.[4]

To turn from the memoirs of the combat soldier of World War II to the autobiographies of his Vietnam descendents, is to be struck by a powerful mediating presence: Hollywood. The two indelible movie memories are *Sands of Iwo Jima* (1949) and *To Hell and Back* (1955), but rare is the Vietnam memoir that does not speak of Hollywood combat or name particular films and scenes as formulative inspiration. "I can't help thinking of the kids who got wiped out by seventeen years of war movies before coming to Vietnam to get wiped out for good," wrote Michael Herr in *Dispatches*. "We'd all seen too many war movies, stayed too long in Television City, years of media glut had made certain connections difficult."[5] The title of MacAvoy Layne's 1973 novel captures the media-bound, revisionist spirit of the Vietnam aesthetic, memoir and film alike: *How Audie Murphy Died in Vietnam*.

For the Vietnam generation, the characteristic Damascus moment is the realization, not that war is hell, but that war is not cinema. By his own account, there was no more devoted a student of Hollywood combat than Ron Kovic. In *Born on the Fourth of July*, his mind's eye unspools whole scenes from, what else, *Sands of Iwo Jima* and *To Hell and Back*. "John Wayne in *Sands of Iwo Jima* became one of my heroes," Kovic rhapsodizes, and:

> I'll never forget Audie Murphy in *To Hell and Back*. At the end he jumps on top of a flaming tank that's just about to explode and grabs the machine gun blasting it into the German lines. He was so brave I had chills running up and down my back, wishing it were me up there. There were gasoline flames roaring around his legs, but he just kept firing the machine gun. It was the greatest movie I ever saw in my life.[6]

When Kovic's own war movie goes tragically wrong, his moral confusion is couched in the ethical terms of Production Code cinema: "He'd never figured it would happen this way. It never did in the movies. There were always the good guys and the bad guys, the cowboys and the Indians." For Kovic, and a good many of his fellows, Hollywood becomes as much a villain and betrayer as the military.

The language and aesthetics of the World War II memoir and film have proven so inapplicable to Vietnam that the more literarily minded leap back a war to the Great War or even further. "We weren't the old soldiers of WWII," wrote Tim O'Brien in *If I Die in a Combat Zone*, a memoir structured around Wilfred Owen's bitter rejoinder to Horace's "Dulce et Decorum est Pro Patria Mori." In Vietnam, as in World War I, it is "just an epitaph for the insane."[7] In the same flash backward, Kovic too retreats to the war that better suits the meaninglessness and existential wreckage of Vietnam. Stone's film pointedly includes glimpses of Kovic poring over Erich Maria Remarque's *All Quiet on the Western Front* and forescreens the paperback book cover of Dalton Trumbo's *Johnny Got His Gun*, a 1939 antiwar novel about a World War I basket case, republished in the 1960s as a Vietnam-relevant metaphor and produced in 1971 as a transparently allegorical movie.

Almost as disillusioning as the experience of real death, pain, and loss was the withdrawal of the celluloid promise of group solidarity. The enduring cliché of the World War II combat film is the American melting pot, a harmonious blend of ethnic flavors. According to Hollywood, one of the compensations of war was the warmth of male camaraderie, the communal connections of brotherhood, shared danger, and manly regard. But as has been widely noted, the experience of the American soldier in Vietnam was a singularly solitary one. Soldiers were not in-country "for the duration," but for "365 days and a wake up." The limited tour of duty was initially conceived as a humane recognition that men under the duress of prolonged combat have their limits. Like so many Pentagon policies, however, it had unintended consequences—namely, a tormenting personal isolation. The Vietnam warrior's story is one of individual survival, not of group solidarity, still less a battle for discernible ideological or military objectives.

Autobiography is an appropriate form to render the sensibilities of the isolated short-timer. The focus on the personal not the public, on identity not society, on self-revelation not social critique suits the isolation of the soldier fighting a very personal war. Though the immediacy of shared danger in combat bridges racial and class barriers—Kovic is rescued by a heroic black trooper whose name he never finds out—little of the casual warmth and unity of the Warner Brothers platoon survives the individual countdown. The conceit cannot be totally obliterated—hence, the woozy, hash-smoking camaraderie of the Motown vignette in *Platoon*—but more typical is an encounter in O'Brien's *If I Die in a Combat Zone*. Newly arrived in-country, he is confronted by a mail clerk: "How many days you got left in Nam? 358, right? 357? Shit, you poor mother. I got twenty three days left, twenty three days and I'm gone! Gone! I'm so short I need a step ladder to hand out mail!" The mail clerk is black, O'Brien Irish, and though their friendly banter washes over the different stateside backgrounds, their different sentence in Vietnam is an unbridgeable gulf. As a group, the

Vietnam narrators are bottled-up, interior types—like O'Brien (and Kovic), they seldom dramatize themselves within the kind of rich social tapestry that was a sine qua non of the World War II combat memoir and war movie.[8]

Rendering the isolation and first-person perspective in the expansive space and multiple eyelines of cinema is a challenge. Stone opts for a Tom-Cruise-in-your-face strategy: the actor is front and center for most of the film and his point of view filters almost all visual information. Curiously, Stone elected to shoot the tightly focused human drama of *Born on the Fourth of July* in widescreen Panavision, the aspect ratio generally associated with the action-adventure genre. (The action-packed *Platoon* by contrast was shot in the standard 1.85 to 1 format.) Though the surplus screen space of Panavision can aptly render the emotional distance between characters, and its extended horizontal plane suits the story of a man who will spend much of his time on his back, the choice may also have been dictated, again, by a desire to twist the Hollywood tradition. *To Hell and Back* and most of the thrilling war movies of the fifties and sixties were shot in CinemaScope. By comparison, Patrick Duncan, director of *84 Charlie Mopic* (1989), realized the private isolation of the Vietnam soldier through a different cinematic tack: "I insisted that for the film to work and convey the sense of the soldier's experience in Vietnam, we had to use a sustained, first-person camera approach."[9] It was, above all, a first-person war.

Where *Platoon* connects itself to the World War II combat film, *Born on the Fourth of July* moves to the next link in the chain, the rehabilitation, or "returning veteran," films of the postwar era. The irony accompanying the technical advance in the arts of destruction is the parallel advance in body-repair work. In Vietnam, helicopter med-evacs and state-of-the-art emergency care made survival from heretofore lethal wounds more certain. As Kovic is told, in any other war he would be dead. As he sees it, this is a mixed blessing.

The wounded warrior faces another, private war. "You are going to have to learn to carry a great burden and most of your learning will be done alone," a priest tells Kovic in his memoir.[10] The burden is doubly heavy. The first affliction is evident—the impact of sophisti-

cated weaponry on human flesh. On screen, the wounds from World
War II were typically fine-cut amputations (*The Best Years of Our
Lives* and *Bad Day at Black Rock* [1955]) or the deprivation of the
sense of sight (*Pride of the Marines* [1945] and *Bright Victory*
[1951]). The wounds from Vietnam have their own horrific symbolism. catatonia and paralysis. As with the combat glory of *To Hell
and Back*, *Born on the Fourth of July* debunks the happy rehabilitation and reintegration of Hollywood's World War II—era veteran.

The ready comparison case is *The Men* (1950), unique among
World War II rehabilitation films in dealing with Kovic's affliction, a
spinal-cord injury. The film's introductory crawl reviews the tradition *Born on the Fourth of July* is up against.

> In all Wars, since the beginning of History, there have been
> men who fought twice. The first time they battled with club,
> sword, or machine gun. The second time they had none of
> these weapons. Yet this by far was the greatest battle. It was
> fought with abiding faith and raw courage and in the end,
> Victory was achieved.

Produced by Stanley Kramer, directed by Fred Zinneman, and
written by soon-to-be-blacklisted Carl Foreman, a veteran of Frank
Capra's 834th Photographic Unit, *The Men* is an earnest melodrama
in the manner of early fifties Hollywood liberalism. Like Kovic, Ken
(Marlon Brando in his first major screen performance) is an embit-
tered paraplegic. Unlike Kovic, Ken has the full support of American culture—concerned and competent doctors, understanding fi-
ancée (Teresa Wright), and a clean and well-regulated VA hospital.
(*The Men* was shot on location at Birmingham Veterans' Administration Hospital and featured forty-five men under treatment.) In all the
rehabilitation films, the best in medical treatment is a matter of
course, but psychological adjustment will prove more difficult.

A revealing expository sequence states the terms of the old
contract. The gruff but caring Doctor Brock (Everett Sloane) lectures to a group of women, wives and girlfriends of his paralyzed
patients. Medical science has no answer to spinal-cord injuries, the
doctor sternly tells the men's women. The lecture is delivered in the

hospital chapel, a suitable setting for the cultural transition away from the expert religious guidance of the man of the cloth to the dress-white expertise of the new priesthood, the technocrat. (During Kovic's convalescence, both types—theological and secular experts—will be discredited.) Dr. Brock implies that the physical adjustments of the paraplegics can be regulated, but that the psychic damage is more tenacious. Called "shell shock" in the Great War and "neuropsychosis" in World War II, it was more unsettling because unseen. In Vietnam the combat backfire would be called "post traumatic stress syndrome," valorized and exploited by the American Psychiatric Association, television movies, and defense attorneys.

If the battle-scarred veteran has a double challenge, the rehabilitation of a battered body and the repair of a shattered psyche, Kovic's mental state is in critical condition. Torturing him are the two unintentional sins he committed in Vietnam, the slaughter of a family of Vietnamese civilians, women and children, and the killing of one of his own men. Together, the acts encompass the two main victims of American policy, the host-country nationals and the young Americans themselves. Paralyzed by enemy bullets and tormented by guilt, Kovic is, at times, quite insane.

The ultimate amputation, never uttered and seldom implied in classical Hollywood cinema, was castration. In *Bright Victory*, the bitter, blinded GI is consoled by a fellow patient. Standing at midwaist by his supine companion, he observes meaningfully, "It could have been worse." *The Men* waltzes around the key question, but in an explicitness rare for Production Code cinema it is frank about bladder and bowel control (verbally if not visually), about the question of having children, and even about the capacity to perform sexually. In his lecture to the wives and girlfriends of the paraplegic men, Dr. Brock voices the doubts of his patients who feel "I'm not a man any longer—I can't make a woman happy." Still, fertility not virility, the ability to reproduce not to give and receive erotic pleasure, is the main textual question; only subtextually does the below-the-waist paralysis concern another member. Ken's own case is ambiguous. When Ken seems to get "return" on his legs, the doctor gauges the extent of his paralysis with a pin ("Look, kid, the legs are gone"), but he fails to confirm or deny animation in the crucial appendage.

Kovic's loss must be spoken—the rationale of the oft-satirized "Penis! Penis! Penis!" scene when he returns home drunk and demented. So too the justification for the extended lost weekend in the brothels of Mexico, another imperialist incursion, and the unflinching exposure of the details of convalescence—enemas, urination, the filth and vermin of the VA, and the bladder and bowel bags that will forever remain a part of his existence. The horror of the veterans' hospital is Kovic's second—rather, third—tour in hell, a clinic miles away not only from the plush facilities of *The Men* but also from the relatively sanitary and benign hospital ward in *Coming Home* (1978). Vietnam itself seems less awful. Nothing in *Born on the Fourth of July* is as horrifying, no indictment as damning, as the treatment accorded the human backwash of the war. None of the comforts of Hollywood's World War II is available to Kovic—not the reconstituted ethnic diversity of the platoon, not the sympathy of a girl back home, not the honor and understanding of an appreciative home front. Massapequa, New York, Kovic's hometown, tries to go through the approved gestures of parades and Independence Day speeches, but the second time around it plays as farce. Unable to utter the patriotic mantra, the local hero breaks down.

But Kovic's suffering, in-country and in-hospital, has one compensation. The castrated Vietnam vet is a powerful antiwarrior. In a wheelchair, wearing torn fatigues and faded insignia, issuing directives with the born-to-lead dispatch of Sergeant Saunders in television's *Combat*, he is the virile point man for a squad of war protesters. The antiwar movement had no more effective protester than the disillusioned former warrior. The members of the Vietnam Veterans Against the War were immune from the usual assaults on their patriotism or courage—the proof was in the uniform, campaign ribbons, medals, and handicaps. Kovic repeatedly uses the potency of his service record to shame and emasculate the hardhat patriotism of the anti-antiwar crowd. (Of course, megastar lead Tom Cruise, Hollywood heartthrob and bravura actor, lends the performance muscle even as it soothes the true horror of the screen character's entrapment. Cruise will walk away to race on another set of wheels; Kovic must remain in place.)

In the extended antiwar protest that is *Born on the Fourth of July*, book and movie, the two veterans want to expose more than insensitive VA administrators. Viewed through the prism of a bitter Kovic and a hardened Stone, America in the Eisenhower fifties and the Camelot sixties is a deeply suppressed and deluded culture. Its childhood games, public rituals, and popular entertainment breed creatures of violence and bloodlust. "We have been a generation of violence and madness, of dead Indians and drunken cowboys, of iron pipes full of matchheads," Kovic observes in a characteristic passage.[11] Cautionary advice from Mom and a pep talk from Coach are sinister foreshadowings. If the British won the Battle of Waterloo on the playing fields of Eton, the Americans stumbled into Vietnam over the wrestling mats at Massapequa High School. More so even than Kovic's book, Stone's film rips into the entire fabric of American culture. In contrast to the evenhanded treatment of the commanders in *Platoon*, the director loses no opportunity to enhance the villainy of the American military. *Born on the Fourth of July* has the usual book-to-movie changes for dramatic purposes (the addition of a gratuitous love interest, a fictional meeting between Kovic and the family of the GI he killed), but the recasting of two pivotal scenes illustrates a Stone-cold dogmaticism where even Kovic modulates the indictment. In the film, the military hierarchy responds to the depredations of Vietnamese civilians and the accidental shooting of Kovic's comrade with complicity and insensitivity. In the book, the marines immediately call in medical aid and Kovic's commander, hearing his confession, gives him an understanding absolution.

To be fully rehabilitated in post-Vietnam Hollywood cinema, the warrior must repent his past misguided patriotism. Unaccountably, the emotional and intellectual passage Kovic underwent in life and articulates in the memoir finds no equivalent in the film, which gives precious little to explain his 180-degree change of heart. The gung ho marine who has enlisted for two tours of duty, endured paralysis, suffered pain and humiliation at the hands of the Veterans' Administration, and found misunderstanding, apathy, and hostility on the homefront—all engendering nary a doubt—snaps to antiwar attention in the space of a jump cut.

But if Kovic rejects the Catholic pieties and patriotic fervor of his youth, another ingrained American faith remains unshaken: the redemptive power of the media. Despite the consistent debunking of the World War II combat movie in the Vietnam War memoir, the power of Hollywood in the American mind is not easily expunged. The Vietnam warrior continues to render his experience in mediated terms—as in the famous one-liner "I hate this movie." Perhaps the most naïve of the Vietnam narrators, Kovic is also the most invincibly media oriented. He consistently compares his experience to the screen—"everything in 3-D," "the glory John Wayne war." Likewise, the climax of his story is a television moment. When he gets two minutes of uninterrupted airtime at the 1972 Republican National Convention, he crows, "It was too good to be true. In a few seconds Roger Mudd and I would be going live all over the country."[12] Paralyzed from the chest down, he is a disembodied spectator, conceiving himself as a living antiwar visual aid—on stages, streets, and television. Stone renders the big moment from Kovic's waist-level perspective. A whirl of hate-filled, contorted faces from the Republican National Convention inflict a calvary of abuse on the honored victim as he, unbending, is wheeled forcibly off the floor. The film's sentimental coda is even better broadcast news, a televised speech from the rostrum at the 1984 Democratic convention. At least in the imaginative projection of themselves as heroes on a screen, Kovic and Stone remain real live nephews of their Uncle Sam.

Against the one-dimensional media vision of Ron Kovic, compare Philip Caputo in *A Rumor of War*, a narrator who knows he and his troops "tend to dramatize ourselves" and renders it with a knowing irony.

> With our helmets cocked to one side and cigarettes hanging out of our mouths, we pose as hard-bitten veterans for the headquarters marines. We are starring in our very own war

movie, and the howitzer battery nearby provides some noisy background music.[13]

But as Kurt Vonnegut says, we have to be very careful who we pretend to be because we *are* who we pretend to be. In *Chickenhawk* Robert Mason recalls a trooper named Simmons whose brother has just received the "proverbial million-dollar wound." It occurs to Mason that since neither brothers nor fathers and sons were supposed to be in the same combat theater at the same time, Simmons could muster out immediately. He refuses.

> "So why don't you tell the CO. He'll get you out of here. You've lost one brother, and another was just wounded. Your family has done enough."
>
> He smiled and said, "No. I'm staying."
>
> "Why?"
>
> "Someone has to do it."

"He really said that," Mason assures us. "I thought I was in a movie. Maybe he did too."[14]

If Vietnam was a war with a movie background that usually refused to follow Hollywood's script, it was also sometimes a war that conformed disconcertingly to generic expectations. In *Guns Up!* Johnnie Clark recalls a spooky, cinematic moment during a night patrol. Walking trail in pitch blackness, he suddenly becomes aware that directly behind his squad is an NVA squad also on night patrol, apparently under the illusion that they are following their own men. "These things don't happen in real life," Clark says. "I remembered the movie about D-Day, the scene where Americans and Germans passed each other without noticing. That was a movie. This was real."[15] The conflations get even more dizzying in the case of Patrick Duncan and the video Vietnam film, *84 Charlie Mopic*. By his own testimony, Duncan's experience in-country followed a dramatic pattern that was eerily in tune with Hollywood expectations. When he arrived in Vietnam, he found that his fellow troops followed the hoariest of war-movie clichés—demographically distributed by race, region, ethnicity, and sensibility. Even at the time, he knew he and his buddies were straight out of a war movie. Twenty years later, when Duncan came to make his own Vietnam movie, he was faced with a surreal aesthetic dilemma: render his real experience and have it look like a movie or falsify his reality so it would look less cinematic.

The favorite linguistic trick of contemporary film criticism is to play on "the real" and "the reel." As fortuitous as the pun is, a glib postmodernist blurring of distinctions between image and reality is not the point here. To say that Vietnam was a war whose imagery and direction was influenced and mediated by Hollywood cinema is neither to compare the two experiences nor to equate the culpability of the executives at Warner Brothers with those in the White House—still less to imply that if Ron Kovic had at an impressionable age seen *The Men* instead of *To Hell and Back, Born on the Fourth of July* would be a different story. It is, rather, to note one of the signature insights and legacies of Vietnam: the special relationships between war and cinema, particularly how the ethos of the World War II combat film proved so devastatingly inappropriate to the Vietnam experience. The notion of a world of simulacra and a "societé du spectacle" fashionable in Continental cinema theory misses a more profound truth communicated in a bumper sticker popular with veterans: "Vietnam was a war not a movie."

Notes

1. In the wake of *Platoon*, such Vietnam veterans as James Carabatsos (*Hamburger Hill*, 1987) and Gustav Hasford (*Full Metal Jacket*, 1987) have begun contributing as screenwriters to popular Vietnam films. But it is a measure of the distance between the sensibilities of contemporary Hollywood and the American military that the union of expertise has been so rare. Generally, the service and testimony of veterans is confined to technical advising and stunt work.

2. For discussions of the "genre work" of the World War II combat film, see Jeanine Basinger, *The World War II Combat Film: Anatomy of a Genre* (New York: Columbia University Press, 1986), and Robert B. Ray, *A Certain Tendency of the Hollywood Cinema, 1930–1980* (Princeton, N.J.: Princeton University Press, 1985) 113–25.

3. Audie Murphy, *To Hell and Back* (New York: Henry Holt, 1949) 5–7.

4. Don Graham, *No Name on the Bullet: A Biography of Audie Murphy* (New York: Viking Press, 1989), confirms the amanuensis but argues that the spirit of the work is true and that some of its most moving writing was done by Murphy himself.

5. Michael Herr, *Dispatches* (New York: Alfred A. Knopf, 1977) 223; also 199–202.

6. Ron Kovic, *Born on the Fourth of July* (New York: McGraw-Hill, 1976) 54. Stone reportedly filmed a version of this scene for the movie but cut it from the final edit.

7. Tim O'Brien, *If I Die in a Combat Zone* (New York: Dell, 1973) 174.

8. Ibid. 77.

9. Lawrence Cohn, "The Long Road for 84 Charlie Mopic; Vietnam Pic Hits N.Y. after 5 Years," *Variety*, 22–28 March 1989: 13.

10. Kovic, *Born on the Fourth* 31.

11. Ibid. 171.

12. Ibid. 179.

13. Philip Caputo, *A Rumor of War* (New York: Ballantine, 1977) 100.

14. Robert Mason, *Chickenhawk* (New York: Penguin Books, 1983) 288.

15. Johnnie Clark, *Guns Up!* (New York: Ballantine, 1984).

Teaching Vietnam
The Politics of Documentary

CHAPTER 14 "Well, you've gone too far this time, Doc." My summer class "World War II and Vietnam on Film" at Missouri Western State College had just finished watching Jean-Luc Godard and Jean-Pierre Gorin's *Letter to Jane* (1972), and, before I could even turn on the lights, one of the Vietnam veterans present was expressing his opinion. But the moment is memorable for its humor and not because of any tension involved. Despite the film's very leftist politics, he was reacting only to its unusual style.

Godard and Gorin's film exemplifies and distills every aspect of film language and is thus a valuable study tool. *Letter to Jane* is the directors' response to a photo of Jane Fonda talking with some North Vietnamese citizens, and it expresses their concerns about the photo's shortcomings as a revolutionary statement. The film contains no actors, action, or camera movement. Editing is done simply by moving still photographs by hand. The filmmakers themselves supply all the dialogue in monotonic, conversational voices, sometimes speaking directly to the viewers by showing only a blank screen while they make their points. Many of these involve discussions of how photographs and film communicate; they examine the focus in the picture of Fonda, the arrangement of the figures in the picture, and the expression on her face.

As Godard and Gorin reveal, stills of Henry Fonda and John Wayne from old movies show these two actors with similar expressions of concern. Thus, the photograph of Jane Fonda becomes only a broad statement of her feelings. It has significance only because she is part of the same "star system" as her father and John Wayne. Therefore, although the film presents two leftists criticizing another for her shortcomings in attempting to serve the cause (also, two men criticizing a woman, the sexist implications of which are discussed in the film), it most importantly reveals the connections of this single photograph to virtually all of Western popular culture and to the way visual images communicate. Recognizing that whatever Fonda accomplished was due only to her celebrity status, Godard and Gorin analyze the photograph not by making a high-budget glossy film of their own but by presenting an exact antithesis to how such films communicate, thereby exposing those methods.

All of which is very admirable, but also very confusing to the average undergraduate who is not used to films that ask him or her to think. That my student's comment was based not on politics (I do not think I even know his political philosophy) but on the film's style was appropriate because it started off an hour-long discussion of how this film, and all films, communicate. As it turned out, this response was characteristic of the entire semester, which ended with a student's remark that he never thought he would enjoy a class that used only documentaries. In fact, none of the students had ever asked when we were going to see a Hollywood production, and, until that closing remark, I had not been conscious of not scheduling any. The course had gone very smoothly.

When students learn to understand what Vietnam War movies "say" and how they communicate, they also gain insight into how powerful messages about America's national identity and its role in international affairs are constructed from a variety of viewpoints. With a better understanding of the film rhetoric of Vietnam documentaries, students will be better prepared to consider the historical and political issues that shaped U.S. involvement in Vietnam.

I like to teach the course in a "politically balanced" way so that students can formulate their own understandings of the Vietnam War. The war continues to be a matter of concern in American politics and in our private lives. In 1988, the nature of Vice-President Quayle's military service became an important campaign issue, and opinions about Vietnam continue to shape the way lawmakers and citizens think about foreign-policy issues. A few examples from my own experience suggest that many people are still dealing with the war's effects: in 1989 and 1990, I attended a meeting to help veterans and their families cope with post-traumatic stress disorder, participated in the debate over placing a statue to women veterans at the Vietnam Memorial in Washington, D.C., and worked with students whose families were strongly affected by the war. Vietnam documentaries can help students in particular to take an active part in the ongoing debates about the war. This chapter is intended to encourage instructors and schools to bring such films into their classrooms.

When I first taught this course in the spring of 1987, *Platoon* was leading a new spate of Vietnam movies into the theaters. The topic was "hot" and seemed to be influencing distributors to remove their Vietnam movies from circulation temporarily to increase the prices. Although the selection was limited, it was adequate for my purposes. The PBS *Vietnam* (1983) series, owned by our college, and Accuracy in Media's response, *Television's Vietnam*, also broadcast on PBS (1985), and produced by Peter C. Rollins, could form the basis of my course, presenting the liberal and conservative perspectives and covering a key period in the war, the Tet offensive. I also wanted to use the well-known left-wing documentary *Hearts and Minds* (Peter Davis, 1974), and, searching for a counterpoint from early in the war, found *A Face of War* (Eugene Jones, 1967). Though not extremely conservative, Jones's film presents a far different picture of American soldiers than Davis's, and subsequently I have found that it serves as a very good introduction to the course.

I always begin by stating that the focus will be on film, not history or political science. I recognize that many of my students are more interested in history than in film, and they have to be able to seek answers to their questions, which tend to be basic ones about how the United States got into Vietnam, which side we fought on, when and how the war ended, and what kind of government Vietnam has now. In discussing such issues, I try to present several points of view. For example, I explain that conservatives locate the origins of the war in America's desire to protect South Vietnam from Communism, while liberals tend to emphasize America's continuation of the failed imperialist efforts of the French. I encourage students to pursue these questions with their own research so that they can reach their own conclusions. By making the effort to answer their own questions, they will begin to consider the larger issue of why studying this subject is important and how it might have some impact on their lives.

Those who have strong opinions about the war certainly are encouraged to express them, but keeping the focus on the films prevents the course from devolving into a political debate. For example, one of the course's major themes is how each film relates to its own era. I contrast Eugene Jones's *Face of War*, which contains the strong element of hope that was still possible when Americans were hearing about the "light at the end of the tunnel," with *Hearts and Minds*, which speaks very specifically about how Americans should view themselves in the postwar era. The "Tet" episodes of *Vietnam* and *Television's Vietnam* relate to the continuing importance of how Americans have understood and responded to the Tet offensive. By analyzing how each of these films relates to its own times, students should be able to gain a better understanding of the origins, strengths, and weaknesses of their own views, as well as those of others. Thus, the class can engage in vigorous discussion, but students do not feel pressured into accepting opinions they find unpersuasive.

I like to begin the course with *A Face of War*. David James criticizes this film for its use of World War II as "a master metaphor,"[1] and I use it as an introduction precisely because it expresses the view of the war that prevailed in 1966. When the film was shot, U.S. involvement in Vietnam was seen as an extension of the work begun in World War II, as spreading American benevolence throughout the world; even liberal intellectuals and politicians endorsed a consensus view of American foreign policy with regard to fighting Communism. Jones's use of World War II as a model also clearly relates the film to a time before political passions had become so aroused that it seemed impossible for filmmakers to present American soldiers in anything like a detached manner.

In all the war films they study, students focus on how soldiers are presented and on what the film states as America's war aims. Unlike most other films about Vietnam, *A Face of War* presents the war from the soldiers' perspective rather than using them to support a political position on what America's role was. David James writes, "*A Face of War* does succeed in making available what is probably the most densely texture version of the GI's experience of the war and of the day-to-day conditions under which it was fought."[2] Jones and his crew lived with the company of marines they filmed for more than three months. Jones was wounded twice during the filming and therefore had to rely on them. So it is not surprising that the first battle scene focuses on the wounded being treated and that Jones presents the men positively.

Another film that takes this unusual approach is John Huston's World War II documentary, *The Battle of San Pietro* (1945), which also presents soldiers' concerns as basically nonideological. They are heroic not for making superhuman sacrifices in support of a just cause but for continuing in their jobs despite the drudgery, boredom, and inhumanity of war. Both directors place the camera at the front line, demythologizing death, showing it to be real, sudden, and shocking. As one soldier in *A Face of War* explains, "If one of those snipers gets you, it isn't because of skill, but only because of luck." Throughout Jones's film, periods of calm are shattered by sudden outbursts of shooting or explosions, the most dramatic occurring when the soldiers' medical work with some villagers is interrupted by a transport truck running over a mine, killing and severely wounding several men. Jones uses this opportunity to show that wounded soldiers react with statements that they want to save their legs or want to go home, not with brave patriotic speeches. In such times, the lucky ones who have been spared injury display great resourcefulness and leadership, immediately taking control to provide aid and bring in the evacuating helicopters.

Jones always uses the suddenness of the attacks to comment on the setting. Several times, as the men are walking through the jungle, the camera will assume the soldiers' perspective, imparting a sense of wariness at what might be behind any tree. At the same time, the jungle also seems to provide protection; only when the troops move out into the open do attacks occur. I instruct students to notice how each war film represents the enemy. In *A Face of War*, the enemy is mainly unseen; we do see Americans looking at a Vietnamese man they have killed and interrogating a prisoner, but even at these times we cannot be sure we are seeing the enemy, and neither are the soldiers. By representing the enemy as an unseen presence, the film heightens our sense of the precariousness of the American situation in Vietnam. The soldier who commented on snipers remarks, "The only thing we really control is this hill we're standing on, and that's only during the day. At night, Charlie [the enemy] has complete freedom to do whatever he wants." The mission presented in the film was to root out all the Vietcong in the region, but, instead of being the attackers, the Americans appear to be only targets.

The soldiers find ways of coping. The two who talk about their precarious situation go on to discuss their hometowns and what they plan to do once they get back. While providing medical care to the Vietnamese villagers, the Americans tell them to return for a checkup the next day, though none is certain to be alive then. Jones shows soldiers trying to continue lives as normally as possible under extreme circumstances. Conversations over evening coffee around the fire, a game of mud football, and swimming and clowning in a waterhole bear witness to the special camaraderie that war can develop and that veterans recall as among the best experiences of their lives.

As a film transition from World War II to Vietnam, *A Face of War* is also interesting for its presentation of race relations. Whereas World War II documentaries sometimes spliced in shots of black soldiers to create an image of equality in the armed forces, Jones did not have to resort to any such contrivances. *A Face of War* shows unmanipulated scenes of black and white soldiers playing together and taking care of each other. While this footage was not doctored, it does not reveal the whole story. The military was no longer segregated, but racial conflicts among Americans in Vietnam existed, and these scenes could be criticized as masking an embarrassing truth. Their similarity to the falsely integrated scenes of World War II films places *A Face of War* squarely within a period in which many Americans did not question the essential goodness of our intentions in Vietnam or the possibility of a speedy and positive end to the war. The film's first reel concludes with a shot of a rainbow after a monsoon, and the second begins with the men helping in the birth of a Vietnamese baby. These images coming at the film's center stress the persistence of hope amid all the death and gloom.

David James aptly points out that these scenes use standard conventions from Hollywood World War II films, providing *A Face of War* with a metaphoric structure. But his claim that "their silent intent is to rewrite imperialist invasion as the anti-fascist liberation of Asia from the Japanese, of Europe from the Nazis"[3] sees the film's structure narrowly in relation to its presentation of American soldiers. The film's reticence with regard to American war aims, however, clearly contrasts with the conventions of World War II films. Jones begins and ends the film in evening darkness, thus setting a gloomy tone that is maintained at the end when the troops again move out on an unknown mission against an unseen enemy. This is no *Why We Fight* (1942–45) film. Jones begins with close-ups of weapons and then moves to shots of the men, making the same point as Huston in *The Battle of San Pietro*, that the men are simply another tool of war. Also, like Huston, Jones shoots entirely from the soldiers' perspective so that we understand their main concern: survival, not politics or ideology. Although the men are admirable for the compassion they display for both each other and the Vietnamese people, if they perform any altruistic service it is as a byproduct of their efforts to survive.

Jones identifies the viewer even more closely with the soldiers' perspective than does Huston because he provides no voice-over narration to inform the audience about what is happening. Jones omits an opening title or credits, starting directly with the action and drawing the viewer into an unfolding event and into the men's anxiety and uncertainty. He uses sound to keep the viewer oriented. Communications come through clearly, though he sometimes has to make special interventions, as when the walkie-talkies are nowhere near the action being shown and could not possibly be heard over the roar of battle and shouts of the men. Thus, Jones preserves the viewer's status as a participant-observer, somewhat above the action. Despite the sudden and shocking nature of much of the film, the viewer is still in a safer position and has a better sense of what is happening than most of the soldiers probably did. Huston was able to accomplish this by describing the setting as similar to a stage on which the drama would take place. He was able to use maps and shots of communications from headquarters so that the viewer clearly understood the strategic importance of the battle and the chain of command. Jones's inability to do that is an important mark of the difference between the two wars.

The notion of American innocence—that we never ask for war, we only fight to protect peace and freedom, and we always act out of benevolence—animated most World War II films. This issue is crucial because it has wide-ranging implications for popular attitudes on defense and foreign-policy decisions. If we only fight to protect freedom, while guilt rests entirely with the other side, then we are justified in building our defenses as much as possible while trying to keep our adversaries' weapons at a minimum. Among the World War II films that relied on heavy-handed assertions of American innocence is the multi–award winning television documentary series *Victory at Sea*, which is still presented on television and used in schools around the country. In the ninety-minute compilation film from the series, the innocence theme is evident in the presentation of the GIs' sexual attitudes. The men visualize returning home to the important women in their lives—wives, the Statue of Liberty, and "Pearl" (Pearl Harbor). The narrator remarks that on the night before a battle, a sailor's thoughts are on home and clean, white sheets. From the vantage point of the 1990s such naïveté seems comical, but it was an accepted (perhaps not a fully persuasive) commonplace of 1950s films. Any audience would find an inconsistency in presenting such innocent "boys" as killers, so the filmmakers never show them wounding or killing the enemy. America's big and powerful guns are never shown hitting anything, and the narrative addresses the destruction of objects only—"over ninety German submarines went to their graves."[4]

A Face of War works to debunk such myths in several ways. When the leader of a small patrol tells his men they are going out to kill the sniper who has been harassing them, he makes no apologies—he wants that guy dead. At another time, the company comes across the body of a man they have killed; they are uncertain that he was the enemy. Jones shows both the body and a group of local women weeping horribly; the men try to justify the killing by saying that they have seen other Vietnamese women put on acts like that before. It is all they can do. In other scenes, the Americans are interrogating a blindfolded and bound prisoner and evacuating a village in huge personnel carriers. Though the soldiers do what they can to console the people, Jones's low-angle shots emphasize the fear that the American military equipment produces.

Although Jones does borrow some standard sequences from World War II films, his approach cannot be labeled as an attempt to justify the war. His film makes an excellent introduction to the course because it reflects the deep divisions in popular attitudes about the war in America during the mid sixties and challenges those with strong attitudes either for or against America's efforts in Vietnam.[5]

In summing up the analysis of *A Face of War*, I remind the students that editing is an integral part of documentary filmmaking. Eugene Jones condensed more than ninety days' worth of shooting into a seventy-minute film, just as every director has to select the images that best convey the point of the film. To demonstrate how crucial such a selection is to supporting a political viewpoint in Vietnam documentaries, I continue the course by focusing on the conflicting viewpoints in the "Tet" episodes of the PBS series *Vietnam* and Accuracy in Media's *Television's Vietnam*.

The discussions compare key aspects of creating the film's political perspectives: images of American fighting men and technology; images of our South Vietnamese allies; images of the enemy; interpretation of the media's role; the method of interpretation for important battles and incidents; the use of on-camera spokespeople; and the use of the narrator.

The PBS film re-creates the original popular perception of American troops beleaguered and confused during the Tet offensive by including several television reports from that time without providing any additional context. For example, in a brief interview during the battle for the ancient imperial capital of Hue, a soldier takes a break from firing to tell a correspondent that the whole situation stinks and he would rather be home in school. Having reloaded, he then wearily resumes fighting. The response is an honest one from a man in battle, but it implies that the soldier is representative of many who regard the whole war effort as worthless. The battle for Hue, the first building-to-building urban fighting of the war, lasted for twenty-six days, enough to fatigue anyone, before American and South Vietnamese forces prevailed. Setting the soldier's remarks in the context of these facts would considerably alter their effect, and it is apparent that their effect was consistent with PBS's entire presentation of Tet, which, as the Accuracy in Media film states, is one of "gloom and doom."

American commanders are presented as either hopelessly inept or liars or both. One of the commanders, Myron Harrington, tells the filmmakers that he used heavy firepower during the battle for Hue with as much caution as possible, hitting houses only when necessary. The filmmakers then cut to a shot of a tank flamethrower apparently firing indiscriminately at large buildings.[6] Shots of General William Westmoreland, the head of American forces in Vietnam, show him nervously explaining the situation to the press in such official-sounding language as "the enemy has deceitfully attempted to take advantage of the holiday cease-fire to launch a major assault on the urban areas with the apparent aim of causing maximum consternation." During his long-winded reassurances that everything is under control, there is an explosion, which Westmoreland attempts to laugh off as test firing. While he was probably being honest, the visual images communicate powerfully that he is claiming control he does not have.

While PBS does explain that Tet was a major military defeat for the Communist forces, effectively removing the Vietcong from most of the fighting for the rest of the war, the documentary also conveys an explanation that reflects negatively on the Americans. The images of U.S. firepower in the PBS film, such as the flamethrowers in Hue, recall a statement, reputedly made by an American officer, that "sometimes it's necessary to destroy a country in order to save it."[7] Early scenes show American personnel and tanks parked around a couple of isolated huts, lazily taking potshots, and a large gun in some type of aquatic vehicle apparently using a corpse in a rice paddy for target practice. Later, the film explains the eventual American victory at the battle for Khe Sanh as the result of "the largest bombing assault in military history," and the celebration of the victory at Hue is marked by a few South Vietnamese soldiers raising their flag over a lot of rubble.

In response to PBS's *Vietnam*, the conservative Accuracy in Media organization produced a two-part film series intended to correct what it viewed as the false implications of the original news reports and the PBS series. The first AIM program, *Television's Vietnam: The Real Story*, appeared on PBS on 26 June 1985. In a prologue to the show, producer Peter C. Rollins stated that the "truth" about Vietnam probably resided somewhere between the AIM version and the PBS account and that viewers would have to form their own opinions about the war. The second AIM program, *Television's Vietnam: The Impact of Media*, focuses on the reporting of crucial events during the Tet offensive, providing a useful contrast to the PBS episode; it should be viewed in the context of Rollins's statement, because its refuting of earlier reports about the war and its own conclusions should be similarly challenged.[8]

Naturally, *The Impact of Media*'s account of key events during Tet is quite different from those of *Vietnam*. For example, former National Security Council member Dolf Droge says that the twenty-six Vietcong who blasted their way through the U.S. embassy wall never got past the three marine guards at the door, and Ambassador Ellsworth Bunker was back at his desk by noon on the day of the attack. These facts, he claims, were never reported by the media. AIM uses footage to show that supposedly beleaguered U.S. troops in the battle for Khe Sanh were actually in a strong position, with the marines holding the high ground all around the base. The film further uses testimony by journalist Peter Braestrup (author of *Big Story*, a two-volume analysis of the reporting of Tet), a veteran of the battle, and Westmoreland to explain the inaccuracies in the continual reports of doom coming from the base.

AIM's presentation of General Westmoreland is also in sharp contrast to PBS's. *The Impact of Media* shows Westmoreland in a relaxed postwar interview, sitting in a leather easy chair, and wearing a suit. Comfortable but formal, he holds a copy of his own book, *A Soldier Reports*, on his lap and appears firmly in command of the facts. His white hair, no longer with a military cut, adds to his image as a wise and tolerant leader, patiently refuting all the charges that have been laid against him. The contrast itself rather than the trustworthiness of the two portrayals is the point; each film carefully presents him in a way that supports its own viewpoint.

The Impact of Media does not depict American firepower, nor does it show the impact of the American presence on the Vietnamese (compare fearful villagers being moved by American personnel carriers, as in *A Face of War*, or Vietnamese children suffering from napalm burns in *Hearts and Minds*). It does acknowledge that horrible incidents occurred—notably, the My Lai massacre and the infamous shooting of a bound Vietcong suspect by South Vietnam's Chief of Police, General Loan, during the Tet offensive. But the film also insists that these events be seen in "proper" perspective. The unfortunate killing of a few hundred innocent civilians by some confused and misguided Americans is compared with the Communists' deliberate and systematic massacre of approximately three thousand citizens following their initial victory at Hue. The film explains the General Loan incident as a misguided but understandable act by an officer seeking revenge for the loss of his men and American soldiers during the heat of battle. Viewers are therefore able to retain some notion of American innocence.

PBS, on the other hand, explains that those killed at Hue were former government officials, intellectuals, and priests—people whom the Communists might legitimately suspect as opposed to their policies. They also present a Communist spokeswoman who claims that victims of the Americans' indiscriminate firing during the battle were old people, pregnant women, and children. Thus, despite a large, calculated massacre by the Communists, the Americans appear only slightly less brutal.

Comparisons of the other important images from these two films reveal similarly strong contrasts. PBS presents the enemy as dedicated fighters, willing to forfeit their lives for their cause, while our South Vietnamese allies are nothing but cheap pickpockets, willing to fight only when their homes are directly threatened. AIM shows the enemy sneaking through the jungle, while the South Vietnamese forces are performing efficiently. In PBS's "Tet," Johnson administration officials are presented as liars, while original network reports are allowed once again to speak for themselves, without comment. In *Television's Vietnam*, every news report is exposed as misleading, reporters are shown goofing off during press briefings, and former journalists criticize their onetime colleagues for not trusting administration sources enough.

Another contrast lies in the style of narration of each film. PBS used a voice-over narrator throughout its series, while AIM employed the actor Charlton Heston as an on-camera narrator. An inherent pitfall of documentaries, to which PBS fell victim, is that all images are used simply to prove the narrator's statements. The filmmakers simply select footage that appears to support their ideas without providing any commentary on the original context of the material. Instead, the images are allowed to "speak for themselves." This same technique (also used in *Victory at Sea*) reduces documentaries to the level of choosing an opinion and finding the footage to support it.

Images contain powerful messages that, when combined with

the statements of an authoritative narrator, can seem irrefutable. But, as Charlton Heston points out near the end of *The Impact of Media*, "It used to be said that a picture could say a thousand words. But, what we are learning now is that it takes a thousand words to explain a single picture."

The statement should, however, also be used to consider how Heston functions as a narrator and why AIM chose to present him on-screen. As a result of his most famous roles as Moses and Ben Hur, Heston is a trusted figure who carries about him an aura of honesty and authority. The makers of *The Impact of Media* have exploited these qualities through their choice of setting and their placement of the actor. Heston sits in a stiff leather chair, looks directly into the camera, and provides the facts cleansed of the journalistic errors in the reporting of Vietnam from the sixties to the eighties. The desk behind him with some papers on it suggests scholarship and that he is relating what he has learned through research.[9] However, the implication that he has just moved from desk to chair, that he is seated, and the huge plant behind the desk lend a casual air that slightly undercuts Heston's authoritativeness. He is, as he says, a concerned citizen, as any good American should be.

By presenting their narrator on-screen, the filmmakers use a style that supports their claim of being open and honest. But their "truths" are certainly subject to question, particularly in the conclusions drawn. The film opens with a shot of President Reagan at the dedication of the Vietnam Veterans' Memorial in Washington, D.C., followed by statements from a retired black officer, Major General George B. Price, and a Democratic congressman from Michigan, David Boniar, honoring the men who fought. Then, over footage of the evacuation of Saigon in 1975 and of subsequent North Vietnamese brutality, Heston states, "After seeing the horrible consequences of communist rule in Indochina—the holocaust in Cambodia and the flights of the boat people from Vietnam—Americans came to recognize that this was a war we should have fought to win." Whether any such national consensus has ever been reached is highly questionable, but the shots of Reagan, Price, and Boniar quickly imply that a broad spectrum of the population has come to this conclusion. Furthermore, their presence, along with the shots of the fall/liberation of Saigon and several shots of the flag, make fighting to "win" appear to be the only humane and patriotic choice that could have been made.

But the filmmakers never state America's reason for being in Vietnam; that aspect of their argument was covered earlier in *The Real Story*, but such broad statements about American attitudes as the ones made in *The Impact of Media* would seem to require more immediate support than the images provided. Recall that PBS had thirteen hours over thirteen weeks to discuss the war, while Accuracy in Media had two hours. While PBS was certainly generous in allowing any kind of broadcast opposing its own documentary on its own network, a complete rebuttal could not be made in so short a time. Nevertheless, *The Impact of Media* fails to address some key points. It exposes many inaccurate news reports, but never suggests the reason that so many journalistic mistakes were made. They make no direct claim that a conspiracy existed, but that implication is allowed to stand in the absence of citing any history of government lies, cover-ups, or uncertainties about American goals and methods. Viewers also have to question and investigate the accuracy of this picture of the entire media coverage of the war. Though the majority of reports from the Tet offensive were negative, reportage before or after Tet was more varied.[10] The CBS video series *The Vietnam War with Walter Cronkite*, for example, contains several reports from throughout the war showing Americans performing honorably. Moreover, *The Impact of Media* makes no mention of special reports and interview programs that might give greater depth and balance to the picture. Such omissions undermine the film's thesis, which blames the media for disastrously swaying public opinion against the war.[11]

I wrap up my course with Peter Davis's *Hearts and Minds*, which may seem to slant matters a little too heavily in the direction of the political Left, but which nevertheless provides, among a number of other things, a useful way of demonstrating how—in this case, in a compilation film—filmmakers manipulate images to support their perspectives. Made in 1975, *Hearts and Minds* has a distinctly postwar theme and reinforces the fact that films about Vietnam (as with all historical films) reveal more about the time in which they were made than about the time to which they refer. *Hearts and Minds*, for example, sets out to prove that America was fighting a counterrevolutionary war in Vietnam and brought massive destruction to the country. But, more important, the movie argues that the superpatriotic attitudes produced by World War II were responsible for getting the United States into the war, that they were still being promoted in 1975, and that such attitudes must be rejected.

In a number of documentary scenes, *Hearts and Minds* shows how fighting and flag waving are often tied together in colorful public events. One specific focus is the pageantry of a high-school football game. At halftime of this "important" contest, one team is obviously losing badly. But the coach still gives his players an emotionally extreme locker-room talk, telling them to keep fighting. Preaching the same message, but much more calmly, is former POW George Coker. In his welcome-home ceremony at Linden, New Jersey, featuring a marching band and a multitude of flags, Coker tells a very receptive crowd that they must be ready to send him to war again, should the need arise.

Hearts and Minds always follows such messages with contrasting shots of American destruction in Vietnam that make the supporters of the war effort look like ignorant hypocrites and attempts to encourage viewers to reject the "patriotic" images and messages. The film hammers its message home during the final parade sequence, in which a group of protesters is being jeered and attacked by the paraders and other spectators. A young veteran complains to the camera, "What is this? I was a platoon leader in Vietnam. What do these people know about the war?" The filmmakers want viewers to pity this poor guy. He obviously does not know the "truth" about the war. They have concluded that public attitudes need to change, which for them means that this veteran's perspective should not even be considered. But the filmmakers do not encourage viewers to question their own presentation, which involves blatant manipulation.

I have focused on my own experience in teaching a course on films about Vietnam, recognizing that my approach may be varied and improved upon in many ways. In an ideal situation, the school would already own or be able to rent all the films (and, for television programs, videos) the instructor wants to use. The class would be held at least one evening a week for viewing, with two additional meetings during the week for discussion, and the film would be available throughout the week for use during discussion sessions and for individual assignments or tests. My own class meets only once a week, and my school owns only one or two of the films I use. To deal with these constraints, I have considered several options.

One is to see and discuss a film during each class session, but the length of some films leaves very little time for class discussion. Delaying discussion until the next meeting may be difficult for students, even if they are good note takers, because they will not easily remember the details of content and structure. Instructors minimize such problems by introducing every film, by providing students with guidelines of what to look for, and by providing study questions that students are to complete as soon as possible after seeing the film. Related readings can be placed on reserve at the school library, along with a set of study questions for the students to complete before seeing the film.[12] Instructors can also assist students by providing short lectures either before or after discussion.

Another option—one that students tend to dislike but that can be useful—is to not watch parts of a film. The instructor can select sections for specific study or start from the beginning and stop for discussion after each sequence. When time is short, the instructor can provide a running commentary to point out immediately what students need to notice; students say this is helpful for connecting the text to any analysis. The students who take the course because they think watching movies will be fun and easy are likely to be frustrated by not seeing an entire film, but after carefully examining portions of films even they might begin to appreciate the complexity of visual language and the need for careful study. In schools that make video equipment and films accessible to students, individuals or groups can study a specific production and prepare either essays or class presentations.

Because the Vietnam War is an issue of strong general interest, I highly recommend making this course part of a continuing-education program and publicizing it in the community, particularly among veterans' groups. In my experience, veterans enrich the discussion with their comments on the authenticity and political perspectives of the films. A representative from a local Vietnam veterans' group might be willing to hold a discussion with the class. In one of my classes, a local veteran presented his synchronized slide show of pictures taken during his tour of duty. Furthermore, modern technology allows instructors to reach beyond their local communities. In conference calls, students in my classes have talked with producer, film instructor, and veteran Peter C. Rollins, who has graciously stayed on the phone for as long as two hours to talk about film language, the role of the media in Vietnam and other national affairs, and a broad range of related topics. For my students, the understanding that the issues raised in the class have importance far beyond the campus grows as they draw on community resources, so I involve the community as much as possible.

A final comment on involvement: I have not been very successful in attracting women to the course. Few enroll, and some of them drop out. Several who dropped said that the films upset them too much, and perhaps students—male and female—regard war as a man's topic. Because the course focuses on issues that concern everyone, special efforts might be necessary to recruit women. Promotional flyers might be used to discourage the idea that the course is some type of macho exercise, and history, political science, English, and theater departments might be encouraged to cross-list the course. As women's studies courses are increasingly exploring women's roles in war, we can expect that women instructors more generally will undertake courses on Vietnam. As with community involvement, increasing women's participation in these courses promotes the understanding that we all have a voice and a role in making sense of the war.

Notes

1. David James, "Presence of Discourse/Discourse of Presence: Representing Vietnam," *Wide Angle* 7.4 (1985): 43.

2. Ibid.

3. Ibid.

4. Director Stanley Kubrick, of course, accurately satirizes this perverse idea of American sexual energy being redirected into military technology in *Dr. Strangelove, or How I Learned to Stop Worrying and Love the Bomb* (1964). Peter C. Rollins, in *"Victory at Sea*: Cold War Epic," *Journal of American Culture* 6 (1972): 463–82, provides a thorough discussion of the documentary's popular success, influence, and critical failures.

5. I try to avoid the terms "pro-war" and "anti-war," feeling that it is unfair to label those who support America's role in Vietnam as lovers of war. This distinction helps create a congenial classroom atmosphere in which students are unafraid to share their opinions. They can learn that it is definitely possible to be strongly opposed to American efforts in Vietnam and still admire the men and women who served there, an important lesson at a time when thousands of Vietnam veterans are still trying to cope with the war's effects.

6. Stanley Karnow's companion volume to the series, *Vietnam: A History* (New York: Viking Press, 1983), is often much fairer to the Americans. Describing the battle for Hue, Karnow writes, "The marines could now direct artillery against the Citadel, their forward observer giving the batteries such precise readings that the shells often fell within twenty-five yards of their position inside the fortress" (533). Later, he quotes Harrington as saying: "Did we have to destroy the town in order to save it? Well, I don't think that the North Vietnamese and Vietcong were about to give it up even if we'd surrounded Hue and tried to starve them out. We had to go in and get them. There was no other way, except to dig them out. But we didn't go in there simply to show how great our weapons were, how much destructive power we possessed. We did our best to avoid malicious damage. Yet, when we had to destroy a house, we destroyed it" (534).

7. Accuracy in Media film producer Peter C. Rollins, in a conference-call discussion with my class, stated that Reed Irvine, director of Accuracy in Media, has repeatedly challenged Peter Arnett, the reporter of that statement, to name his source, but Arnett has refused. Therefore, it is possible that no American officer actually made it, and that the media are again responsible for a powerful, but misleading, idea.

8. According to Peter C. Rollins, *The Impact of Media* has been broadcast by more than two hundred independent PBS stations, by the Turner Broadcasting System, and by the United States Armed Forces Television. AIM secretary Debbie Lambert estimates that five thousand copies of the Vietnam programs have been sold to colleges, secondary schools, and other buyers.

9. As explained, this image adds depth to Heston's role as narrator, lending a sense of animation and intellectual authenticity. But it should not be taken as entirely misleading. Heston is well known as an active supporter of conservative causes, which he apparently takes up through a real sense of civic concern. As Peter C. Rollins told my class, visitors to Heston's house are first taken to see his library, which is not there merely for appearance. Heston is a scholar in his own right. However, George C. Herring, in reviewing both the AIM and PBS productions, finds the PBS narration much more subtle and its commentators more authoritative (*Journal of American History* 74.3 [1987]: 1123–25).

10. See Daniel C. Hallin, *The "Uncensored War:" Vietnam and the Media* (New York: Oxford University Press, 1986).

11. Peter C. Rollins indicated several possible reasons to my class for the inaccurate reports consistently coming out of Vietnam, and particularly from Khe Sanh. First, some of the reporters, in Rollins's opinion, were certainly so opposed to American efforts in Vietnam that they would always seek to portray them as negatively as possible. Another point, as Peter Braestrup asserts in *Television's Vietnam*, is that reporters often flew in for a few days and gave a report based on no more specific information about the situation than what was already pervading the media. By sticking with that story, they would not have to risk proposing a new thesis. The problem was that the accepted "line" on Khe Sanh labeled the battle a replay of the French disaster at Dien Bien Phu in 1954. In *The Impact of Media*, Charlton Heston reports that Bernard Fall's account of the earlier battle, *Hell in a Very Small Place*, became required reading for journalists going to cover Khe Sanh. (However, Stanley Karnow, *Vietnam* 541, asserts that the military itself promoted the Dien Bien Phu analogy.)

A further reason for the misreporting, in Rollins's opinion, was the ineptness of the American commander at Khe Sanh in dealing with the press. Wisecracks about impending disaster were not taken humorously by reporters. This ineptness parallels the entire Johnson administration's failure to make effective use of the press in presenting its own case following the Tet offensive. (For a brief account of the administration's efforts, see Kathleen J. Turner, *Lyndon Johnson's Dual War: Vietnam and the Press* [Chicago: University of Chicago Press, 1985] 219–25.)

Finally, some facts in war simply have to be kept from the press. At Khe Sanh, sensors in the surrounding jungle created an electronic battlefield for American commanders to observe, giving them clear indications of any large enemy movements. Certainly, however, the military could not risk letting the enemy know about the presence of these devices.

Therefore, reporters were not entirely to blame for the inaccuracies, and no conspiracy existed among them. However, that does not account for the failure to report American successes at Khe Sanh (Peter C. Rollins, "Television's Vietnam: The Visual Language of Television News," *Journal of American Culture* 4 [1981]: 124–28) or for the other misleading accounts documented in the Accuracy in Media film. Once again, though, Karnow dismisses the effects of the media's representations by claiming that American public opinion had already turned against the war before Tet. In his view: "Public opinion surveys conducted at the time made it plain that, whatever the quality of the reporting from Vietnam, the momentous Tet episode scarcely altered American attitudes toward the war. . . . For a brief moment after the Tet offensive began, Americans rallied 'round the flag in a predictable display of patriotic fervor. But their mood of despair quickly returned as the fighting dragged on, and their endorsement of the conflict resumed its downward spiral" (*Vietnam* 545).

Other writers confirm that reporting during Tet had little impact on popular opinion. Kathleen Turner states that "the Gallup poll indicated that the percentage of self-described hawks had jumped to 61% in the wake of Tet" (*Lyndon Johnson's Dual War* 219). Even Peter Braestrup, one of *The Impact of Media*'s chief commentators, concluded: "There is no evidence of a direct relationship between the dominant media themes in 1968 and changes in American mass public opinion vis-à-vis the Vietnam War itself. Indeed, public support for the war effort remained remarkably steady in February–March 1968, even as LBJ's popularity hit a new low, as measured by pollsters" (*Big Story: How the American Press and Television Reported and Interpreted the Crisis of Tet 1968 in Vietnam and Washington*, abridged ed. [New Haven, Conn.: Yale University Press, 1983] 505).

Finally, Daniel C. Hallin argues that not only did the media have little impact, they also basically supported American policy and administration positions, though with increased skepticism, even after Tet (*The "Uncensored War"* 174). Hallin observes: "The administration retained considerable power to manage the news: it should not be forgotten that

Richard Nixon was able to keep public support for his handling of the war through four years and more than a hundred thousand American casualties. And many potentially explosive issues never penetrated television's relatively narrow agenda" (163).

12. Readings I would suggest include works by David James ("Presence of Discourse") and Peter C. Rollins ("Television's Vietnam" and "*Victory at Sea*: Cold War Epic"). Other valuable pieces include Stanley Karnow's chapter "Tet" (*Vietnam* 523–66) and Andrew Sarris's review of *Hearts and Minds* in *Politics and Cinema* (New York: Columbia University Press, 1978) 102–4. For instructors wishing to refer to World War II films to provide an introduction to the course, a broad context, and a point of contrast, the introduction and first chapter of J. Fred MacDonald's *Television and the Red Menace: The Video Road to Vietnam* (New York: Praeger, 1985) provide a valuable and concise discussion (vi–12).

Selected Bibliography

Adair, Gilbert. *Vietnam on Film.* New York: Proteus, 1981.

Alexander, William. "Teaching Vietnam: An Appropriate Pedagogy." *Jump Cut* 31 (1986): 59–72.

Auster, Albert, and Leonard Quart. "Hollywood and Vietnam: The Triumph of the Will." *Cineaste* 9 (1979): 4–9.

———. *How the War Was Remembered: Hollywood and Vietnam.* New York: Praeger, 1988.

Baritz, Loren. *Backfire: A History of How American Culture Led Us into Vietnam and Made Us Fight the Way We Did.* New York: William Morrow, 1985.

Bayles, Martha. "The Road to Rambo III." *New Republic* (18 and 25 July 1988): 30–35.

Berg, Rick. "Losing Vietnam: Covering the War in an Age of Technology." *Cultural Critique* 3 (1986): 92–125.

Biskind, Peter. "What Price Balance? On 'Vietnam: A Television History.'" *Race and Class* 25.4 (1984): 61–69.

Bogue, Ronald L. "The Heartless Darkness of *Apocalypse Now.*" *Georgia Review* 35 (1981): 611–26.

Boyd, David. "*The Deer Hunter*: The Hero and the Tradition." *Australasian Journal of American Studies* 1 (1980): 41–51.

Britton, Andrew. "Sideshows: Hollywood in Vietnam." *Movie* 27–28 (1980–81): 2–23.

Burke, Frank. "In Defense of *The Deer Hunter*; or, The Knee Jerk Is Quicker than the Eye." *Literature/Film Quarterly* 11 (1983): 22–27.

―――. "The Dear Hunter and the Jaundiced Angel." *Canadian Journal of Political and Social Theory* 4 (1980): 123–31.

Calloway, Catherine. "Vietnam War Literature and Film: A Bibliography of Secondary Sources." *Bulletin of Bibliography* 43 (1986): 149–58.

Caputo, Philip. *A Rumor of War.* New York: Ballantine, 1977.

Chabal, P., and P. Joannides. "Copping Out with Coppola." *Cambridge Quarterly* 13 (1984): 187–203.

Clark, Michael. "Remembering Vietnam." *Cultural Critique* 3 (1986): 46–78.

―――. "Vietnam: Representations of Self and War." *Wide Angle* 7.4 (1985): 4–11.

Conlon, James. "Making Love, Not War: The Soldier Male in *Top Gun* and *Coming Home*." *Journal of Popular Film and Television* 18 (1990): 18–27.

de Furia, R. D. "*Apocalypse Now*: The Ritual Murder of Art." *Western Humanities Review* 34 (1980): 85–89.

Dempsey, Michael. "*Apocalypse Now*." *Sight and Sound* 49 (1979–80): 5–9.

Dempsey, Michael; Marsha Kinder; David Axeen; and Ernest Callenbach. "Four Shots at *The Deer Hunter*." *Film Quarterly* 32.4 (1979): 10–22.

Dickstein, Morris. "Bringing It All Back Home." *Partisan Review* 45 (1978): 627–33.

Dittmar, Linda, and Gene Michaud. *From Hanoi to Hollywood: The Vietnam War in American Film.* New Brunswick, N.J., and London: Rutgers University Press, 1990.

Doherty, Thomas. "Full Metal Genre: Kubrick's Vietnam Combat Movie." *Film Quarterly* 42.2 (1988–89): 24–30.

Eberwein, Robert T. "Ceremonies of Survival: The Structure of *The Deer Hunter*." *Journal of Popular Film and Television* 7 (1980): 352–64.

Edelman, Rob. "A Second Look: *Go Tell the Spartans*." *Cineaste* 13 (1983): 18–19, 54.

Fore, Steve. "Kuntzel's Law and *Uncommon Valor*; or, Reshaping the National Consciousness in Six Minutes Flat." *Wide Angle* 7.4 (1985): 23–32.

Francis, Don. "The Regeneration of America: Uses of Landscape in *The Deer Hunter.*" *Literature/Film Quarterly* 11 (1983): 16–21.

Galperin, William. "History into Allegory: *The Wild Bunch* as Vietnam Movie." *Western Humanities Review* 35 (1981): 165–72.

Gilman, Owen, and Lorrie Smith. *America Rediscovered: Critical Essays on Literature and Film of the Vietnam War.* New York: Garland, 1990.

Greenberg, Harvey R. "Dangerous Recuperations: *Red Dawn, Rambo,* and the New Decaturism." *Journal of Popular Film and Television* 15 (1987): 60–70.

Hagen, William M. "Apocalypse Now (1979): Joseph Conrad and the Television War." In *Hollywood as Historian: American Film in a Cultural Context,* ed. Peter C. Rollins. Lexington: University Press of Kentucky, 1983. 230–45.

Hansen, Miriam. "Traces of Transgression in *Apocalypse Now.*" *Social Text* 3 (Fall 1980): 123–35.

Hanson, Cynthia A. "The Women of China Beach." *Journal of Popular Film and Television* 17 (1990): 154–63.

Hasford, Gustav. *The Short-Timers.* New York: Harper and Row, 1979.

Heilbronn, Lisa M. "Coming Home a Hero: The Changing Image of the Vietnam Vet on Prime Time Television." *Journal of Popular Film and Television* 13 (1985): 25–30.

Hellmann, John. *American Myth and the Legacy of Vietnam.* New York: Columbia University Press, 1986.

———. "Vietnam and the Hollywood Genre Film: Inversions of American Mythology in *The Deer Hunter* and *Apocalypse Now.*" *American Quarterly* 34 (Fall 1982): 418–39.

Herr, Michael. *Dispatches.* New York: Alfred A. Knopf, 1977.

James, David. "Presence of Discourse/Discourse of Presence: Representing Vietnam." *Wide Angle* 7.4 (1985): 41–51.

———. "Rock and Roll in Representations of the Invasion of Vietnam." *Representations* 29 (1990): 78–98.

James, David, and Rick Berg. "College Course File: Representing the Vietnam War." *Journal of Film and Video* 41.4 (1989): 60–74.

Jeffords, Susan. "Friendly Civilians: Images of Women and the Feminization of the Audience in Vietnam Films." *Wide Angle* 7.4 (1985): 13–22.

———. "Masculinity as Excess in Vietnam Films: The Father/Son Dynamic of American Culture." *Genre* 21 (1988): 487–515.

————. "The New Vietnam Films: Is the Movie Over?" *Journal of Popular Film and Television* 13 (1986): 186–94.

————. *The Remasculinization of America: Gender and the Vietnam War.* Bloomington: Indiana University Press, 1989.

————. "Women, Gender, and the War." *Critical Studies in Mass Communications* 6 (1989): 83–90.

Kelly, William P. "*Apocalypse Now*: Vietnam as a Generative Ritual." In *Rituals and Ceremonies in Popular Culture*, ed. Ray B. Browne. Bowling Green, Ohio: Bowling Green University Popular Press, 1980.

Kerr, Paul. "The Vietnam Subtext." *Screen* 21.2 (1980): 67–72.

Kinder, Marsha. "The Power of Adaptation in *Apocalypse Now*." *Film Quarterly* 33.2 (1979–80): 12–20.

Kinney, Judy Lee. "The Mythical Method: Fictionalizing the Vietnam War." *Wide Angle* 7.4 (1985): 35–40.

Kovic, Ron. *Born on the Fourth of July.* New York: McGraw-Hill, 1976.

Kranz, R. C. "*Apocalypse Now* and *The Deer Hunter*: The Lies Aren't Over." *Jump Cut* 23 (1980): 18–20.

Lehman, Peter. "'Well, what's it like over there? Can you tell us anything?': Looking for Vietnam in *The Deer Hunter*." *North Dakota Quarterly* 51.3 (1983): 131–41.

Lewis, Lloyd B. *The Tainted War: Culture and Identity in the Vietnam War Narratives.* Westport, Conn.: Greenwood Press, 1985.

Lichty, Lawrence W., and Raymond L. Carroll, "Fragments of War: *Platoon* (1986)." In *American History/American Film: Interpreting the Hollywood Image*, ed. John E. O'Connor and Martin A. Jackson. New York: Continuum, 1979; new expanded edition, 1988. 273–87.

Louvre, Alf, and Jeffrey Walsh, eds. *Tell Me Lies about Vietnam: Cultural Battles for the Meaning of the War.* Milton Keynes, Eng.: Open University Press, 1988.

McInerney, Peter. "Apocalypse Then: Hollywood Looks Back at Vietnam." *Film Quarterly* 33.2 (1979–80): 21–32.

Modleski, Tania. "A Father Is Being Beaten: Male Feminism and the War Film." *Discourse* 10.2 (1988): 62–77.

Norden, Martin F. "The Disabled Vietnam Veteran in Hollywood Films." *Journal of Popular Film and Television* 13 (1985): 16–23.

O'Brien, Tim. *Going after Cacciato* (New York: Delacorte Press, 1978).

————. *If I Die in a Combat Zone.* New York: Delacorte Press, 1973.

Palmer, R. Barton. "The Darker Heart of Coppola's *Apocalypse Now*." *Persistence of Vision* 1 (Summer 1984): 5–12.

Palmer, William J. "The Vietnam War Films." *Film Library Quarterly* 13.4 (1980): 4–14.

Paris, Michael. "The American Film Industry and Vietnam." *History Today* 37 (April 1987): 19–26.

Pursell, Michael. "*Full Metal Jacket*: The Unraveling of Patriarchy." *Literature/Film Quarterly* 16 (1988): 218–25.

Pym, John. "*Apocalypse Now*: An Errand Boy's Journey." *Sight and Sound* 49 (1979–80): 9–10.

———. "A Bullet in the Head: Vietnam Remembered." *Sight and Sound* 48 (1979): 82–84, 115.

Quart, Leonard, and Albert Auster. "The Wounded Vet in Postwar Film." *Social Policy* 13 (1982): 24–31.

Rafferty, Terrence. "Remote Control" [on *Full Metal Jacket*]. *Sight and Sound* 56 (1987): 256–59.

Ray, Robert B. *A Certain Tendency of the Hollywood Cinema, 1930–1980.* Princeton, N.J.: Princeton University Press, 1985.

Reaves, Gerri. "From Hasford's *The Short-Timers* to Kubrick's *Full Metal Jacket*." *Literature/Film Quarterly* 16 (1988): 232–37.

Renov, Michael. "Imaging the Other: Representations of Vietnam in '60s Political Documentary." *Afterimage* 16.5 (1988): 10–12.

Rist, Peter. "Standard Hollywood Fare: The World War II Combat Film Revisited." *CineAction!* 12 (1988): 23–26.

Rowe, John Carlos. "'Bringing It All Back Home': American Recyclings of the Vietnam War." In *The Violence of Representation: Literature and the History of Violence*, ed. Nancy Armstrong and Leonard Tennenhouse. London and New York: Routledge, 1989. 197–218.

———. "Eye-Witness: Documentary Styles in the American Representations of Vietnam." *Cultural Critique* 3 (1986): 126–50.

———. "From Documentary to Docudrama: Vietnam on Television in the 1980s." *Genre* 21 (1988): 451–77.

Searle, William J., ed. *Search and Clear: Critical Responses to Selected Literature and Films of the Vietnam War.* Bowling Green, Ohio: Bowling Green State University Popular Press, 1988.

Sklar, Robert, Pat Aufderheide, Larry Ceplair, Leonard Quart, Clyde Taylor, and Bruce Weigl. "*Platoon* on Inspection: A Critical Symposium." *Cineaste* 15 (1987): 4–11.

Smith, Claude J., Jr. "*Full Metal Jacket* and the Beast Within." *Literature/Film Quarterly* 16 (1988): 226–31.

Smith, Julian. *Looking Away: Hollywood and Vietnam*. New York: Charles Scribner's Sons, 1975.

Springer, Claudia. "Antiwar Film as Spectacle: Contradictions of the Combat Sequence." *Genre* 21 (1988): 479–86.

———. "Rebellious Sons in Vietnam Combat Films: A Response." *Genre* 21 (1988): 517–22.

———. *"Vietnam: A Television History* and the Equivocal Nature of Objectivity." *Wide Angle* 7.4 (1985): 53–60.

Steier, Saul. "Make Friends with Horror and Terror: *Apocalypse Now*." *Social Text* 3 (Fall 1980): 114–22.

Stevenson, James A. "Beyond Stephen Crane: *Full Metal Jacket*." *Literature/Film Quarterly* 16 (1988): 238–43.

Stewart, Garrett. "Coppola's Conrad: The Repetitions of Complicity." *Critical Inquiry* 7 (1981): 455–74.

Stone, Robert. *Dog Soldiers*. New York: Houghton Mifflin, 1976.

Studlar, Gaylyn, and David Desser. "Never Having to Say You're Sorry: *Rambo*'s Rewriting of the Vietnam War." *Film Quarterly* 42.1 (1988): 9–16.

Sturken, Marita. "The Camera as Witness: Documentaries on the Vietnam War." *Film Library Quarterly* 13.4 (1980): 15–20.

Suid, Lawrence. "Hollywood and Vietnam." *Film Comment* 15.5 (1979): 20–25.

———. "The Making of *The Green Berets*." *Journal of Popular Film* 6 (1977): 106–25.

Thompson, Lawrence, Richard Welch, and Philip Stephens. "A Vietnam Filmography." *Journal of Popular Film and Television* 9 (1981): 61–67.

Traube, Elizabeth G. "Redeeming Images: The Wild Man Comes Home." *Persistence of Vision* 3–4 (Summer 1986): 71–94.

Tuch, Ronald. "Peter Davis' *Hearts and Minds*." *Film Library Quarterly* 10.1–2 (1977): 45–50.

Walsh, Jeffrey, and James Aulich, eds. *Vietnam Images: War and Representation*. London: Macmillan, 1989.

Walter, Krista. "Charlie Is a She: Kubrick's *Full Metal Jacket* and the Female Spectacle of Vietnam." *CineAction!* 12 (1988): 19–22.

Weiner, Bernard. "Hearts and Minds." *Film Quarterly* 28.2 (1974–75): 60–63.

Whillock, David Everett. "Defining the Fictive American Vietnam War

Film: In Search of a Genre." *Literature/Film Quarterly* 16 (1988): 244–50.

White, Susan. "Male Bonding, Hollywood Orientalism, and the Repression of the Feminine in Kubrick's *Full Metal Jacket*." *Arizona Quarterly* 44 (1988): 120–44.

Wilson, James C. *Vietnam in Prose and Film*. Jefferson, N.C.: McFarland, 1982.

Wood, Denis. "All the Words We Cannot Say: A Critical Commentary on *The Deer Hunter*." *Journal of Popular Film and Television* 7 (1980): 366–82.

Selected Filmography
and Videography

This is a highly selective list of those films and television programs discussed in the text or of special significance to the arguments presented therein. General Vietnam filmographies can be found in Gilbert Adair, *Vietnam on Film* (New York: Proteus, 1981), and in Linda Dittmar and Gene Michaud, *From Hanoi to Hollywood* (New Brunswick, N.J., and London: Rutgers University Press, 1990).

Aliens. USA 1986. 20th Century–Fox. Produced by Gale Ann Hurd. Directed by James Cameron. Written by James Cameron, David Giler, and Walter Hill. Photographed by Adrian Biddle. Music by James Horner. Edited by Ray Lovejoy. Cast: Sigourney Weaver, Carrie Henn, Michael Biehn, Paul Reiser, Lance Henriksen, Bill Paxton.

Apocalypse Now. USA 1979. Omni Zoetrope/United Artists. Produced by Francis Ford Coppola. Directed by Francis Ford Coppola. Written by John Milius, Francis Ford Coppola, and Michael Herr. Photographed by Vittorio Storaro. Music by Carmine Coppola and Francis Ford Coppola. Edited by Richard Marks. Cast: Marlon Brando, Robert Duvall, Martin Sheen, Harrison Ford, Dennis Hopper, Sam Bottoms, Frederic Forrest, and Albert Hall.

Born on the Fourth of July. USA 1989. Universal. Produced by A. Kitman Ho and Oliver Stone. Directed by Oliver Stone. Written by Oliver Stone and Ron Kovic, from Kovic's memoir. Photographed by Robert Richardson. Music by John Williams. Edited by David Brenner. Cast: Tom Cruise, Kyra Sedgwick, Raymond J. Barry, Caroline Kava, Jerry Levine, Frank Whaley, and Willem Dafoe.

The Boys in Company C. USA–Hong Kong 1978. Columbia. Produced by Andre Morgan. Directed by Sidney Furie. Written by Rick Natkin. Photographed by Godfrey A. Godar. Music by Jaime Mendoza-Nava. Edited by Michael Berman. Cast: Stan Shaw, Michael Lembeck, James Canning, Craig Wasson, Andrew Stevens, and Lee Ermey.

Casualties of War. USA 1989. Columbia Pictures. Produced by Art Linson. Directed by Brian De Palma. Written by David Rabe. Photographed by Stephen H. Burum. Music by Ennio Morricone. Edited by Bill Pankow. Cast: Michael J. Fox, Sean Penn, Don Harvey, John C. Reilly, and John Leguizamo.

China Beach. ABC-TV/Sacret Inc.–Warner Bros. TV 1988. Produced by John Wells. Created by William Broyles, Jr., and John Sacret Young. Cast regulars and semiregulars: Dana Delany, Nan Woods, Michael Boatman, Marg Helgenberger, Robert Picardo, Tim Ryan, Concetta Tomei, and Brian Winner.

Coming Home. USA 1978. United Artists. Produced by Jerome Hellman. Directed by Hal Ashby. Written by Waldo Salt and Robert C. Jones. Photographed by Haskell Wexler. Edited by Don Zimmerman. Cast: Jane Fonda, Jon Voight, Bruce Dern, Penelope Milford, Robert Carradine, and Robert Ginty.

Cutter's Way. USA 1981. United Artists Classics. Produced by Paul Gurian. Directed by Ivan Passer. Written by Jeffrey Allan Fiskin from the novel *Cutter and Bone* by Newton Thornburg. Photographed by Jordan Cronenweth. Music by Jack Nitzsche. Edited by Caroline Ferriol. Cast: Jeff Bridges, John Heard, Lisa Eichhorn, Ann Dusenberry, Stephen Elliott, and Nina Van Pallandt.

The Deer Hunter. USA 1978. Universal Pictures. Produced by Barry Spikings, Michael Deeley, John Peverall, and Michael Cimino. Directed by Michael Cimino. Written by Michael Cimino, Deric Washburn, Louis Garfinkle, and Quinn Redeker. Photographed by Vilmos Zsigmond. Music by Stanley Myers. Edited by Peter Zinner. Cast: Robert De Niro, John Cazale, John Savage, Christopher Walken, Meryl Streep, George Dzundza, and Chuck Aspegren.

A Face of War. USA 1967. Commonwealth United Entertainment. Produced by Eugene S. Jones in association with Eli Landau–Oliver Unger. Directed by Eugene S. Jones. Photographed by J. Baxter Peters, Christopher Sargent, and Eugene S. Jones. Sound by Robert Peck. Edited by Jono Roberts.

First Blood. USA 1982. Orion Pictures. Produced by Buzz Feitshans. Directed by Ted Kotcheff. Written by Michael Kozoll, William Sachkeim, and Sylvester Stallone from a novel by David Morrell. Photographed by Andrew Lazlo. Music by Jerry Goldsmith. Edited by Joan Chapman. Cast: Sylvester Stallone, Richard Crenna, Brian Dennehy, David Caruso, Jack Starrett, Michael Talbot, and David Crowley.

Full Metal Jacket. USA 1987. Warner Bros. Produced by Stanley Kubrick and Phillip Hobbs. Directed by Stanley Kubrick. Written by Stanley Kubrick, Michael Herr, and Gustav Hasford from Hasford's novel *The Short-Timers.* Photographed by Douglas Milsome. Music by Abigail Mead. Edited by Martin Hunter. Cast: Matthew Modine, Adam Baldwin, Vincent D'Onofrio, Lee Ermey, Dorian Harewood, and Arliss Howard.

Gardens of Stone. USA 1987. Tri-Star Productions. Produced by Michael I. Levy and Francis Coppola. Directed by Francis Coppola. Written by Ronald Bass from the novel by Nicholas Proffitt. Photographed by Jordan Cronenweth. Music by Carmine Coppola. Edited by Barry Malkin. Cast: James Caan, Anjelica Huston, James Earl Jones, D. B. Sweeny, Dean Stockwell, Mary Stuart Masterson, and Dick Anthony Williams.

Good Morning, Vietnam. USA 1987. Touchstone Pictures. Produced by Mark Johnson and Larry Brezner. Directed by Barry Levinson. Written by Mitch Markowitz. Photographed by Peter Sova. Music by Alex North. Edited by Stu Linder. Cast: Robin Williams, Forest Whitaker, Tung Thanh Tran, Chintara Sukaptana, Bruno Kirby, Robert Wuhl, J. T. Walsh, and Noble Willingham.

Go Tell the Spartans. USA 1978. Avco-Embassy. Produced by Allan F. Boddoh and Mitchell Cannold. Directed by Ted Post. Written by Wendell Mayes from the novel *Incident at Muc Wa* by Daniel Ford. Photographed by Harry Stradling, Jr. Music by Dick Halligan. Edited by Millie Moore. Cast: Burt Lancaster, Craig Wasson, Jonathan Goldsmith, Marc Singer, Joe Unger, and Dennis Howard.

The Green Berets. USA 1968. Warner Bros. Produced by Michael Wayne. Directed by John Wayne. Written by James Lee Barrett from the novel by Robin Moore. Photographed by Winston Hoch. Music by Miklos Rozsa. Edited by Otho Lovering. Cast: John Wayne, David Janssen, Jim Hutton, Aldo Ray, Raymond St. Jacques, Bruce Cabot, Jack Soo, Jason Evers, Luke Askew, and Irene Tsu.

Hamburger Hill. USA 1987. Paramount/RKO. Produced by Marcia Nasatir and Jim Carabatsos. Directed by John Irvin. Written by Jim Carabatsos. Photographed by Peter MacDonald. Music by Philip Glass. Edited by Peter Tanner. Cast: Anthony Barrile, Michael Patrick Boatman, Don Cheadle, Michael Dolan, Dylan McDermott, M. A. Nickles, Harry O'Reilly, Daniel O'Shea, and Tim Quill.

Hanoi Hilton. USA 1987. Cannon Films. Produced by Menahem Golan and Yoram Globus. Directed by Lionel Chetwynd. Written by Lionel Chetwynd. Photographed by Mark Irwin. Music by Jimmy Webb. Edited by Penelope Shaw. Cast: Michael Moriarity, Paul Le Mat, Jeffrey Jones, Lawrence Pressman, Stephen Davis, and David Soul.

Hearts and Minds. USA 1974. Touchstone/Warner Bros. Produced by Bert Schneider and Peter Davis. Directed by Peter Davis. Photographed by Richard Pearce. Edited by Lynzee Klingman and Susan Martin.

Letter to Jane. France 1972. Produced, written, and directed by Jean-Luc Godard and Jean-Pierre Gorin.

Missing in Action. USA 1984. Cannon Films. Produced by Menahem Golan and Yoram Globus. Directed by Joseph Zito. Written by James Bruner, John Crowther, and Lance Hool. Photographed by Joao Fernandes. Music by Jay Chattaway. Edited by Joel Goodman and Daniel Loewenthal. Cast: Chuck Norris, M. Emmet Walsh, David Tress, Leonore Kasdorff, James Hong, and Ernie Ortega.

Off Limits. USA 1988. 20th Century–Fox. Produced by Alan Barnette. Directed by Christopher Crowe. Written by Christopher Crowe and Jack Thibeau. Photographed by David Gribble. Music by James Newton Howard. Edited by Douglas Ibold. Cast: Willem Dafoe, Gregory Hines, Fred Ward, Amanda Pays, Kay Tong Lim, and Scott Glenn.

Platoon. USA 1986. Orion Pictures/Hemdale. Produced by Arnold Kopelson. Directed by Oliver Stone. Written by Oliver Stone. Photographed by Robert Richardson. Music by Georges Delerue. Edited by Claire Simpson. Cast: Tom Berenger, Willem Dafoe, Charlie Sheen, Forest Whitaker, Francesco Quinn, John C. McGinley, Richard Edson, Kevin Dillon, Reggie Johnson, and Keith David.

Predator. USA 1987. 20th Century–Fox. Produced by Lawrence Gordon, Joel Silver, and John Davis. Directed by John McTiernan. Written by

Jim Thomas and John Tohma. Photographed by Donald McAlpine. Music by Alan Silvestri. Edited by John F. Link and Mark Helfrich. Cast: Arnold Schwarzenegger, Carl Weathers, Elpidia Carillo, Bill Duke, Jesse Ventura, and Sonny Landham.

Rambo: First Blood, Part II. USA 1985. Tri-Star Pictures. Produced by Buzz Feitshans. Directed by George Pan Cosmatos. Written by Sylvester Stallone and James Cameron from a story by Kevin Jarre. Photographed by Jack Cardiff. Music by Jerry Goldsmith. Edited by Mark Goldblatt and Mark Helfrich. Cast: Sylvester Stallone, Richard Crenna, Charles Napier, Julia Nickson, Steven Berkoff, Martin Kove, George Kee Cheung, Andy Wood.

Rolling Thunder. USA 1977. American International. Produced by Norman T. Herman. Directed by John Flynn. Written by Paul Schrader and Heywood Gould. Photographed by Jordan Cronenweth. Music by Barry Devorzon. Edited by Frank P. Keller. Cast: William Devane, Tommy Lee Jones, Linda Haynes, James Best, and Luke Askew.

Taxi Driver. USA 1976. Columbia Pictures. Produced by Michael Phillips and Julia Phillips. Directed by Martin Scorsese. Written by Paul Schrader. Photographed by Michael Chapman. Music by Bernard Herrmann. Edited by Tom Rolf and Melvin Shapiro. Cast: Robert De Niro, Cybill Shepherd, Jodie Foster, Peter Boyle, and Harvey Keitel.

Television's Vietnam. Part I: *The Real Story*; Part II: *The Impact of Media*. Accuracy in Media 1985. Produced by Peter Rollins.

Tour of Duty. CBS/New World Television 1987. Produced by Zev Braun. Created by L. Travis Clark and Steve Duncan. Cast regulars and semiregulars: Terence Knox, Stephen Caffrey, Tony Becker, Stan Foster, Ramon Franco, and Miguel A. Nunez, Jr.

Twilight's Last Gleaming. USA–West Germany 1977. Geria-Lorimar-Bavaria Studios. Produced by Merv Adelson. Directed by Robert Aldrich. Written by Ronald Cohen and Edward Huebsch from the novel *Vipers Three* by Walter Wager. Photographed by Robert Hauser. Music by Jerry Goldsmith. Edited by Michael Luciano and Maury Weintrobe. Cast: Burt Lancaster, Richard Widmark, Charles Durning, Melvyn Douglas, Paul Winfield, Burt Young, Joseph Cotten, and Roscoe Lee Browne.

Uncommon Valor. USA 1983. Paramount. Produced by John Milius and Buzz Feitshans. Directed by Ted Kotcheff. Written by Joe Gayton. Photographed by Stephen H. Burum. Music by James Horner. Edited by Mark Melnick. Cast: Gene Hackman, Robert Stack, Fred Ward, Reb Brown, Randall "Tex" Cobb, Patrick Swayze, and Harold Sylvester.

Vietnam: A Television History. USA. WGBH-TV/Public Television Network 1983. Thirteen parts. Produced by Judith Vecchione.

Who'll Stop the Rain. USA 1978, United Artists. Produced by Herb Jaffe and Gabriel Katzka. Directed by Karel Reisz. Written by Judith Rascoe and Robert Stone from Stone's novel *Dog Soldiers.* Photographed by Richard H. Kline. Music by Laurence Rosenthal. Edited by John Bloom. Cast: Nick Nolte, Tuesday Weld, Michael Moriarity, Anthony Zerbe, Richard Masur, Ray Sharkey, and Gail Strickland.

The Contributors

Michael Anderegg teaches film and literature at the University of North Dakota. He is the author of *William Wyler* and *David Lean* and has contributed articles on film to *Film Quarterly, Persistence of Vision,* and *Cinema Journal.*

David Desser teaches film in the Unit for Cinema Studies and the Department of Speech Communications at the University of Illinois, Urbana-Champaign. He is the author of *The Samurai Films of Akira Kurosawa* and *Eros plus Massacre: An Introduction to the Japanese New Wave Cinema* and has also written on films about the Vietnam War.

Thomas Doherty teaches in the American Studies program at Brandeis University. He is the author of *Teenagers and Teenpics: The Juvenilization of American Movies in the 1950s,* and his film criticism has appeared in *Cinefantastique, Cineaste, Film Quarterly, Film and History,* and the *Journal of Film and Video.*

Ellen Draper teaches film at Simmons College in Boston. She has published articles and reviews in *Wide Angle, Film Quarterly,* and the *Quar-*

terly Review of Film and Video. An essay on *Le livre de Marie* is forthcoming in a book on Godard's *Je vous salue, Marie.*

Cynthia J. Fuchs teaches film in the English department at George Mason University.

Owen W. Gilman, Jr., teaches at Saint Joseph's University in Philadelphia. He has written on various aspects of American literature and is currently preparing an article on Barry Hannah for a collection of essays, *Writers of the Modern South.* His essay "Vietnam and the South" recently appeared in the *Encyclopedia of Southern Culture.*

John Hellmann is the author of *Fables of Fact: The New Journalism as New Fiction* and *American Myth and the Legacy of Vietnam.* He is an associate professor of English at the Ohio State University at Lima.

Judy Lee Kinney received her Ph.D. from UCLA in English and has written on film in *Quarterly Review of Film Studies* and *Wide Angle.* She has taught at Emory University and now resides in Denver, where she divides her time between completing a book on Vietnam War films and managing her real-estate-development company.

Daniel Miller teaches at the University of Maryland, College Park, and also produces documentary film and video. Critical studies and cross-cultural minority issues constitute the major areas of concern in both his academic and film-production work.

Thomas J. Slater teaches at Indiana University of Pennsylvania. His publications include *Milos Forman: A Bio-Bibliography,* and he is currently working as editor and coauthor of *A Handbook of Soviet and Eastern European Film and Filmmakers.*

Carolyn Reed Vartanian is a Ph.D. candidate in the critical-studies division of the School of Cinema/Television at the University of Southern California. Her dissertation concerns the representation of women in the film and television texts about the U.S.–Vietnam War.

Susan White is an assistant professor of English at the University of Arizona. Her book on the representation of women in the films of Max Ophuls is forthcoming.

Tony Williams is an associate professor of Cinema Studies in the Department of Cinema and Photography, Southern Illinois University at Carbondale. He regularly teaches a graduate seminar, "Vietnam in Literature and Hollywood Film."

Index